BUSTER

A LEGEND IN LAUGHTER

Joseph Francis "Buster" Keaton
1895-1966

BUSTER

A LEGEND IN LAUGHTER

LARRY EDWARDS

McGuinn & McGuire
PUBLISHING, INC.
Bradenton, Florida

BUSTER: A LEGEND IN LAUGHTER. Copyright 1995 by Larry Edwards. Printed and bound in the United States of America. All rights reserved. No part of this book may be reproduced or transmitted in any form or by any means, electronic or mechanical, including photocopying, recording, or by any information storage or retrieval system without permission in writing from the publisher, except by a reviewer who may quote brief passages in a review to be printed in a magazine or newspaper. For information, contact McGuinn & McGuire Publishing, Inc., Post Office Box 20603, Bradenton, Florida 34203.

Excerpts from *Keaton: The Man Who Wouldn't Lie Down* by Tom Dardis used with permission of Proscenium Publishers Inc., New York.

Excerpts from *The Parade's Gone By* by Kevin Brownlow © 1968 Alfred A. Knopf, Inc.

Excerpts from *Rushes and Retakes* by John Eastman. Copyright © 1987 by John Eastman. Reprinted with permission of Ballantine Books, a Division of Random House, Inc.

Keaton Filmography © 1960 used with the permission of Alan Twyman Presents The Rohauer Collection.

Excerpts from *The Movie Star* by Elizabeth Weis © 1981 reprinted with permission of Penguin Books USA Inc.

Library of Congress Cataloging-in-Publication Data

FARCA

Edwards, Larry, 1957-
   Buster: a legend in laughter / Larry Edwards.
      p.   cm.
   Filmography: p.
   Includes bibliographical references and index.
   ISBN 1-881117-10-3 – ISBN 1-881117-07-3 (pbk.)
   1. Keaton, Buster, 1895-1966. 2. Comedians – United States –
Biography. 3. Motion picture actors and actresses – United States –
Biography. I. Title.
PN2287.K4E38 1995
791.43'028'092–dc20
[B]   94-41838

Printed in the United States of America

This book is dedicated to all of the Hollywood funny people who, through their art, have helped us forget our problems. If laughter is indeed the greatest medicine, they are the world's greatest physicians.

To my son Mathew: May the great spirit of laughter be with you always (and thanks for putting up with the silent and black and white films).

And most importantly, to the memory of Joseph Francis Keaton, without a doubt the greatest comedic talent there ever was and ever will be. Though you never smiled, the ones you caused still light up the world.

CONTENTS

. . . AND THEN THERE WAS VAUDEVILLE!   1

BUSTER AND FATTY   17

THE KEATON STUDIO   41

THE GENERAL   75

A STAR BEGINS TO FALL   97

FADE TO BLACK   127

FILMOGRAPHY   173

BIBLIOGRAPHY   205

INDEX   207

For who would not wish to live a hundred years in a world where there are so many people who remember with gratitude and affection a little man with a frozen face who made them laugh a bit long years ago when they and I were both young.

Buster Keaton
Actor, Director, Writer
1895 - 1966

1

... AND THEN THERE WAS VAUDEVILLE!

The Mohawk Indian Medicine company traveled through the Midwest entertaining and selling their snake-oils and cure-alls during the fall of 1895. Two of the performers with this old west medicine show were Myra and Joseph Keaton. When the Mohawk Indian Medicine company hit the small town of Piqua, Kansas, on October 4, 1895, Myra Keaton gave birth to a son, Joseph Francis Keaton, or as he would later be known, Buster.

Myra Keaton was a pipe smoking, bourbon drinking, little dynamo. Standing only four-feet eleven-inches and weighing about ninety pounds, she was a strong influence on all three of her children, especially her eldest, Buster. Myra was the daughter of F.L. Cutler, a co-owner of a traveling minstrel show called the Cutler-Bryant 10-Cent Show. Myra had an affinity for musical instruments and, before she reached her teens, was considered an excellent fiddle, piano, and cornet player. Later, when the saxophone was introduced, she became the first female performer to play this newfangled instrument. Myra Keaton's first love was card playing and she was an ace pinochle and bridge player. While on the road during her medicine show days, Myra often emptied the pockets of her fellow performers with her cardsharp ways.

Joseph Keaton was a tall, lanky, good looking man. He was born in 1867 in a rural area near Terre Haute, Indiana, called Dogwatch. Young Joseph Keaton would perform little skits for his family and any bystanders who would pay him attention. These skits always included a variety of pratfalls that amazed his receptive audiences.

In 1889, at the age of twenty-two, Joseph Keaton departed the friendly confines of Dogwatch. Bidding his family good-bye, he decided to go west to become a prospector. In his later years, Joseph related this story to anyone who would listen: "I took off with a total of eight dollars in my pocket. One dollar was intended for bacon and eggs, and the other seven dollars was for ammunition as a defense against claim-jumpers." His thoughts of "striking it rich" did not last long and, by 1890, he gave into his childhood fantasy of show business.

Getting into show business was not easy for Joseph Keaton. In the late 1800's, show business was a rough and tumble career to enter. If you didn't know anyone in the field, your chances of making it were slim. This was a very closed community and did not look kindly toward outsiders. This was nothing new to Joseph Keaton since nothing in his life had ever come easily. He was a fighter in every sense of the word and proud of it.

While attempting to make his mark in the world of show business, Joseph Keaton met some seasoned veterans, including Will Rogers, George M. Cohen, and Al Jolson. During this time he became friends with another newcomer, Harry Houdini. Houdini was a rather stocky man with pure and unadulterated mystery in his eyes as well as a gait of pure cockiness.

As Joseph Keaton and Harry Houdini became close friends, they also became business partners and started up their own medicine show, the Mohawk Indian Medicine Company.

In 1894, Joseph Keaton married Myra Cutler, who was ten years his junior. During the first few years of their marriage, they weren't wallowing in the riches of their show business success, as fame and fortune evaded them. The birth of their first child, Joseph Francis Keaton, did not help matters in 1895. Their income depended on the economy of the towns where they were playing. They were a small troupe and only played small, rural communities, so they barely made enough money to buy food, let alone think about expenses.

Money, during these times, was something they only talked about, wished upon, and prayed for.

Once word started to get around about the medicine show's star performer, Harry Houdini — master escapologist, the crowds started to show up in droves and more money began to flow in. The whole medicine show was rather simple: Joseph Keaton would do his act of telling a few jokes and stories, dancing around in a "tribal" fashion and dazzling the audience with pratfalls and acrobatics.

Next, Myra would perform with her saxophone playing and facial contortions. The next segment of the show had Harry Houdini performing a couple of magic tricks, some slight of hand card tricks, and then amazing the throng of people with his uncanny ability to escape easily from the local authorities' handcuffs. After his act, he became Doctor Harry Houdini and sold bottles of Kickapoo Elixir, a typical snake-oil and cure-all, to the more than willing customers at the price of one dollar per bottle. Doctor Houdini would bark, "Kickapoo Elixir will cure everything from barber's itch to the galloping consumption!"

"My birth in Piqua, Kansas, on October 4, 1895, was comparatively uneventful, though Piqua itself not so long afterward was blown away during a cyclone," Buster was once quoted. "In addition to the humiliation of having my birthplace blown right off the face of the map, I had to share mom's milk with a papoose of a Kickapoo squaw who had none of her own."

How Joseph Francis Keaton (he was not a junior) become known as Buster is a story which pretty well wraps up not only his youth, but his career as well.

At six months of age, while his family was staying at a performers boarding house, Buster fell down a flight of stairs. As he came to a tumbling stop, he let out an ear-shattering wail. While rehearsing his craft, Harry Houdini heard the wailing child. Running to him, Houdini scooped him up, took him to Myra and Joseph, and stated, "My, you have yourself a real little buster here!" A *buster* in vaudeville jargon means a person who can take hard falls and not sustain bodily injury, which Buster did not.

Joseph Keaton decided this was the name his son would go by. . . Buster. For many years, most people thought Buster was really his

3

first name, including his second wife, Mae Scribbins. It was rumored that she never knew his real first name was Joseph.

"As far as I've been able to learn," Buster mused, "I was the first man given that nickname. Even Buster Brown, R.F. Outcault's comic strip, was born a few years after I came into the world."

Falling down the boarding house stairs was actually the second of many frightening experiences for baby Buster, not to mention his ever-worrying parents.

The first frightening experience occurred when Buster was four months old. Sleeping in a wardrobe chest which was being used as a crib while Myra and Joseph were performing, the lid of the chest slammed shut nearly suffocating Buster. When Myra ran backstage to retrieve a forgotten prop, she noticed the chest was closed. She opened it, checked to make sure Buster was still breathing, and then ran back onstage to join her husband. If Myra would've been a few minutes later with her check, Buster would have surely died.

The strangest of all incidents of his youth occurred when Buster was three years of age. Actually it was a series of three incidents which occurred over a twelve hour period.

While vacationing at the family boarding house in Kansas, three-year-old Buster Keaton was in the backyard watching a maid wash clothes in a wringer-type washer. Being a typical three-year-old boy, curiosity got the best of him and he decided to investigate this strange looking mechanical device. While playing with the machine, his right index finger was crushed in the wringer. When the doctor arrived, he amputated the finger above the first joint (Buster always attempted to hide this handicap in all of his films).

A few hours later, Buster was once again trampling in the back-yard. Looking up at a large peach tree, he decided he was hungry. Being too small to reach up and grab the peach hanging over his head, he found a brick and threw it up at the peach, hoping to knock it down. He missed. When the brick came down, it hit him on top of his head, splitting his head open. Once again the doctor was summoned. After receiving five stitches, Buster was ordered to bed.

During the late afternoon of the same day, Buster was awakened by a strange noise coming from outside his bedroom window. He walked over to the window and saw a cyclone twisting its way toward the boarding house. Wanting to get a better look at this mysterious swirling wind, Buster opened the bedroom window wide and was at once sucked out! A neighbor found him four blocks away and carried him back to his parents.

Just before his first birthday, Buster made his show business debut by crawling out onto the stage where Joseph Keaton was performing. Seeing little Buster crawling out onto the stage, the audience went into fits of laughter. Joseph Keaton was thinking the audiences' reaction was to his performance and smiled broadly. He did not know Buster was on the stage until he felt a tug on the leg of his pants. Joseph picked up Buster, took a bow, and walked off the stage to a standing ovation. This was Buster's first taste of show business but it was not the beginning of his career; that occurred three years later.

In the latter part of 1899, the minstrel and medicine shows were giving way to a new entertainment rage dubbed *vaudeville*. Joseph Keaton knew vaudeville was going to be successful and lucrative which is why he decided this was going to be the direction he and Myra were going to take. The vaudeville act Joseph designed relied on nothing more than roughhousing. In this act, Buster played "The Human Mop" and this was the start of his career. In the course of a scripted scenario, Joseph and Myra played a married couple with a problem child played by Buster. During this performance, Joseph picked up three-year-old Buster and literally mopped the floor with him, whence came the billing "The Human Mop."

The vaudeville audiences loved the Keatons, and Buster in particular. Before long, the act was being billed as "The Three Keatons" and, due to the rave critical reviews they were receiving, they were soon the most requested act on the vaudeville circuit. Joseph Keaton knew their success was due to their rough-and-tumble ways and, with this in mind, their act became more rough, or as one critic put it, "violent."

On any given night, it was not uncommon to see Joseph Keaton dropping young Buster on the stage with Buster pretending to bounce, or picking Buster up and throwing him through whatever scenery they were using. One of the favorite routines of The Three Keatons was one in which Joseph Keaton picked Buster up and threw him into the orchestra pit. Buster would land on the bass drum causing a thunderous "BOOM!" One of the most famous gags Joseph and Buster performed had Joseph hitting Buster in the face with a broom. Buster's response to this assault was to stand facing the audience with no expression or emotion registered upon his face. After a few seconds of silence, Buster all of a sudden would yell "OUCH!" and the audience would erupt in uncontrollable laughter.

"The people were amazed because I didn't cry," Buster recalled. "I didn't cry because I wasn't hurt. All little boys like to be rough-housed by their fathers. There is one more thing; little kids when they fall down haven't very far to go. I suppose a psychologist would call it a case of self-hypnosis."

As for Buster showing no emotion, this "stone face" was to become his trademark. There are many stories regarding Buster's acquired ability to never smile or register emotion. One of these stories tells of how he would bite his lower lip with his upper teeth until it would bleed. As the blood seeped into his mouth, it would cause him to have a look of sickly bewilderment or, as it was phrased at the time, "the Buster Keaton look."

Another story, which has never been proven, is that if Buster smiled, Joseph would beat him. On one occasion when Buster was asked about this, he politely avoided the question.

In the latter years of his life when he was being rediscovered as both a comedic genius and living legend, he relayed a couple of different variations on how he acquired his "stone face."

"I developed the stone face thing quite naturally. I just happened to be, even as a small kid, the type of comic that couldn't laugh at his own material. I soon learned at an awful early age that when I laughed, the audience didn't."

Another version: "If something tickled me and I started to grin, the old man would hiss 'face, face!' That meant freeze the puss. The longer I held it, why, if we got a laugh the blank pan or puzzled puss would double it. He kept after me, 'never let up,' and in a few years it was automatic. Then when I stepped on stage or in front of a movie camera, I couldn't smile."

Still another version: "I noticed that whenever I smiled or let the audience suspect how much I was enjoying myself, they didn't seem to laugh as much as usual. It was on purpose that I started looking miserable, humiliated, hounded, and haunted, bewildered, and at my wit's end."

Finally, in an interview with the British Broadcasting Company, Buster stated: "I had learned at a very early age that I had to be the type of comedian that could not laugh at anything he was doing. And I also learned that the more serious I took everything and how serious life was in general, the better laughs I got."

No matter what the actual account is, one fact is undeniable. The amount of dedication, self-control, and agony which went into his facial muscle control, which obviously covered up pain as well as joy, took an inhuman amount of self-discipline. This would be extraordinary for any adult, but when you consider Buster was not yet ten years of age when he perfected this look, it is truly amazing.

Because of the way Buster acted on stage, there were those who did not believe he was a child. As one critic put it, "There is not a child on this earth who could take these nightly beatings, throwings, and falls without at least once breaking into tears." Perhaps it was this critic's remark that initiated the rumor of Buster not being a child but a midget.

For Joseph Keaton, the rumor of Buster being a midget was one which he supported. He wanted everyone to believe Buster was a midget because The Society for the Prevention of Cruelty to Children (later known as the Gerry Society) began to bear down on him. Joseph even worked to strengthen the rumor by dressing Buster to be a miniature mirror image of himself, including a dark wig with a bald plate and sideburns, a dark suit with white waistcoat, and spats.

Though Joseph Keaton promoted this rumor and transformed it into a money-making publicity stunt, he was still a very proud father. To make this point, Joseph put ads in all of the theatrical papers and trade magazines stating: "Buster is not a midget, but a revelation in eccentric juvenile talent, properly directed to produce the lasting comedy effect! The most unique character in vaudeville. A miniature comedian, who presents irresistible comedy, with gigantic effects, making ladies hold their sides too!"

The Society for the Prevention of Cruelty to Children never let up on Joseph Keaton and never bought the rumors of Buster being a midget.

"The Society for the Prevention of Cruelty to Children accused my father of mistreating me on the stage," Buster remembered. "They made such an issue out of it that Mayor R.A. Van Wych, a Tammany man, ordered me brought to his office and stripped so that he could see for himself if I had any bruises or black-and-blue marks.

"'Why is he free of hurt as one of my own boys?' said his honor, dismissing charges."

This was not the last time this type of action was taken. Even though Joseph Keaton was cleared after Buster appeared before Mayor Van Wych, in each city thereafter Buster was forced to a Mayor's office, social workers' offices, judges' chambers, and, on one occasion, a Governor's office. At no time was there any physical evidence that Buster was being abused by his father.

"The undiscouraged child-savers continued their battle. When Seth Low, a reform Mayor, succeeded Van Wych, they brought me before him to be stripped and examined, also before one New York Governor. They had age limits raised (those for child performers), but our lawyers beat them in court by pointing out that the law barred children only from performing on high or low wire, a trapeze, bicycle, and the like. There was not one word that made it illegal for my father to display me on stage as 'The Human Mop' or to kick me in the face."

Never being able to prove their accusations against Joseph Keaton, The Society for the Prevention of Cruelty to Children ended their *witch-hunt* and The Three Keatons continued full-force their renowned vaudeville act.

The year 1910 saw vaudeville reach its peak. On any given night, you might see the talents of Bert Lahr (later to be immortalized in *The Wizard of OZ* as the Cowardly Lion), the Marx Brothers (Groucho, Harpo, Chico, Gummo, and Zeppo), George Jessle, or George Burns. If you were lucky and could get a ticket, there was W.C. Fields, Will Rogers, Al Jolson, and the hottest ticket in the business . . . The Three Keatons.

While The Three Keatons were performing at Pastor's in New York City, one of their opening acts was a young singing piano player named Izzy Balin. Izzy was nothing more than an in-house piano player who had a catchy way with the words and tunes he penned. Joseph Keaton, a man never to mince words, told Izzy, "You're never going to go anywhere with a name like Izzy!" Apparently Izzy took this advice to heart. He changed his name to Irving Berlin and the rest, as they say, is history.

Figure 1-1 – One of the few known portraits of The Three Keatons. At five years old, Buster appears to be a miniature version of his father. It is no wonder that people thought he was a midget instead of a little boy.

In Rudi Blesh's writings on Buster Keaton, he recreates a typical week of acts performed by The Three Keatons.

"Monday might be twenty minutes of up-tempo mayhem relieved by 'My Gal Sal' on the alto-saxophone, practical jokes and counter jokes, slips, tumbles, trips, slides, and the unbelievable comic falls. Tuesday night develops into one long comic routine, all in off-the-cuff pantomime and not a word spoken. Wednesday would perhaps unfold as recitation time, with merciless parodies of Bernhardt, Eva Tanguay, or Sothern and Marlowe's Romeo and Juliet, with balcony and Buster falling upon Joseph.

"Thursday night might be devoted to one long outrageous burlesque of some popular melodrama. Or all these things and more might be cross-stitched into a Keaton sampler of the modes of madness. Not only was this Keystone Comedy long before Mack Sennett met the movie camera, it was surrealism before Salvador Dali was even born and pop art before the first Campbell's soup can sat before Andy Warhol."

One of the funniest and most popular routines Joseph and Buster Keaton would perform was also one of their most violent. This routine consisted of Buster hitting Joseph with a broom while Joseph was slapping Buster on his forehead. It all started out with the two of them doing this for fun, a sort of weird love exchange between father and son. Before long they got carried away as the orchestra started to play The Anvil Chorus. As the music played, Buster and Joseph kept time by continuing to pound each other to the beat of the music. As the orchestra played faster, father and son pounded each other faster. This went on until everything was in a frenzy.

Throughout his vaudeville career, Buster sustained very few injuries. This is incredible when you consider the rough and violent nature of the routines in which he participated.

One routine in which an injury occurred had Buster and Joseph roughhousing in a kitchen motif, hitting each other with pots, pans, and whatever else they could get their hands on. Joseph then picked Buster up and threw him through the background scenery. This was a routine they performed often and had down pat, or so they thought. Because they did not rehearse in one particular theater, they didn't know the way the stage and its surroundings were constructed. When Joseph picked Buster up and threw him through the scenery,

Figure 1-2 – The Three Keaton's in action. This is a rare photo, one of only two times when Buster was caught with a smile.

there was a loud "THUD!" Neither Joseph nor Buster was aware that behind the scenery there was a solid wall, instead taking for granted the scenery was just a hanging curtain with more backstage area behind it. Buster was knocked out cold. Being the "show must go on" type of performer he was, Buster was back on the stage by the time the curtain rose for their next performance. The reason there was no rehearsal for this skit was because Joseph felt rehearsals were the same as performing for free and this was something which went against everything he stood for and believed in.

Only once did Buster ever miss a performance because of an injury. Joseph Keaton had just written and choreographed a new routine which showcased his talents as an acrobat and skilled trick-kicker. The scenario for this routine was as follows: Buster stood behind a door. The only thing visible to the audience was his head with a pair of hands gripping his neck as if strangling him. Joseph saw this and rushed over to fight off this unseen assailant and performed a sweeping kick in an effort to protect Buster. He missed his target and kicked Buster behind the head.

"When he kicked over my head, he misjudged and his knee kicked me right behind my neck," Buster recalled. "I stiffened, went out, and fell back. He didn't realize what went wrong. My head hit the floor and I'm out eighteen hours."

On one occasion there was a member of the audience who got hurt.

Ma was on stage playing a song on her saxophone while Pop and I were backstage getting ready for one of our skits. While putting on his makeup, Pop was hearing some yelling going on out front. Poking his head out the curtains, he saw a young man sitting about five rows back who was heckling Ma. Without saying a word to me, Pop grabbed me by the collar and dragged me out to the stage where we joined Ma.

As we got out onto the stage, Pop told Ma to stop playing. Glaring at the guy who was heckling Ma, Pop told the guy "shut up or get the hell out of the theater." The guy made a dangerous mistake when he started to give Pop a bad time. Not missing a beat, Pop picked me up and threw me at the guy. Like a knife thrower tossing at his target, Pop's aim was perfect. I ended up landing on the heckler's lap, breaking a few of his ribs. I wasn't hurt at all. After I landed, I jumped right up and ran back up onto the stage. I'll tell you this, there was never anymore heckling during our shows once word of what Pop did got out.

With Buster being on the road during his entire childhood, there was not much time for a formal education. Whereas most people can look back to their school days, Buster never could, as his formal education lasted only one day.

While performing in Jersey City, it was recommended to Joseph and Myra that it might be a good idea for Buster to attend school. Since their engagement in Jersey City was going to be a long one, they agreed and enrolled Buster in a local school. Buster loved this idea, as now he would be around children his own age. Here is how Buster once recalled his first, last, and only day of schooling.

I brought some jokes and decided to bring joy into the classroom by telling them. The teacher called roll:

"Smith?"

"Here!"

"Johnson?"

"Here!"

"Keaton?"

"I couldn't come today!"

During geography class our teacher asked, "What is an island?" I shot up my hand. When the teacher gave me the nod, I said, "an island, ma'am, is a wart on the ocean."

Next came grammar. One of the questions was, "give me a sentence with the word delight in it?"

Once again my hand shot up first. My answer was, "the vind blew in the vindow and blew out de light."

The teacher sent me home with a note that read: "Do not sent this boy to our school anymore!"

Even though Buster received no formal education, his show business education was taught to him by the best teachers in the world. Two of these teachers Buster grew to love and respect. One was Bill "Bojangles" Robinson and the other was Harry Houdini.

I was about seven years old when we first worked on a bill with Bojangles. By Tuesday of that week, Robinson was broke and had borrowed money from all the grown-ups on the bill.

His face lit up on hearing that, small though I was, I always had money in my pockets. On Wednesday, he borrowed two dollars from me. He promised to pay it back but neglected to mention I'd have to wait until Saturday when he got his weeks pay.

Nobody else had ever borrowed money from me, and I was very impressed by the transaction. But at every performance after that I asked Robinson, "Mr. Bill, where is my two dollars?"

This depressed him more and more, but he managed to take it until Friday. Then, unable to stand anymore donning, he approached Pop and said, "Mr. Joe, I don't know whether you will approve of this, but I borrowed two dollars from Buster. He has been asking me for it every minute since. Mr. Joe, could you please let me have two dollars until tomorrow night so I can pay Buster and not have him asking me for his money anymore?" Pop gave Bill the two dollars, and he gave it to me and paid back my father the next day.

About thirty years later when Bill was playing with Shirley Temple at Twentieth-Century-Fox, he encountered me on the lot. He was walking with Darryl Zanuck, then the studio's production chief. We stopped to chat. Suddenly Bill turned to Zanuck and said, "Mr. Zanuck, don't ever borrow any money from that man!"

Harry Houdini was another of Buster's heroes as well as a teacher. Aside from the typical *hero-worship*, Buster was also in awe of Houdini. Whenever the great magician and master escapologist was on stage mystifying his audience, young Buster was eyeing his every move and taking precise and exact mental notes. Houdini would amaze Buster with his trickery and Buster Keaton did not like being amazed in such a way unless he could figure out what it was which was amazing him. On many occasions, Buster was asked to name the greatest showman he had ever seen and he always answered the same . . . "Harry Houdini."

As The Three Keatons reached their popularity peak, things started to happen that spelled the downfall of vaudeville's greatest comedy act.

Martin Beck was virtually the *lord* of the vaudeville circuit. He owned a couple of the largest theaters which featured the best vaudeville acts and on his word alone, he could make or break the biggest acts in the business. Joseph Keaton hated Martin Beck and Beck's feelings toward Joseph Keaton were the same.

One night while Joseph Keaton was performing in one of Martin Beck's theaters, their mutual hatred toward each other came to a head in front of a sell-out audience. Just as Joseph Keaton was ending his solo part of the act, he heard Martin Beck shout from the stage wings, "Make me laugh Keaton, make me laugh!" Stopping his act cold, Joseph Keaton went after Beck and ended up chasing him out of his own theater. Because of this, Beck used his immense power and blackballed The Three Keatons from the major vaudeville houses throughout the United States.

It was now as if they were starting all over again. They went back to small towns and no-talent roadshows. Instead of two shows a day in swanky first-class theaters, it was now three, four, and sometimes five shows a day in theaters resembling nothing more than barns on the back lot. The Three Keatons, once one of the top acts in show business, was now begging for work. What this professional slap-in-the-face did to Joseph Keaton was nothing short of self-ruin. Because of this professional demotion, Joseph Keaton's best ally was no loner his son and partner; it was now his ever present bottle of whiskey.

By 1916, Buster could take it no longer. He was now five-feet four- inches tall and weighed one hundred and forty pounds. In the condition Joseph Keaton was in most of the time, their act, which relied on precise timing and perfect physical conditioning, was becoming nothing more than a very unfunny parody of what they once were. There were now times when Joseph was so drunk he could barely walk onto the stage. For the first time in his professional life, Buster was frightened of performing. He was well aware that a half second off in their timing of throwing a kick or ducking a punch could very easily result in a serious injury . . . his!

While in the midst of an engagement at the Orpheum Theater in San Francisco, Joseph Keaton got drunk one time too often. After their final performance in San Francisco, Buster decided it was time to break up the act. Once he came to this conclusion, he phoned Myra, who had left the act in 1916, and informed her of his decision. Myra had no objections and told Buster, "You lasted longer than I thought you would. I understand your reasoning."

Buster packed his belongings and headed for New York City. Being hurt, disillusioned, and confused, Buster never informed Joseph of his decision. Joseph found out about the breakup when he arrived in Los Angeles for what was supposed to be the opening of their show at the Pantages Theater.

The end of The Three Keatons came at a very interesting time for Buster, as the popularity of vaudeville was giving way to another form of entertainment, a somewhat new medium called *moving pictures*.

2

BUSTER AND FATTY

In 1912, when nickelodeons were the rage, Joseph, Myra, and Buster Keaton were invited to perform their vaudeville act on film. Joseph Keaton, speaking for the family, refused this offer, as he looked upon the budding film industry as having no future and no aim other than to destroy vaudeville. Buster did not feel the same way.

When Buster was twelve, he dropped his first coin into a nickelodeon and it was love at first sight. By the time he was twenty-one, Buster claimed to have seen every film released up to that date. Even though this is, in all probability, an exaggeration, Buster did spend much of his free time watching these flickering lighted images of movement on film.

By 1914, nickelodeons were giving way to large scale movies being shown in large theaters. One of the largest of these theaters was the Mark Strand Theater in New York City which had a seating capacity of three thousand. By the time the Mark Strand Theater opened, average receipts from movie theaters during any given week was well into the millions of dollars. Whereas Buster Keaton fell in love with the film industry when he was twelve, it was now all of America that was falling in love.

If a finger is to be pointed toward the one person who did the most to bring films to popularity, this finger would have to be pointed in the direction of D.W. Griffith.

D.W. (David Wark) Griffith was born in Kentucky in 1875.

Attempting a career as a stage actor, he failed. He then tried his hand at writing and failed in that endeavor as well. Feeling he was born to be in some facet of show business, he turned to a new form of show business that was just beginning to take hold . . . filmmaking.

Griffith's initial break was given to him by Biograph Studios, where he directed his first film, *The Adventures of Dollie* (1908). Before his time with Biograph was complete, he made history by directing the first *feature film* ever produced, *Judith of Bethulia* (1914).

Leaving Biograph, Griffith joined the ranks at Reliance Majestic Studio as Head of Production. It was at Reliance Majestic where he took Thomas Dixon's novel *The Klansman* and turned it into the feature film *The Birth of a Nation*. With *The Birth of a Nation*, (controversial then and even more so now) Griffith single-handily proved that film could be an art form.

His next film was *Intolerance* (1916), which is considered equal to Buster Keaton's *The General* as one of the greatest films ever produced. With *Intolerance*, Griffith recounted man's inhumanity to man in four parts.

In 1919, with Mary Pickford, Douglas Fairbanks, and Charlie Chaplin, Griffith founded United Artists Incorporated.

In 1936, Griffith was awarded a special Academy Award "for his distinguished creative achievements as director and producer, and his invaluable initiative and lasting contributions to the progress of the motion picture arts."

In 1948, D.W. Griffith died in a Hollywood *flea-bag* motel, a bitter and broken alcoholic who had been forgotten by the community he had built almost single-handily.

With The Three Keaton's now nothing more than a part of vaudeville history, Buster found himself alone in New York City — unemployed, but not unwanted.

At twenty-one years of age, Buster's reputation of being a "one-and-only" was getting him plenty of offers. One offer that Buster considered was to be the headliner in a Shubert Revue getting ready to play the Winter Garden Theater in New York City. The money he was being offered was never divulged, but according to some people

Figure 2-1 – Roscoe "Fatty" Arbuckle. Once the highest paid entertainer in the world, Fatty gained notoriety during the Arbuckle Scandal. Buster often stated that Fatty taught him everything he knew about filmmaking.

who were involved with putting this deal together, it was a very large sum.

While contemplating the Shubert offer, Buster decided to take a walk to clear his head. It was this walk which changed his life and gave birth to the golden age of film comedy.

There are various stories surrounding this walk. The most famous had Buster walking down Broadway on a snowy day in 1917 and bumping into Roscoe "Fatty" Arbuckle. As he was talking to Fatty, Buster mentioned the breakup of The Three Keatons and the fact he was currently out of work. Fatty then, the story goes, offered Buster a role in his film *The Butcher Boy* which Buster accepted and thus started his film career.

Even though the above story sounds good, it isn't true. The truth is, Buster did not know Fatty personally at that time, he had only seen him in some of Mack Sennett's Keystone Cop comedy shorts. The actual story of Buster breaking into films is more businesslike and less Hollywoodish.

While walking down Broadway in New York City and mulling over his offer from the Shubert Revue, Buster did not bump into Fatty Arbuckle; he bumped into Joseph Schenck, an old show business acquaintance, walking to his office.

As the two men were talking about Buster's Shubert offer, Schenck mentioned to Buster the possibility of working on film. Seeing that this piqued Buster's curiosity, Schenck continued talking. What Buster did not know at this time was that Joseph Schenck was producing Fatty Arbuckle films.

As they continued walking, Schenck led Buster to the Talmadge Studios on 48th Street, where Fatty Arbuckle was working and where Buster's life would begin to change. It was at the Talmadge Studios where Buster met Fatty Arbuckle for the first time. As the two men shook hands, a bond was created, a bond which would last until Arbuckle's untimely death.

Arbuckle had been a fan of Buster's ever since he first saw The Three Keatons and was thrilled to finally meet him. When Fatty asked Buster if he had ever performed on film, Buster answered," no." With a smile on his rotund face, Fatty told Buster to come back to the studio the next day and he would use him in his film *The Butcher Boy*.

Roscoe "Fatty" Arbuckle was born on March 24, 1887, in Smith Center, Kansas. At a very young age, the family moved to Northern California where they settled in the farming community of Santa Clara, about fifty miles south of San Francisco.

Arbuckle's childhood, in some respects, paralleled Buster's. As a child, Arbuckle was physically abused by his father (though unlike Buster, these were not show business staged beatings) for his constant truancy from school. To Fatty, school was not as important as being a *class clown* on the playgrounds or school yards.

Because he felt it was a waste of time, Fatty quit school and found jobs in vaudeville, carnivals, burlesque, and, strangely enough, on the opera circuit as a comedic singer before finding his infamous niche in films.

In 1907, Fatty started his film career with the Selig Poli Scope Company. He stayed with Selig Poli until he was discovered by silent film comedy production master, Mack Sennett, in 1913. Signed by Sennett, Fatty was immediately put into Sennett's Keystone comedies and reached stardom later as one of the original Keystone Cops. Early in 1917, Arbuckle left Sennett and went into a film partnership with Joseph Schenck which lasted until 1919, when he signed a contract with Famous-Players-Lasky. This contract, at seven thousand dollars a week, made him one of the highest paid performers in the world.

In his first film with Mack Sennett, Fatty's job was not acting, it was dancing. The script called for Fatty to come dancing up some stairs leading to the top of a porch where a couple was cavorting. Fatty did the scene as scripted and added a few back-flips. The sight of a two hundred and eighty pound, five-foot ten-inch tall Fatty Arbuckle doing back-flips amazed Sennett. Mack Sennett, being a man never to let opportunity slip by, decided right then and there that audiences would love a "fat cop" who was agile enough for pratfalls and signed Fatty as one of the Keystone Cops at three dollars a day. By the time Fatty was finished with Sennet, he was the most popular film comedian in the world.

All of Arbuckle's films have one common denominator: they are all violent in their comedy. As great and original as Fatty was, his films are in no way comparable to those of Charlie Chaplin or Buster Keaton.

The day after their initial meeting, Buster took Fatty up on his offer and went back to the Talmadge Studios. Upon entering the studios on 48th Street, Buster could feel a rush of excitement building within him. That feeling stayed with Buster for his entire career, which was to last the rest of his life.

The film Fatty Arbuckle was working on, *The Butcher Boy*, was the first for his and Joseph Schenck's film company, Comique Film Corporation. As soon as Fatty saw Buster walk through the door, a huge smile graced his face. Greeting Buster with a mighty handshake and a solid pat on the back, Fatty asked, "are you ready?"

Not knowing what Fatty was talking about, Buster responded, "sure." Buster did not know that Fatty was talking about being "ready" to start filming.

The Butcher Boy is a rather simple film. Fatty plays a worker in a general store and, as he goes about his daily duties, he creates a series of very funny errors. Buster did not know that when he walked into the studio he was going to be the center of two of the films funniest scenes. As Fatty once said, "Buster stole the show the moment he got in front of the camera. He was actually sort of poetry in motion."

The first scene Buster ever appeared in is now considered to be a classic in film comedy. The scene is simple and uses molasses as the main prop. Buster sees a barrel of molasses sitting in the corner of the general store. As he walks over to it and looks inside, one of his feet gets stick in a puddle of the sweet, gooey brown syrup. As he attempts to free his stuck foot, he gets some molasses on one of his fingers, then licks it off. From the look on his face, it is obvious he likes the taste and then he decides to buy a small twenty-five cent bucket of it. As Fatty is filling a tin bucket for Buster, some of the molasses spills into Buster's pork-pie hat, which is sitting on the counter next to the bucket.

"When I put my hat back on to leave and get the bucket," Buster remembered, "he tipped his hat to say good-bye and when I tried to do the same thing, mine wouldn't move. Then I spilled the molasses all over and got both my feet caught in it."

To watch Buster free himself from this sticky mess, with the help of Arbuckle, is to witness an uproarious series of comedic events unparalleled in film comedy. This entire scene was accomplished in one take, something that Buster was profoundly proud of.

"My first scene in The Butcher Boy is the only movie comedy scene ever made with a newcomer that was photographed only once. In other words, my film debut was made without a single retake."

Another famous scene from The Butcher Boy has Fatty hitting Buster in the face with a bag of flour. To perform this scene, Buster had to be tutored by Fatty. This was the first of many film lessons the "fabulous fat man" gave Buster and was one of the reasons Buster always said, "Fatty was not just my best friend, he was also my best teacher."

The flour scene starts with Fatty and Al St. John (a co-star in the film) in the general store tossing around bags of flour. While this is going on, Buster is waiting in the wings for his entrance cue.

22

Roscoe had brown bags filled with flour, tied up, and ready for use. He lost no time in putting me to work. "As you come in the store," he explained, "I will be throwing some of these bags at St. John. He will duck and you will get one right in the face." It seemed like nothing after all the punishment I'd been taking from Pop all those years.

I asked Fatty, "How am I going to keep from flinching?" and he says, "Look away from me. When I say turn, it'll be there!"

It was!

Fatty Arbuckle was deadly accurate with everything he would throw and Buster found this out the hard way. As the bag of flour hit Buster when he walked through the door, the force literally upended him and as Buster put it, "he put my head where my feet should've been but weren't."

Buster was dazed, yet not injured. "Enough flour went up my nostrils and into my mouth to make one of mothers old-fashioned cakes. Because I was new to this business, I was politely picked up and dusted off. But it was fifteen minutes before I could breath freely again.

"Between one thing and another, I would say that my long career as 'The Human Mop' proved most useful from the start of my career as a movie actor. Everything about this new business I found exciting and fascinating."

By the time 1917 rolled around, Buster's new career as a "movie star" was a reality as The Butcher Boy opened in theaters across the nation. A total of two hundred theaters were showing the film, with thirty-five of those theaters in New York City alone. Even though the film received lukewarm reviews, Buster was given his share of kudos. As the trade magazine Moving Picture World wrote: "Buster Keaton does some excellent comedy falls . . . a whale of a comedy." The term "whale of a comedy" was directed toward Arbuckle who, at Paramount Studios, was known as the "Prince of Whales," a reference to his size and not to the royal family of Great Britain.

A couple of days after filming The Butcher Boy, Fatty took Buster back to the Talmadge Studios for a look at how moving pictures were made, from a technical point of view.

The first thing I did in the studio was to tear that camera to pieces. I had to know how that film got into the cutting room, what you did with it in there and how you made things match and now you finally got the picture together. I just watched Arbuckle do it and that's all there was to it.

Roscoe, no one who knew him on a personal basis called him Fatty, knew more about making movies than anyone I've ever known and because of his knowledge, I received a complete course in the art of filmmaking.

The main thing Buster was interested in was trick photography. Though he never used trick photography methods where his stunts were concerned, he did use it often to get a certain effect he was looking for in his films.

The money Buster was being paid working with Fatty Arbuckle was considerably less than what he was making on the vaudeville circuit, yet at no time did he ever complain about his forty dollar a week salary, a small salary which didn't last long. A couple of weeks after filming *The Butcher Boy*, Buster was given a raise to seventy-five dollars a week and soon after, another raise to one hundred and twenty-five dollars a week.

"Money," as Buster once put it, "is really nothing when you consider the fact that although you're working for peanuts, you're finding your goal, your niche in life."

From April to October of 1917, Buster Keaton made five films with Fatty Arbuckle. These films included *A Reckless Romeo*, *The Rough House*, *His Wedding Night*, *Oh Doctor*, and *Fatty at Coney Island*. All of these films, with the exception of *Fatty at Coney Island*, were filmed at the Talmadge Studios. *Fatty at Coney Island* was shot on location at Coney Island. One point of historical interest regarding *Fatty at Coney Island*: this is the first and only time Buster Keaton ever smiled on film.

During the filming of *The Rough House*, Buster received not another raise, but an artistic promotion. "I was only with Roscoe about three pictures when I became his assistant director. That was the guy who sat alongside the camera and watched scenes that he was in and I ended up just about co-directing with him."

Figure 2-2 – Buster, Fatty, and Al St. John in a still from the 1918 comedy short, Out West. *Fatty's films were known for their violent nature.*

During the latter part of October 1917, Fatty Arbuckle, Buster Keaton, and the entire Comique Film Corporation departed New York City for the sunny skies and palm tree-lined streets of California and a rising new community called Long Beach. They took over a small studio being run by the Horkheimer Brothers located on the corner of Sixth and Alimitos Streets. Within days of getting settled, the studio was renamed the Comique Film Corporation Studio. The new California show business community was elated at Fatty's arrival in the land of sunshine and hype. All the stars who were participating in the making of Hollywood were stopping by to bestow their blessings on the "fat man" of film comedy.

The most famous of these stars was Charlie Chaplin, one of Fatty's best friends and a former Mack Sennett stable-mate. On meeting Chaplin for the first time, Buster said he was "awestruck." To commemorate their meeting, Buster had a photo taken of himself with the "little tramp."

Upon moving to Southern California, Buster took more than his clothes and personal belongings; he also took his parents, brother, and sister. Even though Joseph Keaton still believed moving pictures to be "degrading to truly talented performers," whenever Buster would offer him a role in one of his and Fatty's films, Joseph would accept saying, "movie acting is all right if Buster is directing me."

By 1918, three-fourths of all films were being produced in Southern California. By 1920, the fifth largest industry in the United States was filmmaking.

Buster made about nine films with Fatty Arbuckle in California; the actual count is unknown due to some being lost and others destroyed. The films accounted for are: *A Country Hero*, *Out West*, *The Bell Boy*, *Moonshine*, *Good Night Nurse!*, *The Crook*, *Back Stage*, *The Hayseed*, and *The Garage*. All of these films are in the typical Arbuckle style of pure energetic hilarity.

The working arrangements Buster and Fatty made for themselves were grueling as their contracts stated they were to make one film every eight weeks. None of their films was scripted, everything was ad-libbed. They would simply start with an idea and go from there. As an example, if Buster and Fatty were working on a film and suddenly changed their mind regarding the locale, they would change in midfilming. This is evident while watching some of the films made in Long Beach when all of a sudden one film turns into another. This change is done gracefully and is not really noticeable unless you are aware of it. Buster continued this manner of filming after he left Arbuckle and ventured out on his own.

The film *Moonshine* proved to be a pivotal point in the career of Buster Keaton. Though he received no credit as the director of the film, this was in fact his directorial debut and the result is the best of the Arbuckle/Keaton films.

Moonshine was filmed on location at the Mad Dog Gulch in the San Gabriel Canyon of Los Angeles. Buster and Fatty portray two G-men who are searching for a family of moonshiners. As director of *Moonshine*, Buster put his new knowledge of film technique and trick photography to use. At one point in the film, Buster opens the door of a large touring car and his fellow agents get out. Fifty-four men issue forth, one right after the other. The sight of this seemingly never-ending stream of agents sent the audiences into fits of laughter. This trick was accomplished by a not overly complicated method of masking over one half of the camera lens, shooting, rewinding the film to its starting point, then masking the other portion of the lens and shooting again. Buster also utilized a car which had been cleverly prepared in advance in order to display the necessary jiggling quality which would convince the audience that what they were seeing was real. The audience loved these tricks and the critics raved about their ingenuity. This was also the first time trick photography was used in the art of the cinema.

Working together as closely as they did, it is amazing that Fatty and Buster never had a major clash, either personally or artistically.

"I can only remember one thing he ever said that I disagreed with," Buster said of his working relationship with Arbuckle. " 'You must never forget,' he told me, 'that the average mentality of our movie audience is twelve years old!'"

Fatty Arbuckle and Buster Keaton loved to play practical jokes on unsuspecting people. Perhaps the most famous of these practical jokes was one which was played on the diminutive Adolph Zukor of Paramount Studios. Zukor was invited to an intimate supper party given by Arbuckle for some of his close friends. In order for the complete plot to work, all of the guests had to be perfectly aware of what was going to happen. Among the guests were young ladies then appearing in films: Anna Q. Nilsson, Bebe Daniels, and Buster's friends Alice Lake and Viola Dana. No one seems to remember the names of the male guests, with the exception of Sid Graumen, the founder of the Chinese Theater on Hollywood Boulevard which bore his name for many years. Buster was always very proud of the way this practical joke turned out and was always more than willing to recount it.

The way we had it planned, I was to play a bumbling butler. Everything I did was wrong and everything I touched I'd ruin. We had no worry of Zukor recognizing me as I was not yet that recognizable but to be on the safe side, we had the lights dimmed slightly.

When it came time for me to serve dinner is when the fun really began. The first course I served was shrimp. Against proper protocol, I served the men first. Seeing this, Roscoe screamed, "You stupid numbskull, don't you know better than to serve the men first?" So I collected the shrimp from the men, some half-eaten, and gave them to the ladies. The look on Zukor's face as I was doing this was of pure shock.

Next was the soup. As Roscoe was telling everyone how good the soup was going to be, I went into the kitchen. After silently counting to twenty, I started to throw some pots, pans, and silverware around the kitchen. Once this noise died down, I took pots of water and soaked myself. Dripping from head to toe, I went back into the dining room and without saying a word, I removed some soup bowls. The guests who knew what was going on continued eating their shrimp but Zukor looked like he was in a state of shock. As I was taking the bowls away, Roscoe was screaming at me, "You idiot! You stupid idiot! It is impossible to get decent help in this town! I've had it! I'm quitting pictures and moving as far away from here as possible!" When Zukor heard this, he turned white as a sheet. You see, he had just signed Roscoe to a contract and had invested a lot of money in him.

Once Roscoe's acting tirade was over, I came back into the dining room. Bebe Daniels, who was sitting next to Roscoe, asked me if I would pour her some ice water. Taking the pitcher off the table, I walked over to where she was sitting. While pouring the water, I feigned to be flirting and not paying attention to what I was doing. Instead of pouring the water in her glass, I was pouring it on Roscoe's lap. Once again Roscoe started screaming, "Idiot! Idiot! Idiot!"

The *coup de gras* of our joke on Zukor was one that took a lot of planning. As things settled down after the ice water episode, Roscoe announced it was time for the main course which was a huge turkey. As I was coming out of the kitchen with this huge bird, I dropped the towel that was draped over my left arm. Holding the platter with the turkey in one hand, I bent over to pick up the towel. Just as I bent over, another culprit in our scheme pushed open the swinging kitchen door and knocked me and the bird on the floor. What transpired next was nothing short of a greased pig contest. Both of us were trying to grab the turkey and what with its oily skin, it was damned near impossible. The real funny thing here was not our trying to get a grasp on the bird, it was the look on everyone's faces. Even those who were in on the joke were watching with wide eyes and open mouths. You talk about slapstick comedy, this was it at its best.

Once we got the turkey back onto the platter, I did what came naturally. I started to wipe it off. Of course I was wiping it off with the dirty towel that fell off my arm that started this mess in the first place. At this point Roscoe jumped out of his seat, grabbed me around my neck as if he was going to choke me and dragged me into the kitchen where we both started to laugh uncontrollably. Once we gained control of ourselves we both started to throw pots, pans, and other stuff around and Roscoe began yelling threats at me. To everyone in the dining room it sounded as if I was being killed, which is the point we were trying to get across. After a couple of minutes, Roscoe went to join his guests and in a calm and satisfied voice told them, "The idiot will no longer be a problem."

After a couple of minutes, I sneaked up the back stairs to one of the guest rooms to clean up and change clothes. About two hours later, I picked up a telephone and called downstairs to Roscoe. Keeping the act going for Zukor, Roscoe invited me over for some dessert, to which I happily accepted. Appearing at the front door, I was greeted like a long lost cousin and I could tell from the look on Zukor's face that he didn't recognize me as being the bumbling butler. Finally, Sid Grauman pointed out to Zukor how much I resembled the butler and then the cat was out of the bag. Throughout his entire life, Adolph Zukor never let me forget this night.

Not long after the Zukor party, it was Marcus Loew's turn to be the butt of an Arbuckle/Keaton practical joke. As Buster told the story, it involved his pretending to be Roscoe's chauffeur. The occasion of this deception arose when Loew, on one of his rare visits to Los Angeles from New York, ran into Arbuckle as he was leaving the Metro Studios.

Arbuckle offered him a ride back to his hotel. Loew accepted gladly and, with Buster at the wheel, the car took off on an incredibly high speed tour of the entire area around Hollywood. The main point of this exercise was for Buster to stall the car at the exact point on the trolley tracks where it could easily remain while the express trolleys whizzed by it on both sides.

The pranksters had carefully checked out the length of Arbuckle's car and knew to an inch exactly where it could be stalled for maximum safety and terror. Loew was even more frightened of getting out of the car than of staying in it as the trolley's screamed past. Arbuckle occupied the time abusing his stupid lout of a chauffeur for choosing "this place of all places" to stall the car. Eventually, Buster started the car up and drove to Loew's hotel by every crooked, bumpy road he could find, at a full sixty miles an hour. Loew was completely shaken up by the mad drive, and Arbuckle kept offering his profuse apologies for his idiot of a chauffeur. When they finally got to his hotel, Loew and Arbuckle relaxed a bit over a drink in Loew's room. There was soon a knock on the door and Buster, minus his fake mustache and without his driving goggles, entered the room with a broad knowing smile.

In June of 1918, Buster took his act back on the road in the service of the United States Army. As a soldier, Buster's first and only stop was France. While stationed in France, his main duty was entertaining the troops, which he did with great joy and gusto. Buster never felt the army was interested in him because when they handed him his uniform, it was two sizes too big. For his size six feet, they gave him size eight shoes. As Buster once noted, "My army days were a complete farce."

Even though his army career lasted only seven months, there were some eventful times. Due to reasons which have never been explained, as Buster was serving his hitch with Uncle Sam, he received an ear infection which rendered him almost completely deaf. It was his lack of hearing which almost got him killed before the army sent him home.

On a stormy Parisian night as he was walking on the base, a guard yelled at him to "Halt!" Buster did not hear the guard and kept walking. Again the guard yelled, "Halt!" As before, Buster did not hear him and continued on his way. Finally the guard fired a warning shot. This caught Buster's attention as the warning shot just missed his head. Three days after this episode, the army thought it advantageous to both them and Buster to send him home. Buster did not object.

Upon his return to America, Buster was engulfed with film offers and contracts. Two of the most lucrative offers came from Jack Warner of Warner Brothers and William Fox from Twentieth-Century Fox. Both of these offers were for the same amount, one thousand dollars a week. Buster turned both offers down and returned to Fatty Arbuckle, Joseph Schenck, and the Comique Film Corporation at a salary of two hundred and fifty dollars per week.

After making three more films, the team of Fatty Arbuckle and Buster Keaton broke up. Joseph Schenck sold Fatty's contract to Famous-Players-Lasky, which was headed by Adolph Zukor. Keaton didn't shed any tears over this development because Joseph Schenck, on a deal consummated with a handshake, offered Buster his own film company and studio: the old Chaplin Studios, later renamed the Keaton Studios.

When one thinks back on the great comedy teams in film history, a couple of names always come to mind: Laurel & Hardy, Abbott & Costello, Martin & Lewis, the Marx Brothers, and the Ritz Brothers. Without a doubt, though, the funniest and most original comedy team in the history of the American cinema was Roscoe "Fatty" Arbuckle and Buster Keaton. To prove this point, all it takes is a onetime viewing of these two comedic legends who perfected the fine art of film comedy.

In September of 1921, a scandal brought Hollywood to its knees and changed the life of Joseph Francis "Buster" Keaton. This was an event Keaton termed "the day the laughter died." To this day, the scandal of 1921 is still referred to as "the Arbuckle scandal."

With Famous-Players-Lasky (later becoming Paramount), Fatty Arbuckle became an unhappy superstar. In his autobiography titled *I Blow My Own Horn*, Jesse Lasky said of Arbuckle, "he was conscientious, hard-working, intelligent, always agreeable and anxious to please." Some, including Buster, believed the "always agreeable and anxious to please" is what caused Fatty Arbuckle's demise and un-timely death.

Everyone who deals with trivia, studies Hollywood lore, or con-siders himself a film historian, has heard or read of the infamous Arbuckle scandal. There are as many stories regarding this incident as there are neon lights on Broadway.

The Arbuckle scandal took place on Labor Day, September 5, 1921, in San Francisco. To understand and comprehend this scandal, requires going back four years to March 6, 1918, at Mishawn Manor in Boston, Massachusetts. On this night there was a party to celebrates Fatty's signing of a huge contract with Jesse Lasky and his company, Famous-Players-Lasky. The party, or blowout as it was referred to, was held at Brownie Kennedy's Roadhouse, where a multitude of female *wanna-be's* were employed to provide "entertainment."

At this party, Fatty spied a girl he found to be to his liking. With bootlegged liquor flowing and inhibitions disappearing, Fatty grabbed this girl and started to dance with her. Within minutes Fatty and "his" girl were dancing on a table while taking off their clothes, all of this to the delight of the guests including Adolph Zukor, Jesse Lasky, and Joseph Schenck.

As the revelers got louder and more than a little destructive, the police were summoned. When the police arrived on the scene, they were witnesses to what has been described as an orgy. Nobody was arrested, but citations were handed out.

With Fatty Arbuckle considered to be a "family act," Jesse Lasky was terrified about what would happen if word of the Boston inci-dent leaked out to the press. Because of his fear, Lasky got together with Adolph Zukor and Joseph Schenck and came up with one hundred thousand dollars to pay off Boston's District Attorney and the Mayor, James Curly. Even though charges were dropped, lessons were not learned.

Because the Boston party was squashed with Lasky's "hush mon-ey," the events were never brought up during the trials in San Francisco four years later.

Buster Keaton's reaction to the Arbuckle scandal was pure disbe-lief. Did Roscoe "Fatty" Arbuckle rape and kill actress Virginia Rappe? To his dying day, Buster Keaton loudly proclaimed, "No!" Was this an effort on Buster's part to cover-up a best friend's memory? Or was it that Buster didn't know all the facts behind the incident and was going on gut instinct and what he'd been told? The answer to these questions seems to be all of the above. The only thing Buster knew about the Arbuckle scandal was what he'd been told by friends who were at the Labor Day party in San Francisco. Buster was not at the party. He was invited but, due to filming schedules, he was unable to attend.

The following is how Buster relayed the incident on the many times he was asked about this infamous Hollywood scandal. The story he always recounted differed in words, yet had the same basic content, time after time. It is what Keaton believed to be the truth.

Roscoe had just completed his third consecutive film with Famous-Players-Lasky and hadn't had a day off in months. Wanting to get away from anything resembling a studio or film location, Roscoe decided he needed a little playtime, a short vacation. Gathering a few of his buddies, including Lowell Sherman and Fred Fishbach, Roscoe drove up to San Francisco for a long Labor Day weekend of partying.

In San Francisco, Roscoe got a suite at his favorite hotel, the St. Francis. Since Roscoe knew a lot of people in this area, he had many contacts who were willing to supply him with bootlegged liquor. While in his suite with Sherman and Fishbach, he heard Virginia Rappe and some of her friends were also in town and staying at another hotel. Roscoe wanted to get a party going and invited Rappe, her girlfriends, and her manager, Al Seminacher, to his St. Francis suite.

Virginia Rappe did not have the best reputation in Hollywood. She was a bit player known for getting drunk, going crazy, and taking off her clothes. She was by no means petite at five-feet seven-inches tall and weighing one hundred and thirty-five pounds. She was untalented and would do anything to get any part in any film.

While Roscoe and the guys were drinking their whiskey, Rappe was guzzling down orange juice and gin, a drink known as an Orange Blossom. Living up to her reputation, after a couple of drinks, she started to strip. Before long she got sick and was, at Roscoe's request, put into the bedroom by a couple of her friends.

A little while later, being the caring person he was, Roscoe went into the bedroom to check up on her. Rappe always had a crush on Roscoe, so to make sure she wasn't feigning an illness to get him into the bedroom, he took a piece of ice from his drink and placed it against her thigh to see if he could get a reaction. When she didn't show any emotion, Roscoe called the hotel doctor while Rappe's friends undressed her and put her in the bathtub.

After the hotel doctor checked Rappe out, she was taken to a hospital where she died a few days later. Before she died, according to one of her friends, Rappe said, "Roscoe hurt me, he hurt me!"

On her friends' word, the San Francisco District Attorney brought charges against Roscoe for murder.

"I'll tell you this," Buster said, "Roscoe was as guilty of that murder as I was."

The jury acquitted him of the murder, but for whatever reasons, Hollywood did not. Because of this District Attorney's zeal to make a name for himself by prosecuting a big Hollywood movie star, he ruined Roscoe's life. Roscoe was blackballed from the very industry he dedicated his life to.

This was Buster's account of the Arbuckle scandal from the information he received from friends, including Lowell Sherman, Fred Fishback, and Roscoe himself.

The true facts of the Arbuckle scandal differ greatly from Buster's account. According to court transcripts and some never before released documents, the facts regarding the infamous scandal are as follows.

Regarding Buster's version, he was correct about Fatty getting away after months of making full-length films without a break. However, as far as facts are concerned, Buster's story ends there.

The facts show that, in an effort to enjoy himself for a few days, Fatty Arbuckle decided to take a few friends with him to San Francisco for a Labor Day weekend. This was also a chance for Fatty to try out his new Pierce-Arrow automobile. The friends accompanying Fatty were Lowell Sherman, Fred Fishbach, Virginia Rappe, Bambina Maude Delmont, and about five Famous-Player-Lasky showgirls. As the men jumped into Fatty's Pierce-Arrow, the women clamored into a second car and then they all drove from Los Angeles to San Francisco – a full days drive.

Contrary to Buster's account, Fatty did know Virginia Rappe and knew her well. Fatty was enamored with Rappe and often offered her starring roles in many of his films. Virginia Rappe turned down Fatty professionally as well as personally. Rejection was not easy for Fatty Arbuckle to take, as his ego matched his girth in size.

Virginia Rappe was not at all the ogre Buster made her out to be. Virginia Rappe was a very beautiful young lady with flowing brown hair, eyes which pleaded "take me" and a smile both warn and genuine. She was known as a "bedhopper," doing this only to advance her career (a common practice for fledgling starlets) and, as rumor had it, she gave most of the crew at Mack Sennett Studios the crabs to such a point that Sennett himself ordered the entire company shut down and fumigated.

Virginia Rappe, at the time of the Arbuckle scandal, was well on her way to stardom, as she was to return to Hollywood after this infamous Labor Day weekend to get her first starring role in a major motion picture from Twentieth-Century Fox.

Upon their arrival in San Francisco, Fatty Arbuckle, Lowell Sherman, and Fred Fishbach checked into the St. Francis Hotel. Arbuckle sent the ladies to the Palace Hotel (now the Sheraton-Palace Hotel). At the St. Francis, Fatty reserved a couple of suites on the twelfth floor. Soon after being escorted to the suites by the bellboy, Fatty made some calls to his connections for bootlegged liquor and the partying began. This was all on Saturday, September 3, two days before Labor Day.

On Labor Day, September 5, the party was still going full-force. For the entire weekend, Fatty's suites on the twelfth floor resembled an open-house. The party-goers realized this was their last day of frolicking before heading back to Hollywood and they were letting loose with the liquor flowing at a very rapid pace. While the men were drinking whiskey and scotch, Rappe and the other ladies were drinking Orange Blossoms. With the party getting more rambunctious, the women began to take their clothes off and dance from one suite to another.

A little after noon, Fatty, who was feeling no pain, grabbed Rappe and danced her into the bedroom of suite 1221. Waltzing into the bedroom with the giggling Rappe in his arms, Fatty looked to where some of his friends were sitting and said, "this is the chance I've waited for, for a long time." Grinning from ear to ear, he closed the bedroom door and locked it.

What went on behind the locked bedroom door only Fatty

Arbuckle and Virginia Rappe knew for sure. However, what was overheard going on in the bedroom is part of the official court transcripts. According to Bambina Maude Delmont, Rappe's friend, "screams rang out and there was some rather weird noises coming from the bedroom."

When Fatty came out of the bedroom, his clothes were ripped and in an agitated voice he told Delmont, "go in and get her dressed and take her back to the Palace Hotel." As Fatty was talking to Delmont, loud crying and screaming was coming from Rappe in the bedroom. "Tell her," Fatty shouted, "to shut up or I'll throw her out the window!"

When Delmont and another friend, Alice Blake, entered the room, they found it to be a mess. In court, Alice Blake testified: "We tried to dress her, but found her clothing torn to shreds. Her shirtwaist, under clothes and even her stockings were ripped and torn so that one could hardly recognize what garments they were."

In Delmont's testimony, she stated: "She was on the bed nude and in a great deal of pain. She kept telling me, 'I'm dying, I'm dying! He hurt me!'"

One of the ladies called for a doctor using the telephone in the suite bedroom (it is uncertain whether Delmont or Blake made the call as neither could remember when questioned in court, however, one of them did make the call; it was not Fatty). Rappe was rushed to the hospital. At the hospital, Virginia Rappe lapsed into a coma and never regained consciousness. Once again, according to court transcripts, the last words Rappe spoke were to one of the nurses and those words were, "Fatty Arbuckle did this to me. Please make sure he doesn't get away with it!"

On September 10, 1921, Virginia Rappe died.

According to San Francisco Deputy Coroner, Michael Brown, the autopsy showed no visible signs of rape. This did not mean a rape did not occur, it simply meant there were no traces of semen found. The cause of death was attributed to peritonitis (inflammation of the internal surface of the abdomen and viscera within). This could have been caused, according to Deputy Coroner Brown, by a perverse sexual act. (The rumor has always been that Fatty raped with a cola or champagne bottle. In a statement not in the court transcripts but attributed to one of Fatty's wives, he had been "sexually impotent since 1917." This has never been substantiated as being either a true or false statement).

Deputy Coroner Brown's determination of the "cause of death" from peritonitis was not a simple determination to come by. Brown was not initially the coroner doing the autopsy; that job was being done by another coroner (name unknown). Brown got involved after receiving a strange phone call (the caller believed to have been Adolph Zukor) regarding the autopsy of Virginia Rappe's body. This call was actually an attempt to cover up the whole incident (as what had happened four years prior in Boston). As Brown was leaving his office to confer with his immediate supervisor, Chief Coroner T.B. LeLand, he came across an orderly carrying a jar containing the mangled bladder of Virginia Rappe. The orderly was on his way to the hospital incinerator.

San Francisco Police Detectives Tom Regan and Griffith Kennedy were the detectives assigned to the case. After doing their preliminary investigating and interviews, they charged Roscoe "Fatty" Arbuckle with the crimes of first degree murder and, for good measure, rape.

Once the newspapers got hold of the story, the banner headlines were as if printed in neon. From the Sunday, September 12, 1921, *Los Angeles Examiner*: ARBUCKLE HELD FOR MURDER!

Another newspaper headline blared: ARBUCKLE ORGY! RAPER DANCES WHILE VICTIM DIES!

One part of Buster's recollection of the Arbuckle scandal is definitely true, this was in fact "the day the laughter died." There is only one word to express how Hollywood was feeling . . . shocked!

The movie-going public was outraged. In theaters all across the country which were showing Arbuckle films, people were throwing things at the screen, climbing up onto the stages and trying to rip Fatty's flickering image, and, in one case, a man fired a gun at the screen every time Fatty appeared. All theaters were being vandalized in one form or another. It was determined to be the best move for all involved to withdraw Arbuckle's films until everything in San Francisco was over. It never really was over and these were the last times Fatty Arbuckle ever appeared on the silver screen.

As the Arbuckle case came to trial, the *Los Angeles Examiner* gave this account of their first page:

FATTY'S SMILING GAIETY
TURNS TO SULLEN GLOOM!

Fatty Arbuckle, known the world over for his grin and antics, is smiling no more. In his cell and in court at San Francisco, where he faces a first degree murder charge following the death of Virginia Rappe, pretty film actress, Arbuckle is living in gloom. Here are extracts from the story of his appearance yesterday in court proceedings that show how life has changed for the debonair comedian.

Arbuckle came into court, faultlessly groomed, but unable to conceal under a mask of "well-dressed leisure" the concern written largely on his features.

Dressed in a natty blue suit, freshly barbered and wearing a new tie and fresh shirt, he arrived at the inquest room at 2:15 P.M. A detective walked on either side of him and he was seated in the rear of the room with other witnesses.

He tried to avoid the court order to stand trial, begging that he be allowed to remain in his cell and away from the crowds, but the court was obdurate.

As he entered the courtroom through a side door, a battery of flashlight guns went off having somewhat of the staccato cadence of a machine gun battery.

Arbuckle was mindful of this, but when the court advised him that he would have to stand trial on a charge of murder, his head dropped and he could not keep his hands from trembling.

Arbuckle's lawyer attempted to plea bargain the charge of first degree murder to manslaughter. When San Francisco District Attorney, Matt Brady, hesitated on this move, Adolph Zukor called him and offered him one million dollars to drop all charges against Arbuckle. This attempted bribe made Brady all the more intent on getting a conviction of Fatty for both the rape and first degree murder charges.

There were three trials with the first one beginning in November of 1921. After numerous testimonies and forty hours of jury deliberation in the first trial, the jury voted ten-to-two in favor of an acquittal. The judge declared a mistrial.

In the second trial, the jury came back with another ten-to-two verdict, this time for a conviction. The judge for this trial dismissed the jury.

The third and final trial was a judicial joke. The judge in this third trial dismissed most of the evidence and made it a part of his instructions to the jury to take into serious consideration the fact there was no murder weapon to be introduced into evidence and that each witness who testified against Arbuckle was a member of the Labor Day party and all were drinking, thus their accountability could only be taken with a grain of salt.

When the third jury came back with their verdict, it was unanimous. Roscoe "Fatty" Arbuckle was innocent of all charges. The foreman of the jury read this statement after the trial:

"Acquittal is not enough for Roscoe Arbuckle. We feel a grave injustice has been done him and there was not the slightest proof to connect him in any way with the commission of any crime."

Arbuckle's reaction to the acquittal was, "This is a most solemn moment in my life. My innocence of the hideous charges preferred against me has been proved. I am truly grateful to my fellow men and women. My life has been devoted to the production of clean pictures for the happiness of children. I shall try to enlarge my field of usefulness so that my art shall have wider service."

Even though Fatty Arbuckle was acquitted for the murder and rape of Virginia Rappe, he was actually the loser in the long run. Paramount immediately cancelled his three million dollar contract and all of his unreleased films were destroyed. Roscoe "Fatty" Arbuckle was free, but he was also destroyed.

Because of the Arbuckle scandal, Hollywood took to the cause of morals and started the Hays Commission under the leadership of Will Hays, a Presbyterian minister. The Hays Commission had to approve every film before it was released. If the film did not live up to the commissions high morals, it was sent back to the studio to have the specific scenes in question reshot. The Hays Commission lasted twenty years and is the forefather of today's motion picture rating process.

When Fatty got back to Hollywood, his name was taboo. All the studios, whether large or small independents, banned him because of what they feared would be retribution by the public.

Buster Keaton succeeded in getting Fatty Arbuckle back into the business by changing his name and putting him behind the camera, not in front of it. The name Fatty used was William B. Goodrich (originally it was to have been Will B. Good, but it was turned down as sounding "too phoney"). Under the Goodrich name, Fatty did direct a few films, but he was not happy and gave it up, essentially going into a forced retirement.

On June 28, 1933, Roscoe "Fatty" Arbuckle died an alcoholic, broke, and a Hollywood has-been.

3

THE KEATON STUDIO

As the 1920's were beginning to roar, Buster Keaton was on his own. Unlike other comedians who attempted to go solo, Buster had a leg up on his competitors (with the exception of Charlie Chaplin) because he, like Chaplin, had his own studio.

The Keaton Studio was purchased for Buster by Joseph Schenck, his best friend, mentor, and future brother-in-law. Throughout his career in Hollywood, Joseph Schenck was considered an honorable and trustworthy man, which, at that time, was a rarity. It can be said the most important person in Buster's career, other than Roscoe "Fatty" Arbuckle, was Joseph Schenck. Whereas Schenck helped create the legend of Buster Keaton, he also helped to destroy him in later years.

Under Joseph Schenck, Buster Keaton became an all-around film man, showing his genius as a writer, director, and comic actor. Much has been written and documented regarding Buster's acting ability, but outside of the Hollywood community, his directorial abilities have been ignored. Buster Keaton, the film director, was a perfectionist. The usual look of his films captured the era of the story, from the locations to the costumes, all of which he designed himself.

Buster understood that filmmaking is a collaborative art and early on assembled a team that worked for him for many years, helping carry out his comedic visions. This team included Clyde Bruckman, a writer and gag man credited as co-director of *The General*; technical wizard Fred Gaboure, who helped Buster construct his brilliant sight gags, such as the house frame in *Steamboat Bill, Jr.* which collapsed on the imperturbable Buster and barely missed crushing him to death; and cameraman Elgin Lessley, who worked with Buster in extending the possibilities of film. Together they created the multiple exposure in *The Playhouse*, in which nine Busters appear in blackface on the screen singing and dancing in unison, and the first combination of live and animated action, which occurred in *The Three Ages*. In *Sherlock, Jr.*, Buster himself used techniques of film, montage, and jump-cuts to demonstrate the hero's shifts between illusion and reality.

As a director, Buster Keaton did not just work with actors and animals, he also worked with the forces of nature in the destructive forms of cyclones, fires, floods, and raging rivers. There was also the mechanical powers of man, including trains, ships, and even whole armies on the march.

Possibly the greatest tribute given to Buster Keaton the film director, comes from David Thomson's book, *A Biographical Dictionary of Film*, in which he writes the following:

> It has been argued, with justice, that his films are beautiful, which means that their comedy is expressed in photography that is creative, witty and excited by the appearance of things.
>
> Perhaps the explanation is Keaton's pleasure in authenticity and the way in which his own supercilious screen persona dominated the direction. Unlike Chaplin who tended to reinvent the world of Victorian melodrama, and unlike those comics who merely dressed up vaudeville routines, Keaton conceived of films specifically American.
>
> That is what strikes us today as the most admirable thing about Keaton: the scene capacity for absorbing frustration and turning a blind eye to fear and failure.

Joseph Schenck had complete faith, trust, and confidence in Buster and to prove this point, Buster had unlimited freedom to do whatever he wished or deemed necessary to make a film successful. At no time, under Schenck, was Buster Keaton ever put on a budget and this was something for which Buster was always grateful.

*Figure 3-1 – Buster Keaton's first studio publicity shot. He was
in his late twenties at the time of this photo.*

The hallmark of a Buster Keaton comedy is the energy of its central character, with all the animation others display on their faces being expressed by Buster in a headlong ballet of acrobatics which he performs himself, in long-shot and without any cuts. There is no trickery about the log-bouncing scene in *The General*, or Buster's high-dive from the top of the ship in *The Navigator*, or the vaulting ease with which he skims down the riverboat decks in *Steamboat Bill, Jr.* and all the way up again a moment later. In *Spite Marriage*, a single shot follows his desperate battle with the villains from one end of a luxury yacht to the other where, flung into the ocean, he is carried by the current back to the lifeboat trailing the yacht at the stern and hauls himself over the side to resume the struggle. During his career, as he often reported in later years, he broke every bone in his body. In *The Paleface*, he dropped eighty-five feet from a suspension bridge into a net, he nearly drowned under a waterfall in *Our Hospitality*, and, during a train sequence in *Sherlock, Jr.*, he actually broke his neck, yet continued stunting and filming despite months of blinding headaches.

However, it is not as a stuntman, but as a unique tragicomic personality that Buster Keaton survives as the most fascinating of the silent screen comedians. As if pursuing a redefinition of his private experiences, his films illustrate the purgatorial struggles of an inconsequential reject, habitually bullied by a scornful father or disdainfully ignored by an unappreciative girl, who by sheer persistence and ingenious courage (physical danger never seemed to occur to him as a possibility) battles his way to social acceptability. In the tenacious war against the forces of evil, his endurance and his enigmatic face give nothing away – no promises, no denials – he is one of the screens great martyrs.

The Buster Keaton legend began on September 7, 1920. This was the date *One Week*, his first starring film, was released. *One Week* proved to be an auspicious debut for Buster, as it is the perfect comedy. The story-line for *One Week* is basic. Buster Keaton and Sybil Seeley play newlyweds. For a wedding present they receive a "do-it-yourself" kit for a house, as well as a lot to build it on. "My former rival," Buster recalled, "for the girl's hand changed the instruction numbers on the crates. When I put the house up, it was the darndest thing you ever saw. After it was finished, I found out I built it on the wrong lot." Buster got the idea for *One Week* after watching a documentary on how you could build a portable home in seven days.

In *One Week*, Buster uses a gag which he again used in a later film, *Steamboat Bill, Jr.* This gag is the one where a house front falls down on him and he is saved because a window is open, leaving him standing and untouched with a look of pure amazement on his somber face.

One Week is also the first film where Buster shows his love of using trains in his films and gags. In one of the most memorable sight gags in *One Week* is when Buster and Sybil are moving their "erected" house from one lot to another via a hook-up on the back of their car. As they cross the railroad tracks, the house breaks free from the car and gets stuck on the tracks. At that moment a train comes speeding down the tracks, heading directly for the house. Just as the train is about to plow right through their dream house, Buster and Sybil close their eyes. As was Buster's way of always wanting to fool his audience, the train and the house are on separate tracks, and the train speeds by doing nothing but creating a strong breeze. Taking a deep breath, the newlyweds are relieved. Unknown to the audience, another train is steaming down the tracks from the opposite direction of the first one. This train plows through the house. The element of surprise here is tremendous (even after viewing it over one hundred times).

There is one scene in *One Week* which really had heads turning and eyes bulging, and it had nothing to do with a famous Buster Keaton stunt. This scene takes place in the bathroom of the "built-by-the-numbers" house. Sybil Seeley is taking a bath while Buster is comically working on the outside of the house. While in the bathtub, items start falling off the walls and from the ceiling causing Seeley to scream in fright. Hearing her screams, Buster climbs a makeshift ladder (which is actually a picket fence) and climbs up the side of the house to the bathroom window. As the scene switches back into the bathroom, we again see Seeley in the bathtub and it is very apparent she is nude from the waist up. In 1920, this scene caused quite a stir and almost resulted in the film being banned.

The first injury Buster suffered in his film career occurred while filming *One Week*. In preparation for one of the gags, a fall from the second story of the house to the ground, a large hole was dug where Buster was to land. The hole was then filled with straw and foam and then grass was put on top of everything to give the area an appearance of normality. When it came time to do the gag, not all went as planned.

As Buster fell and landed on this "fixed" piece of gardening, he fell right through everything and landed with a jolt on the packed dirt at the bottom of the hole. Even though Buster was shaken by the impact of the fall, he still got up and finished the day's filming.

By the end of the day, Buster felt immense pain in his left elbow. He took off his shirt and saw his elbow and the surrounding area had swelled to about twice its normal size. By the time he was ready to go home, his back and both arms were swollen to their maximum girth. On doctors orders, Buster was forced to stop filming for a couple of weeks, something which he frowned upon greatly.

This was the first of numerous injuries Buster suffered in his career, many of which almost proved fatal.

All of the sight gags in *One Week* were engineered by Buster and no trick photography was used, which is amazing when you consider the intricacy of the gags executed. According to many film historians and critic's, *One Week* is the greatest starring film debut by an actor in the history of the American cinema.

A little over a month after the release of *One Week*, Metro released Buster's first full-length film, *The Saphead*. The first review of *The Saphead* appeared in *Variety* and read in part," . . . Buster Keaton's quiet work in this picture is a revelation!"

The Saphead was a film which was rewritten for Buster. Originally it was entitled *The New Henrietta*. The script was brought to the attention of Marcus Loew, owner of Metro Studios and a nationwide chain of movie theaters, by Douglas Fairbanks, Sr. and Mary Pickford. After reading the script for *The New Henrietta*, Loew asked Fairbanks what he thought of it, to which Fairbanks replied, "It's great and you have the perfect man for the lead right here, a fellow named Buster Keaton."

Marcus Loew took Douglas Fairbanks' recommendation to heart, had the script rewritten especially to showcase Buster's talents and changed the title to *The Saphead*. With its release, *The Saphead* became one of Metro's biggest box office hits of 1920.

The Saphead is not one of Buster's better films, but it does introduce the type of character Buster became known for: a helpless, naive man who almost begs to be taken advantage of. Some of Buster's other characters who also display this persona are Rollo Treadway in The Navigator, Alfred Butler in Battling Butler, and the unnamed character he portrays in One Week.

The story-line for The Saphead deals with Bertie (Buster's character) attempting to save his father's brokerage firm from going under as he buys all the "for sale" shares of a gold mine called The New Henrietta Gold Mine. This story line was not understood by the majority of the film-going public due to the fact it deals with Wall Street and the New York Stock Exchange, two items which were foreign to the average film-goer in 1920. Buster's performance in The Saphead proved to the public and critics alike that he was not a "one film wonder."

In addition to One Week and The Saphead, 1920 also saw the release of three other Buster Keaton films. They were Convict 13, The Scarecrow, and Neighbors. All three of these films have the Buster Keaton touch of physical comedy, but, of the three, only The Scarecrow contains a truly memorable scene. In this scene, Buster marries Sybil Seeley (his leading lady in both One Week and Convict 13). After the ceremony, they both hop on a motorcycle, with Seeley getting into the sidecar. They take off for what looks to be a typical "happily-ever-after" honeymoon. As the Buster Keaton scenario often was, the obvious is not the conclusion. In the course of this motorcycle ride, they plunge into a river and . . . end of honeymoon.

Buster's first year on his own, 1920, was both a personal and critical triumph. As 1920 was giving way to 1921, the name Buster Keaton was becoming synonymous with the term "comedy greatness."

The year 1921 was very busy for Buster Keaton. He had seven films released and married the first of what would be three wives, Natalie Talmadge.

Buster's first release of 1921 was The Haunted House. The usual great sight gags are plentiful, but this is not what the movie-going audience took notice of. It was in The Haunted House where Buster's frozen face or "stone face" became his worldwide trademark. Even though his "stone face" was the staple of most of his films with Roscoe "Fatty" Arbuckle, it was more noticeable in his own films.

Between the release of *The Haunted House* and his next film, *Hard Luck*, Buster began filming one of his greatest classics, *The Electric House*. During the filming of *The Electric House*, Buster suffered another injury, this time seriously breaking his leg while performing one of the many sight gags. *The Electric House* centers around a house full of electrical gadgetry. In the scene where he broke his leg, there was an escalator going from the first floor of the house to the second. For whatever reasons, other than to supply laughs, this escalator was malfunctioning and was moving at a rapid pace. As Buster hopped on the escalator, he was rapidly taken to the second floor. When he reached the point where the escalator stairs folded into the conveyor, the sole of one of his shoes got caught and he was catapulted twelve feet into the air and down to the lower section of the house (set). Once again, much to his chagrin, Buster was ordered to stop working for four months by his personal physician. One note of historical interest: the scene where Buster broke his leg, unknown to many, is included in the original release of *The Electric House* (and in the home video version, as well).

Buster's second release of 1921, *Hard Luck*, dealt with a subject matter many in 1921 considered to be taboo . . . suicide. Buster, being a man who liked to buck the system, did not let this taboo hinder him and decided to treat suicide in a comic vein. His gags in *Hard Luck* are not as outlandish as in some of his other films, but their impact is just stunning.

For any person wishing to study the art of the cinema or the golden age of film comedy, *Hard Luck* is a film to be included on the *must see* list.

On April 12, 1921, one of Buster's best loved films, *The High Sign*, was released. There is some confusion about when *The High Sign* was filmed. A great number of film historians claim it was filmed in 1917 and then shelved because Buster didn't like it. Others state it was filmed around 1918 or 1919 and the release was held back due to it being "too good" of a film to be released as his first solo project, thus the film-going public would hold it up against everything which would follow. None of these stories is true. *The High*

Sign was filmed, just as all of Buster's films, a few months before its release date. The actual filming date was in the late 1920's.

The High Sign moves at a torrid pace. The gags Buster engineered for *The High Sign* are all classics and are copied in some of today's major motion pictures. One of these gags, seen in many film compilations featuring Buster, is a scene where he is sitting on a bench and reading a local newspaper. As this scene unfolds, it becomes obvious the newspaper is not separated into pages. It is one larger-than-life sheet of paper and, as Buster unfolds it, he becomes buried within it.

Another scene shows Buster's genius for originality. He rigged a special feature at Tiny Tim's Shooting Gallery. The way this gag was set up, Buster tied his pet dog to a protrusion on a wall. In front of the dog Buster had placed a bone. On one end of the bone was a string which was attached to the trigger of a gun. When the dog grabbed the bone, it pulled the string, released the trigger, fired the gun and, yes, the bullet hit the target right in the bulls-eye!

In *The High Sign*, Buster once again could not help outsmarting his audience. This sight gag centered around the age-old slapstick routine of "the banana peel on the floor." In this scene, we find Buster eating a banana and arguing with the characters being portrayed by Joe Roberts and Virginia Fox. During this argument, Buster inadvertently drops the banana peel on the floor. As Roberts and Fox depart the room, Buster follows. Everyone in the audience knows Buster is going to slip on the banana peel and do one of his resounding pratfalls. He doesn't!

Like most of Buster's films, *The High Sign* has a chase scene. As opposed to most filmed chase scenes, this one takes place inside a house rather than on the outside. The house is actually a cut-away set, meaning the entire set is constructed without a front, thus the audience can see every room at the same time. To film this scene, the cameras were moved as far back as possible so the entire interior could be seen on film. In this chase, the actors are seen running through various doors, falling through hidden trapdoors, tripping up and down stairs, sliding down drainpipes and bouncing off walls. By the time this scene ends, the audience is out of breath from both their laughter and the witnessing of all of the fast-paced action. This whole chase sequence was filmed in one take, something many of today's directors look upon in awe. When *The High Sign* is shown at revivals and film festivals today, this chase scene always garners something unheard of in movie theaters . . . standing ovations!

Buster followed *The High Sign* with his film *The Goat*. The story-line for *The Goat* has Buster playing an accused man who is actually innocent and must prove his innocence to those who believe he is guilty. This film is somewhat ironic as four months after its May 1921 release, Buster's best friend, Roscoe "Fatty" Arbuckle, was being charged for a murder a jury would later conclude he did not commit.

In May 1921, there was another Buster Keaton release; this was not a film, it was something much more personal. This was the release of his bachelorhood. At the summer home of Joseph Schenck on Bayside, Long Island, Buster Keaton married Natalie Talmadge. This marriage produced two children, both boys, James and Robert. Aside from the children, the only other things this marriage produced were pain, heartache, and humiliation.

Buster was not the exact type of husband Natalie Talmadge's parents had in mind for her, even though it is rumored they forced the union. The rumor is that Peg Talmadge, Natalie's mother, talked Joseph Schenck (Schenck was married to actress Norma Talmage, thus was Peg's son-in-law) into talking Buster into marrying Natalie. This was all in an effort to get Natalie out of the house and to keep her from becoming an *old maid*. The fact that Buster was on his way to becoming a very wealthy man didn't hurt matters much. These rumors, in all probability, hold much more fact than fiction.

The first thing Natalie found out about Buster was how much he depended on others for his needs. Since she was now his wife, she had to take the place of all those *other* people. She had to be his secretary, his nurse, his nanny, his dresser, and his chauffeur. This was not the life Natalie Talmadge had envisioned for herself when she agreed to become Mrs. Buster Keaton.

In June of 1922, Buster and Natalie's first son, James, was born. Two years later, the second son, Robert, came into the world. It was after the birth of Robert when their marriage started on the road to disintegration. There was no divorce until years later. What started this disintegration was nothing more than two incompatible people living together. On the advise of her two famous acting sisters,

Norma and Constance Talmadge, Natalie was urged to "kick" Buster out of the bedroom and not to give into his "animalistic behavior," or what is otherwise known as sex. Why a divorce did not come at this time is unknown, as Buster refused to talk about this marriage.

As for the banishment from their bedroom, Buster retained his humor when he once cited, "Having got two boys out of our first three years, frankly, it looked as if my work was done. Lost my amateur standing. They said I was a pro. I was moved into my own bedroom." Even though Buster and Natalie were still in fact married, Buster had no intentions of practicing celibacy just because of Natalie's decision.

Another 1921 change for Buster came when Joseph Schenck found another distributor for Buster's films. No longer was it Metro; it was now First National. With First National, Buster had complete control over everything regarding his films and, with Joseph Schenck as his producer, he also had a *blank check* as far as money was concerned. The first Buster Keaton film released by First National was *The Playhouse.*

The Playhouse is a perfect example of a surrealistic film. The locale is a theater much like the type Buster performed in during his vaudeville days. As the camera pans the audience, the backstage area, and the musicians in the orchestra pit, every face shown is Buster Keaton's. Never before had such a film feat been attempted and, even though Buster masterminded this Hollywood first, he gave the credit to his special effects man, Fred Gaboure. As *The Playhouse* continues, what was once thought impossible occurs. Up on the screen comes a dancing Buster. Then another Buster appears doing something different. Before the sequence is complete, there are nine Busters appearing on film at the same time and each is doing something entirely different. This multi-exposure film trickery had never before been attempted and was thought to be impossible. The idea for this masterpiece in filmmaking came to Buster as he was studying the works of one of Hollywood's greatest directors, Tom Ince. Ince was an egocentric director who would give himself screen credits for everything except the acting roles.

The story line for *The Playhouse* is as close to autobiographical as any Buster Keaton film ever produced. One haunting scene, filmed in dream sequence, gives us a glimpse of what vaudeville life was like for young Buster Keaton. The dream begins with Buster lying on a bed in a cheap inn. Enjoying his slumber, he is awakened by a monster of a man claiming to be a policeman. As Buster is forced out of the room by this ogre, it becomes known this is a part of his dream; there is no room, there are no four walls and a bed, and there is no brutal policeman. What there is, is Buster tripping around the backstage area of an empty theater. According to accounts attributed to Buster regarding his vaudeville days, occurrences such as this dream sequence actually did happen to him, usually when he was worked to the point of total exhaustion.

On November 10, 1921, Buster's film *The Boat* was released. Buster's character in *The Boat* fits his persona to perfection. He is a man attempting to fulfill his dream of building a boat and sailing it, yet at every turn of the plot something goes wrong. Buster's portrayal is the exact definition of the term *comic-gloom*.

The Boat starts out with Buster in his garage building his dream boat, a boat he wants to be bigger than his friend's boat to prove he's successful. When his boat is complete, he brings his two children to see it and they're both spitting images of Buster, right down to their pork-pie hats. What Buster does not comprehend is that he's built the boat too large to get out of the garage, which leads to an uproariously funny sight gag.

When Buster does tow the boat out of the garage, the house slowly starts to collapse. While towing the boat, he never looks back to see this demise. Once the boat is out, he finally looks back to the house and sees it in a heap. The look on Buster's face as he sees the shambles is memorable in its own deadpan way.

The final scene in *The Boat* shows Buster launching the boat he had christened *Damfino*. As he puts the boat onto the ramp leading down into the water, he climbs upon the bow and takes a "Statue of Liberty" pose. As the boat enters the water, it is obvious to all except Buster that it is not going to float. As the boat sinks, Buster does not move from his statuesque position. The final shot shows Buster's ever-present pork-pie hat floating where the boat should've been.

The Boat, like so many of Buster's films, is one which deals with all the emotions of man; the highs, the lows, the good, and the bad. *The Boat* is one of Buster's favorite films and through the years has gained a cult following unsurpassed by any other film.

To close out 1921, a film considered Buster's weakest of the silent film era was released. This film is *The Paleface*. The first three intertitles sum up the weak storyline of this film:

> #1: In the heart of the west, the Indians of today dwell on simple peace.
> #2: But there came a group of oil sharks to steal their land.
> #3: The tribe gets notice to vacate.

The Indians are against the white men and they vow to kill the next one who comes into their camp. The next white man is Buster Keaton in the persona of a timid butterfly collector out to net his daily quota of flutterers. As the Indians spot him, the bedlam begins. The sight gags here are tepid, at best. There is the usual array of Buster's patented pratfalls, some of them amusing, but most in the typical slapstick realm.

Whereas 1921 ended in a professional lull for Buster, 1922 started off with a huge, resounding bang. On February 15, 1922, one of Buster's greatest shorts was released and immediately was hailed as a classic in film comedy. This film is titled *Cops*.

Like most of Buster's films, the first line in *Cops* sums up the story line. As Buster is standing behind the gates of a mansion talking to his girlfriend (played once again by Virginia Fox), she tell's him, "I won't marry you until you become a businessman!" From this point on, *Cops* moves at a consistently accelerating pace and its artistry in slapstick humor has never been excelled.

The action in *Cops* starts out with Buster bumping into a man and in the course of this accidental bumping, which includes some magnificent slight-of-hand gags, Buster ends up with the man's wallet and a large sum of money. One interesting moment in this sequence of scenes concerns Buster and a cabbie. As Buster pays the cabbie his fare, a close look at Buster's face will show the slightest trace of a grin. This is as close to a smile as Buster ever got in any of his own films.

With the money Buster finds in the man's wallet, he buys a horse and wagon from a streetside peddler who, as it turns out, does not really own either the horse or the wagon. Soon, Buster finds himself at the mercy of a con man who steals a load of furniture sitting on the street unattended. When the con man gives Buster a sad story, Buster gives the con man most of the rest of his money in exchange for the furniture. Little does Buster know that the furniture does not belong to the con man but to a policeman who is moving his family and has the furniture sitting on the curb awaiting the moving wagon he had ordered.

With the furniture piled onto his wagon, Buster tries his hand at peddling these goods in an effort to become the businessman his girl wants him to be. Included here are some classic scenes between Buster and the horse. These scenes clearly illustrate Buster's magic in working with animals. It is almost as if Buster and the horse are communicating with each other by the way they play off one another.

Riding along the streets, vainly attempting to sell the furniture he believes he owns, he accidentally rides into the middle of a parade honoring Policeman's Day. While riding in this parade, Buster reaches into his pocket and grabs a cigarette. With the cigarette in his mouth, he searches for a match. From the sad look on his face, it is apparent he has no matches. Just when it looks as if he'll have to forgo his cigarette, from somewhere on the parade route, a "villain" throws a lit bomb. The villains aim is the parade viewing stand where sits the Mayor and Chief of Police. The bomb misses its target and ends up on Buster's lap. Taking the bomb's burning wick, Buster lights his cigarette with it and then tosses the bomb, which he does not realize is a bomb, over his shoulder and it ends up in the reviewing stand where it explodes. Soon Buster is being pursued by every policeman in the city, including the policeman whose furniture he is innocently trying to peddle.

The chase scene between Buster and the police is one of the greatest chase scenes ever filmed. Throughout this chase there are some truly brilliant physical stunts, all performed by Buster without the use of any stunt double. One of the great stunts occurs when Buster is cornered and takes refuge on a wooden plank leaning against a fence. As Buster scales this plank, it becomes a seesaw type apparatus. While avoiding the grabbing hands of the cops on both sides of the fence, Buster is catapulted through the air where he lands on the cop whose furniture he was trying to peddle. This stunt with Buster being catapulted through the air is performed without the use of trick photography and is considered one of the greatest single stunts in the history of the cinema.

As the chase scene and the film comes to its conclusion, Buster is seen running into a large building which is, unknown to Buster, the police station. He is followed into the police station by the entire police force. A few seconds later, a uniformed policeman backs out of the station and as he slowly turns around, we see that it is Buster. In his hands are the keys to the police station, which he uses to lock the real cops inside. As Buster starts to walk away from the station, he throws the keys into a garbage can situated outside the police station door. It is here when Buster incorporated his favorite practice of fooling his audience. Whereas this looks to be the conclusion of the film, it isn't.

As Buster starts to walk away from the police station, he runs into his girlfriend whom he greets as if he's accomplished everything she requested of him. To his great surprise and disbelief, she rejects him and walks away. Feeling all reasons to live are now over, Buster goes back to the garbage can where he threw the keys, retrieves them, unlocks the door to the station, and allows himself to be yanked inside to meet his fate. The final frame of *Cops* shows a tombstone and on top of this tombstone hangs Buster's trademark pork-pie hat.

Buster's film *My Wife's Relations* had the unfortunate task of having to follow *Cops*. With film fans and critics raving over *Cops*, *My Wife's Relations* suffered due to the comparisons people were making between the two films.

When viewing *My Wife's Relations* now it seems as if Buster was trying to tell the public how it was to live with the Talmadge's as part of his family. *My Wife's Relations* is a parody on the home life of a person who is picked up off the streets and made part of a family who treats him like trash. The subtle comedy and realism in this film makes it quite different from Buster's other early works and is one of the reasons it is considered to be a *closet classic*.

On July 21, 1922, a film many consider to be a *sleeper* was released. This film is *The Blacksmith* and, even though it did not gain critical acclaim or set break box office records, it is a film which shows Buster's genius in engineering sight gags. The character Buster portrays in *The Blacksmith* lives under the rule commonly referred to as Murphy's Law (if something can go wrong, it will go wrong).

Two scenes which stand out in this film both center around Buster and horses. One of these scenes shows Buster attempting to fit a horse with a cross between a saddle and a shock absorber. This is in an effort to appease a female rider who doesn't want to be sore after a day's riding. The other horse scene has Buster fitting a horse with new shows. In this scene, Buster treats the horse not like an animal, but like a person who is shopping in a shoe store. The results here are quite original and very funny.

Unlike others of his ilk, Buster Keaton was an artist who got a big thrill out of making fun of his industry and the people within it. With his August 1922 release of *The Frozen North*, Buster satirized one of the cowboy stars of this era, William S. Hart.

As *The Frozen North* opens, we see Buster emerging from a New York City subway station. When he exits the subway to street level, he is all of a sudden standing on a frozen lake. Our first glimpse of Buster has him clad in a cowboy outfit and, instead of his usual pork-pie hat, he is wearing a cowboy hat tied under his chin and a gun hanging from each hip. Looking around at his surroundings, he emulates one of William S. Hart's most famous moves which is rolling a cigarette with one hand. Whereas Hart performed this task with grace, Buster fails miserably and comically.

Even though *The Frozen North* is a very funny film, William S. Hart did not find the film amusing at all. Hart was a proud man and took his cowboy characters seriously. To see Buster mocking him in such a way drove Hart crazy and he contemplated a law suit, but was talked out of it by his legal aides.

One scene which was a direct mocking of Hart's screen persona shows Buster walking through the front door of his house. As he enters, he sees a man and a woman in a romantic embrace. Even though he can only see the woman's back, he is certain the woman is his wife. As the camera goes in for a close-up of Buster's face, there are huge tears rolling down his cheeks. Figuring he is defeated, a loser in the game of love, he does a sharp U-turn and starts to walk out of the house.

Getting to the front door, Buster turns and takes one last look at the couple. They are no longer just hugging, they are now in the throes of a passionate kiss. He now goes over the brink. He unholsters both guns, takes aim at the lovers and shoots them dead.

Figure 3-2 – From the film The Frozen North. *Buster enters a subway and, when he emerges, is in the frozen North. Lake Tahoe, California, one of Buster's favorite locales for filming, was the actual location.*

When Buster sees their faces for the first time and an intertitle comes across the screen in the form of Buster's line: "My God, I'm in the wrong house!"

To close out 1922, there were two more Buster Keaton releases: *Daydreams* and *The Electric House*, released in September and October respectively.

In *Daydreams*, Buster plays a character he was quite used to. He is a man trying to woo a beautiful girl. The one difference in *Daydreams* is that he must win approval of her father, a task he finds impossible. The story line for *Daydreams* can be summed up in the first four intertitles:

#1. Buster: I've come to ask the hand of your daughter. I've thought the matter carefully, and I think I'm a suitable match for her.

#2. Father: Well . . . there's just one question . . . Can you support her?

#3. Buster: I don't know . . . I'll test myself by going

away to the city and performing great deeds . . . If I'm not successful, I'll come back and shoot myself!

#4. Father: Very well, I'll lend you my revolver.

Buster goes away to the city to prove he can be a success. While in the city attempting to prove himself a suitable match for his girl, Buster sends his beloved letters. After reading each letter, she daydreams about his successes; yet, unknown to her, his successes are really failures. There are three letters, thus three daydreams are depicted.

Daydream #1: Buster is working in a pet hospital. There is nothing sensational in this sequence other than the amusing way Buster interacts with the various animals.

Daydream #2: Buster is a street sweeper. This sequence starts off slowly and builds to a climax using great sight gags. Included here is a scene Buster reused in his film *Steamboat Bill, Jr.* showing Buster battling Mother Nature's invisible fury . . . gusting winds.

Daydream #3: Buster is a thespian performing in a Shakespearean play where he is totally inept. The finale of this sequence is reminiscent of *Cops* where Buster is being chased around the town by an entire police force. This chase is nowhere as amusing as the chase in *Cops*, but it is loaded with great pratfalls and sight gags. The police chase Buster onto a paddle-wheel boat where one of his most famous and ingenious sight gags takes place: Buster fighting a rapidly revolving paddle-wheel. To witness this scene is to witness a comedic genius at his best.

The final frames of *Daydreams* show Buster admitting to his girl's father that he has not proven himself worthy of her. To insure that Buster keeps his word of shooting himself for his failures, the father hands Buster his revolver. Being a man of his word, Buster takes the gun and goes to shoot himself. He misses!

As 1922 was turning into 1923, the burning question in the show business community was, "Why is Buster Keaton so great of a comedic talent?" The answer to this question is now an easy one. There are three basic reasons for Buster's rise to fame. First, Buster Keaton was ideal for silent comedy because his movements, expressions, and genius in pantomime gave him the opportunity to express himself better than anyone else.

Second, his comedic timing was absolutely impeccable.

And, finally, Buster was a film fan as well as an actor. This point is very noticeable in all of his films as Buster knew exactly what his audience wanted and never failed to produce it. When Buster left Roscoe "Fatty" Arbuckle and the Comique Film Corporation, there was only one promise he made to himself: to do the best he could and to never sell his audience short.

Buster's eighteenth film, *The Balloonatic*, is one of his most popular. It concerns a man at a country fair who comes across a hot-air balloon ride. As he sneaks onto the balloon, it starts to float away. When the balloon comes to a crash landing, Buster finds himself in the middle of an isolated forest.

It is difficult to pinpoint the best sight gags in *The Balloonatic*, however a couple of great scenes include Buster battling the natural elements of a rapidly flowing river. Another interesting and amusing scene has Buster in a battle of wits with a bear. By the way, this bear is not an actor in a bear suit, it is a real bear!

The conclusion of *The Balloonatic* is as original as the film itself. It is mysterious, eerie, and in the true Buster Keaton style . . . surprising.

The last film Buster made for First National was *Love Nest*. Just about the time *Love Nest* was released, March 6, 1923, Joseph Schenck received a telegram from the President of First National, John D. Williams. The telegram read:

> We do not wish to renew Keaton's contract stop
> We cannot be bothered with his short subjects stop

According to John D. Williams, this telegram was not to be taken literally, it was just First National's way of stating they wanted to renegotiate a new contract. Regardless of Williams' intentions, Buster Keaton and Joseph Schenck did take the telegram literally, and went in search of another company to distribute Buster Keaton films. They did not have to look long. As word reached the Hollywood moguls of Buster being a "free agent," Marcus Loew contacted Joseph Schenck and said he wanted Buster back under contract and he wanted him to make feature-length films. As it would turn out, the two films

Buster made as part of this deal were two of his best: *Three Ages* and *Our Hospitality*.

Three Ages came about due to Buster's admiration of the legendary "father of filmmaking," D.W. Griffith. When Griffith made his classic film *Intolerance*, Buster thought it was the most remarkable film he'd ever seen. Out of respect for Griffith, and to one again poke a little fun at his industry, Buster wrote and filmed *Three Ages* by himself.

Whereas *Intolerance* showed man's inhumanity toward man in four parts, Buster had *Three Ages* show the evolution of man in three parts representing ages. These ages are The Stone Age, The Roman Age, and The Modern Age. *Three Ages* is a feature film, but to be even more precise, it is actually three separate short films edited together to make one feature-length film.

With *Three Ages*, Buster wanted to make a point to his audience as well as to make them laugh. The point he wanted to make was, that since the beginning of time and creation, the relationship between both sexes has never really changed. Did Buster accomplish the feat of making this point to his audience? It is hard to tell, as most people were (and still are) to wrapped up in the comedy to even attempt to find the moral of this very funny and imaginative story.

There is a very important historical note regarding the filming of *Three Ages*. This was the first time in the history of the cinema where animation and live action were combined onto film.

Everyone remembers with great praise and awe Steven Spielberg's dynamic film of 1989, *Who Framed Roger Rabbit*. Not to take anything away from Steven Spielberg, but, sixty-six years earlier, Buster Keaton originated the combination of art forms with *Three Ages*.

In *Our Hospitality*, released on November 19, 1923, Buster once again decided to parody his business, this time making a film which poked fun at the family feud films which were rather popular in 1923. In *Our Hospitality*, Buster cast some very familiar faces, which were also very personal: Natalie Talmadge (who was still legally his wife), his father, Joseph Keaton, and his son James, who for this film was dubbed Buster Keaton, Jr. *Our Hospitality*, unlike Buster's other films, was not played solely for laughs, it also contained some pretty suspenseful and dramatic scenes, as well.

Our Hospitality was not filmed in Hollywood or, for that matter, anywhere near Southern California. It was filmed on location in and around South Lake Tahoe, California, one of Buster's favorite areas. It is a story which takes place around 1831 in an unknown area which is supposed to be "somewhere in the South." The idea for this film is a simple one: this is Buster's version of the Hatfield and McCoy feud. To protect himself from any type of lawsuit or bodily harm from the relatives of either family, Buster changed the names of the families to Canefield and McKay. True, it wasn't a major name change, but Buster did this on purpose; he wanted his audience to know who he was parodying without being blatant. In *Our Hospitality*, Buster plays Willie McKay.

Our Hospitality once again has Buster using trains as an important prop. The train used here is an exact replica of a model known as the *Stephenson Rocket*. After the filming of *Our Hospitality* was completed, Buster donated the train to the Smithsonian Institute in Washington, D.C.

There are two scenes in *Our Hospitality* which almost cost Buster his life. Both of these scenes, as in *The Balloonatic*, occur in a rapidly flowing river and both scenes, interestingly enough, have Buster trying to save the life of the character being portrayed by Natalie Talmadge. Also, both of these scenes are in the film just as they happened. In other words, the accidents which occurred while filming *Our Hospitality* can be witnessed when you watch this film on home video.

The first scene which almost proved fatal took place in the rushing rapids of the Truckee River, a river which flows from Nevada into California. The Truckee's main source of water is the Sierra snowmelt, so the water is always ice cold. With regard to the river's great speed, it crashes against many sharp rocks and, as many rafters will attest, bodily injury while riding the Truckee is often the rule and not the exception.

The setup for this scene is simple: Buster must jump into the rapids to save Natalie. As was always the case, Buster took every precaution where his safety was concerned but as the old adage goes, "accidents do happen."

Before the cameras started to roll, Buster was tied to a sixteen foot piece of security wire. This security wire was thin enough so that it would not be seen on film, yet it was the strength deemed necessary for this very dangerous stunt. As the filming was ready to begin, Buster yelled, "Roll 'em," and jumped into the ice cold rapids. As he was bodily riding the rapids (without any padding whatsoever), it was obvious that he was being punished by the jutting rocks which were in his path. As the camera continued to roll and catch all of the action, the security wire he was attached to suddenly snapped, sending him on a reckless and unguided path toward his possible demise. (When watching this on video, you can actually see the wire break and Buster lose all control of his movements.)

As he continued on his reckless path down the Truckee, co-director, Jack Blystone, made sure the camera stayed on Buster, as all of Buster's films had to follow one stringent rule: the camera never stopped filming until Buster himself yelled, "Cut!"

Just when it looked as if Buster's untimely death was going to be captured on film, he reached out and grabbed for a clump of tree branches which were in his path. Once he had hold of them, he held on for dear life . . . literally. The whole crew, with the exception of the cameramen who were still manning their cameras, rushed to Buster and pulled him back to the shoreline and safety. Buster's body was battered and bruised, his hands ripped apart from the tree branches and his breathing was irregular due to the water in his lungs.

The second incident which almost proved fatal, once again had Buster battling water. This time the water was in the guise of a waterfall. This stunt was also the most physically challenging of his career.

In this scene, the character portrayed by Natalie is on a raft-like device which is going down a river (not the Truckee) and rapidly approaching a waterfall. It is Buster's job to make sure she doesn't go over; he must save this "damsel in distress."

It has often been believed this scene was filmed at an actual waterfall in the Sierra. However, it was in fact filmed at a specially built waterfall on the backlot of the Metro Studios. The determination of using this specially built waterfall over a real one was for safety sake (Buster was still in pretty bad shape from his accident on the Truckee).

As Natalie approached the waterfall, filming stopped and Natalie (who was pregnant with Buster's second child) was taken off the raft and replaced with a dummy. As the dummy and raft were ready to go over the waterfall, Buster, who was once again attached to a security wire, swung across the waterfall and caught the dummy in his arms, and then swung back to the original position from which he had initially jumped. In the course of catching the dummy and swinging through the middle of the waterfall, Buster had inhaled so much water that when he got back to his original position, he was unconscious and emergency first aid had to be given to him by the studio doctor who was on the scene for precautionary reasons. According to personnel on the scene this day, Buster Keaton, once again came very close to drowning as his lungs filled with water. This scene, like the one shot on the Truckee River, was left in the final print of *Our Hospitality* just as it happened.

On April 21, 1924, Metro released one of Buster's most interesting films, *Sherlock, Jr.*, which gave the actor free rein to play with the cameras and execute as many special effects as he wanted.

The story line for *Sherlock, Jr.* is a simple one, as were most of Buster's story lines. In this film, Buster plays a very naive and sleepy movie house projectionist who, while working, falls asleep and, in his dreams, enters the movie which is showing in the theater, *Hearts and Pearls*. In the dream, he is no longer his "boob" self, but instead a valiant "knight in shining armor" who is going after the "bad guy" who has kidnapped his girl. Throughout this film, Buster's character has more than his fair share of trouble separating the screen world he dreams himself in from the real world.

As his dream begins, we see a ghost-like Buster, one who is almost transparent, leave his projection booth, walk down the center aisle of the theater, jump up onto the stage and then, literally, walk right into the screen and the movie as it is being projected. Apparently, Woody Allen is a big fan of Keaton's, as he used the same basis and cinematic tricks in his film *The Purple Rose of Cairo*.

The techniques Buster used in filming *Sherlock, Jr.* are to this day studied in college film courses (and there are even some colleges which have courses on Buster himself) and some of Buster's film techniques are still looked upon in awe by people in the filmmaking business. As Buster was always quick to point out, these film effects would not have been possible without the brilliant mind of his ace cameraman, Elgin Lesley, who Buster vowed was, without a doubt, "the best cameraman in the business." Since the day he had left Mack Sennett and the Sennett Studio, Elgin Lesley had been with Buster's crews.

The amount of film trickery in *Sherlock, Jr.* is endless and is the main reason the film grossed well over a half-million dollars at the box office. By today's standards, that doesn't sound like much, but, in 1924, that half-million dollars made *Sherlock, Jr.* one of Hollywood's biggest monetary hits of the year.

In the fall 1958 issue of the publication *Film Quarterly*, Buster talked about the making of *Sherlock, Jr.*, and in particular about his innovative use of film:

QUESTION: About the dream sequence in *Sherlock, Jr.*, was this something that you thought of on the spur of the moment, or something that had been planned ahead?

ANSWER: No, it was planned out ahead because we had to build a set for that one.

QUESTION: How was that done? Did you have an actual screen beforehand on which the characters were appearing?

ANSWER: No. We built what looked like a motion picture screen and actually built a stage into that frame but lit it in such a way that it looked like a motion picture being projected on a screen. But it was real actors and the lighting effect gave us illusions, so I could go out of semi-darkness into that well lit screen right from the front row of the theater into the picture. Then when it came to the scene changing on me when I got up there, that was a case of timing and on every one of those things we would measure the distance to the fraction of an inch from the camera to where I was standing, also with a surveying outfit to get the exact height and angle so that there wouldn't be a fraction of an inch missing on me, and then we changed the setting to what we wanted it to be and I got back to that same spot and it overlapped the action to get the effect on the scene changing.

While filming *Sherlock, Jr.*, Buster once again suffered a serious injury, but this time he didn't really know it until thirteen years later.

The scene in which Buster suffered this injury had him performing a stunt on a train: the train is rolling down the tracks at a pretty good speed and Buster is seen running along the tops of the cars until, obviously, he reaches the last car. When he reaches this last car and the train is still moving, Buster reaches out for a pipe which is protruding from a railroad water tower. While hanging onto this pipe, it starts to bend under his weight, taking him toward the tracks. As he is descending, the pipe opens up and water from the tower cascades down over him.

Since Buster did not rehearse this scene, he was not aware of the force of this cascading water. As the water smashed down upon him, he lost his grip on the pipe and fell to the tracks, where the back of his neck fell across the steel railroad ties.

Buster didn't know that he broke his neck in this accident, but he did suffer from painful headaches for weeks afterward. He found out that he broke his neck thirteen years later when a doctor noticed it after taking some x-rays during a physical examination. Even though this sounds amazing, from all accounts it is true.

If anyone is interested in viewing a film which is filled with special effects, *Sherlock, Jr.* is the film, as it is one special effect after another. It is truly a marvel of the American cinema.

In 1924, Metro Pictures combined with a couple of other studios and became known as Metro-Goldwyn-Mayer (M-G-M). Since Buster was under contract with Metro for the release of his films, he automatically became an original member of the M-G-M family. This first stint with M-G-M was a dream for Buster; it was his second stint which proved, along with his personal problems, to be his downfall.

To commemorate the birth of M-G-M, Buster gifted the studio with the biggest money-making film of his career, *The Navigator*. Upon its initial showing, *The Navigator* started to receive critical praise. *Photoplay* magazine, in its review chortled, " . . . studded with hilarious moments and a hundred adroit gags." With the release of *The Navigator*, M-G-M burst onto the filmmaking scene with a bang and achieved a status in the community it still has today . . . a giant in the business.

The idea which gave birth to *The Navigator* came to Buster one day when he heard the ship *U.S.S. Buford* was going to be scrapped for metal. The *U.S.S. Buford* was the historical ship which, in 1919, deported those believed to be Bolsheviks to Russia. Buster, being a history buff, could not stand by and watch this ship being turned into scrap metal without trying to save it. He called Joseph Schenck and informed him that he had an idea for a movie and that for the movie he needed the *U.S.S. Buford*. Schenck hesitated at the idea Buster had for buying the ship, so . . . Buster bought it himself with his own money. The price Buster paid has never been divulged as there were never any papers signed.

In *The Navigator*, Buster plays a spoiled millionaire named Rollo Treadway. As the film opens, Rollo finds himself adrift at sea on the *U.S.S. Buford*, where he thinks he is alone and left to die on a sinking ship. Unknown to Rollo, he is not the only person on the ship; his estranged girlfriend is also on board and she, too, thinks she is alone.

As the film continues, Rollo Treadway and his estranged girl-friend (portrayed by Katheryn McGuire) finally run across each other. The scenes with Rollo and his girl are truly classics of the comedy cinema. At one point, Rollo goes into the ships kitchen (galley) and attempts to fix a meal for them. In the course of this culinary action, everything goes wrong. This scene has been copied in films ever since, including the famous kitchen scene in Woody Allen's classic, *Annie Hall*.

The other famous scene in this film shows Buster (as Rollo) battling a folding chair which refuses to cooperate with him. It just folds and folds and folds. During the filming of all of these sight gags, Buster was doing what only he could do with perfection . . . ad-libbing.

While filming *The Navigator*, Buster once again found himself suffering an injury of sorts: Buster almost suffocated himself while costumed in a diver's suit. While putting on a diver's suit in preparation for some underwater scenes, Buster was smoking a ciga-rette. With the diving suits of this era (1924), the helmets were made of heavy steel or metal and were quite heavy. The scene called for Buster to be smoking while the diving helmet was put on him, this being one of the sight gags. As the helmet was put on the smoking Buster, the character portrayed by Katheryn McGuire, accidentally gave the helmet a twist, thus locking it into place. With the helmet

Figure 3-3 – No movie still shows Buster's incredible body strength than this one from The Navigator. *There were no wires used to hold Keaton in this position.*

locked and airtight, Buster started to choke on the cigarette smoke. McGuire tried, unsuccessfully, to remove the helmet, but with its weight and bulk, her attempts proved futile. Buster, locked in the helmet and coughing uncontrollably, could do nothing to help his plight. Finally, Ernie Orsattie, one of the film's crew members, ran over to Buster and removed the diving helmet. According to all of those present at the scene, a few minutes longer and Buster would have suffocated to death.

The underwater scenes in *The Navigator* were firsts for both Buster and the American cinema. Never before had underwater scenes been attempted, so, once again, here was Buster Keaton initiating a new technique in filmmaking. A few years later, during an interview, Buster elaborated on this ground-breaking scene.

First of all, we thought we'd use that big tank down at

Riverside. If we built it up, we could get five or six feet more water in the deep end. So they went down and built it up, and put more water in – and the added weight of the water forced the bottom of the swimming pool out. Crumbled it like it was a cracker. So we had to rebuild the swimming pool.

Next thing, we tested over at Catalina, and we found there was milk in the water – the mating season of the fish around the island causes that. The moment you touch the bottom, it rises up in the mud, rises up and blacks out your scene.

Lake Tahoe is the cleanest water in the world, and it is always cold because it's a mile high, and that's an awful big lake. So we went to Tahoe. I'm actually working in around twenty feet of water in that scene.

You imagine: we built this camera box for two cameras, a little bigger than a square table, with a big iron passage up to the top with a ladder on the inside. It holds two cameras and two cameramen. It was built on planks and sealed good so there was no leakage. But it's wood, and there has to be added weight. Well, I added about a thousand pounds to it. Now we find that the inside's got to be kept at the same temperature as the water outside. So we hung the thermometer out there so the cameraman looking through the glass can read it. And one on the outside.

First thing in the morning, and the night before, we have to put ice in there, and then add more to make sure to keep the temperature of the camera box the same as the water on the outside, so it won't fog up the glass. Either one side or the other will fog up on you, see. The difference was that when two bodies are in there, the body heat means we have to add more ice immediately. So as you put the cameramen in, you roll more ice in as well.

So there's the whole outfit, and me with that deep sea diving suit down there – and the cameraman says, "I'm too close. I want to be back farther."

I moved the camera box. I moved it! That's how much you can lift when you're down around fifteen to twenty feet

Figure 3-4 – Buster Keaton with wife Natalie Talmadge and his two sons. One of the few family photos ever taken, this was for publicity purposes. Buster and Natalie were separated at the time.

deep. The box must have weighed fourteen hundred pounds, something like that, with two cameras, two cameramen, about three hundred pounds of ice, another one thousand pounds of weight – and I picked it up and moved it! I was one month shooting that scene. I could only stay down there about thirty minutes at a time because cold water goes through your kidneys. After about a half hour, you begin to go numb. You want to get up and get out of there.

The best sight gags in *The Navigator* are the ones which take place underwater. These sight gags are vintage Keaton. One of these has Buster working underwater on the *U.S.S. Buford* and, in the course of this work, he gets his hands dirty. To clean his hands, he washes them in a bucket of water (remember, this is going on underwater). Another sight gag which Buster claimed was one of his favorites, consisted of twelve thousand fake fish, suspended in the water by clear fishing lines. These fish were supposed to resemble a school of fish that was passing by him. As the fish are passing, Buster picks up a fake starfish and attaches it to his chest, this to represent a policeman's badge. Now Buster takes on the persona of an underwater traffic cop and directs the traffic of the school of fish.

Even though Buster loved this scene (and it cost a great deal of money to produce), when the final cut of the film was put together, it was edited out. The reason for the editing was that, during the previews, the response from the audience was very poor. (Buster previewed all of his films before test audiences before they were released worldwide.)

Another Buster Keaton film where preview audiences played an important part was his next release, *Seven Chances*, which was released on March 6, 1925.

The story line for *Seven Chances* has Buster's character turning twenty-seven years old and, according to a will in which he is the benefactor, he must wed by seven that night or he will forfeit seven million dollars. His efforts to find a bride are often quite funny, yet it often seems he is bored with his role.

The finale of *Seven Chances* was inspired by the preview audience who first viewed it. During the previews, Buster was amazed that there was hardly a laugh to be heard in the theater. While the film was being shown, there were a few titters now and than, but only one real laugh. This *real* laugh had to do with Buster running down a hill and being chased by a giant boulder. Taking this cue from the preview audience, Buster pulled the film from distribution and reshot the ending for the worldwide release.

For this new ending, Buster had his special effects team build fifteen-hundred rocks, some as big as eighteen feet in diameter. Even though these boulders were fake, they were weighty. Buster was pursued down a mountainside by these boulders and, on more than one occasion, he was hit by one or more. While viewing this scene today on home video, one sees what appears to be some great pratfalls. In all actuality, these are not pratfalls at all, they Buster taking some very hard falls in true attempts to get away from the fake, yet a dangerously heavy, boulders. By the time this scene was finished shooting, Buster's body was a vibrant shade of black and blue.

What Buster was thinking about when he came up with the idea for his next film, *Go West*, no one will ever know. It is a rather strange concept when you consider it is a story about a down-and-out man and his relationship with a cow! Regardless, *Go West* is one of Buster's most beloved silent films.

The character Buster portrays in *Go West* is a hapless, unloved, pathetic creature named Friendless. Besides Buster, the only other significant role in this film belongs to Brown Eyes — a cow.

In reviewing this film, the late film critic/author, James Agee, wrote, ". . . it had a disturbing tension and dreamlike beauty."

Go West was filmed entirely on location in the deserts of Arizona. It was a film whose budget skyrocketed, mostly due to the location filming. The weather in the Arizona deserts often became so hot that it ruined the film and, at times, actually melted it. The cameras were also affected by the heat and more times than not, the cameras had to be nearly buried in ice to keep them in working order. Members of the crew would pass out from the heat, some having to be rushed to a nearby hospital. When someone brought up the idea of going back to Hollywood for filming, Buster said, "No! It not only has to look real, it must *be* real!"

Another problem with the filming had nothing to do with the weather, but with Brown Eyes. Brown Eyes was a female cow and during the filming she went into heat and, according to Buster, "the damned cow fell in love with me, literally." There was some talk about getting another cow, but because there was such a strong *magic* between Buster and Brown Eyes (which is evident when viewing this film), Buster decided to wait the two weeks the cow's heat lasted.

One very interesting scene in *Go West* takes place as a Friendless is playing poker with some cowboys. Noticing a cowboy who was cheating, Friendless voices his displeasure. The cheater then draws his gun and utters the line, "When you say that, smile!" Buster, who was now known worldwide as "the great stone face," obviously could not smile, in character or out. So, what did he do? He put his fingers to his mouth and made one of the most pathetic attempts at a grin ever seen on the silver screen.

Interestingly enough, Buster had mixed emotions regarding *Go West*. "Some parts I liked, but as a picture, in general, I didn't care for it."

On August 30, 1926, Buster had the last film of his M-G-M contract released. This film was *Battling Butler*, and had originally been a Broadway musical starring veteran character actor, Charles Ruggles. The film, however, showed very little resemblance to the stage musical.

In *Battling Butler*, Buster plays a one-time millionaire who becomes a beacon of power, all for the love of a woman. Along the way, the character takes on the persona of a professional boxer and, in these scenes, Buster proves his great physical abilities and creates some of the cinema world's greatest moments of slapstick comedy. As it would turn out, *Battling Butler* was a very profitable swan-song in the initial Buster Keaton and M-G-M relationship.

When it came to his films, Buster Keaton was an architect. He constructed everything from the original idea to every gag, and did it to cinematic perfection. He took great pride in his work and every film was a personal achievement. Because of this personal aspect, Buster never really surpassed Charlie Chaplin as the "king of screen comedy." Looking back, though, Keaton is without a doubt *the* genius of the silent screen era, the greatest comedic actor in cinema history, and a true legend in laughter.

During the 1920's, the comparisons of Buster Keaton and Charlie Chaplin seemed to be the number one pastime for the film-going public and film critics, yet neither Chaplin nor Keaton saw any similarities in their styles or characters. Buster was once quoted as saying, "I was puzzled when people spoke of the similarities in the characters Charlie and I played in the movies. Charlie's little tramp was a bum with a bum's philosophy. Lovable as he was, he would steal if he got the chance. My little fellow was a working man and honest."

An analysis of these two great "clowns" reveals even bigger differences than those pointed out by Keaton.

Buster played a typical everyday sort of guy who tried his best at whatever he attempted, yet, for whatever reasons, very seldom accomplished his goals, at least without various types of adversity. He

Figure 3-5 – Buster in the ring with Snitz Edwards in Battling Butler.
*Another example of a Keaton sight gag: Buster punches himself
in the nose as he tries to protect his face.*

gives us a stare that mesmerizes us with his sad "puppy dog" eyes;
and that great "stone face" told us volumes of what he was thinking
and going through. Buster *was* his films and without him, they
would have simply been frames of celluloid with differing shadows.

Charlie Chaplin, on the other hand, was always a possessed
character who tried more for the artistic approach than the common
folk approach. Chaplin usually maintained one character, that of his
Little Tramp, and was afraid to branch out with his characterizations.

Make no mistake about it: Charlie Chaplin was a great comedian
and one whose style we will never see again. In fact, Buster was once
quoted as saying that, "Charlie Chaplin was the greatest comedian
who ever lived!"

To compare these two giants of film comedy, some might say, is
wrong. But to appreciate Buster Keaton and his tremendous gifts and
talents completely, this comparison must be made.

Probably the most amazing aspect of the film career of Buster
Keaton is the fact that he essentially ad-libbed everything; there was
never a real written script, even though outlines were always used. It

was this filming on pure instinct which was the secret to Hollywood's golden age of comedy.

The magic of Buster Keaton was never more evident than in his early films and the characters he portrayed. "We had to get sympathy," Buster once noted, "to make the story stand up, but the one thing that I made sure of is, I didn't ask for it. If the audience wanted to feel sorry for me, that was up to them. I did not ask for it in actions."

Most film historians marvel at the way Buster's films consistently keep their sense of continuous humor and artistic continuity. The secret of this success is really quite simple: throughout the twenties, when Buster was releasing classic film after classic film, he always had the same crew working with him. This crew consisted of a co-director (Buster directed all of his films, even though at times he was not credited), three writers (not including Buster), a prop man, a unit manager, a film editor, and two cameramen.

Two cameras were used by Buster for one very simple reason. As one camera was filming a print for American release, the other was filming a print for international release. Doing it this way made it possible for the international release to open overseas earlier than normal, thus making more money. Buster was the only comedian of his age to incorporate this method of filmmaking.

4

THE GENERAL

On New Years Eve 1926, movie-making history was made, although no one was aware of it at the time. It was on this day that a film now considered to be one of the greatest ever produced opened, and this film was Buster Keaton's epic . . . *The General.*

The General was the first of three films made by Buster to be released by United Artists, then headed by Joseph Schenck, and also marked the beginning of Keaton's decline as a true superstar, legend, and genius. The other two Keaton films released by United Artists were *College* and *Steamboat Bill, Jr.*

In the history of movie-making and Hollywood, *The General* is the only film ever made around which college courses dealing directly with its production have been created. In 1977, the American Film Institute, with its membership including highly acclaimed members of the Hollywood community, studio moguls, film critics, film historians, and avid fans of films and its history, polled its membership on what they believed were the top fifty films (American made) of all time. Included in this poll were the usual classics such as *Gone With the Wind*, *Citizen Kane*, *The Wizard of Oz* and others. But there was only one film on their list from the silent era: Buster Keaton's *The General.* The interesting thing about *The General* and this poll is that it took fifty-one years for the public to recognize this masterpiece for what it truly was and still is – the best film of its era that the American cinema has to offer.

When *The General* was released in 1926, it was a miserable

failure. The critics of the time, for the most part, panned it, some going so far as to say that it was a bore, a waste of money, a waste of Buster's talents, and just plain unfunny.

> *The New York Times*: "This is by no means as good as Mr. Keaton's previous efforts."
> *Variety*: "*The General* is far from funny!"
> *Life Magazine*: "Many of his gags are in gruesomely bad taste."
> *The New Yorker Magazine*: "It has all the sweet earnestness in the world. It is about trains, frontier America and flowerfaced girls."
> Mordount Hall (famed film critic): "The production itself is singularly well mounted, but the fun is not exactly plentiful. Here he is more the acrobat than the clown, and this vehicle might be described as a mixture of cast iron and jelly."

The General was one of the most expensive films made during the silent era in Hollywood (some insiders have stated it was the most expensive ever made). Point in fact: the train wreck sequence in *The General* cost Joseph Schenck and United Artists $42,000; this is without a doubt the most expensive sequence in the silent film era (and for that matter, the early sound era as well). As far as the film's box office draw, *The General* failed miserably and did not even come to close to breaking even.

There are many stories regarding how Buster came to write *The General*. Some say he just wanted to do a film which showed his love of trains (the *General* is the name of a train), while others believe Buster wanted to do a film which was more serious than his other films because he wanted to be considered as much more than just a comedic actor. All of these speculations have little basis in fact. The truth is, Buster wrote *The General* because of his love of history.

Although Buster's formal education consisted of just one day of schooling, he loved to learn and always took pride in educating himself. In this self education, Buster focused on history. Buster was also an avid reader and one of his favorite subjects was the Civil War. It was while reading about the Civil War that Buster learned the true

Figure 4-1 – From The General: Buster Keaton and his most
theatrically talented leading lady, Marion Mack.

details of what was called "The Great Locomotive Chase" and it is this
story upon which The General is based. While studying the Civil
War, Buster became enamored with the Civil War photographs taken
by Mathew Brady. Combining Brady's photographs with the story of
The Great Locomotive Chase, Buster came up with the idea for The
General.

One of the most gifted photographers in history, Mathew Brady
was a pioneer in the art of photography. The list of people who sat
for Brady is like looking down the corridors of a Hall of Fame for
great American patriots and legends of the arts. Included in this list
are such names as Zachary Taylor, Andrew Jackson, James Polk, John
Tyler, Edgar Allan Poe, John Wilkes Booth, James Audubon, and, his
most famous client, Abraham Lincoln, who made Brady his official
photographer while he was President.

During the Civil War, Brady became what was then known as a picture war correspondent, or what today is called a photojournalist. While photographing the Civil War, Mathew Brady almost single-handedly chronicled this historical era. Because of Brady's untiring efforts, today we can look back on this war which pitted brother against brother.

After the Civil War, Brady's life took a turn for the worse. His later years found him very ill and living in poverty. Mathew Brady died on January 16,1896, and is buried in the Congressional Cemetery in Washington, D.C.

Of all the films which Buster made or was a part of, *The General* was his favorite. He always took great pride in talking about this film and pointing out the fact that, basically, the story of *The General* was an actual event of the Civil War told in detail. It was those details about which Buster was adamant, telling his crew numerous times during the filming, "make it so real it hurts!"

The General was a perfect film for Buster, as he was able to share his love of trains with the whole cinematic world. In *The General*, Buster is not really the star; the star is the *General* itself. Is *The General* a comedy? In every sense of the word, yes, but it is also much more. Most of the sight gags (and they are numerous) are subtle. Buster did not want them to overshadow the historical story that he was telling. There are many dramatic points in this film and each is carried out to complete perfection. For those into the technical aspect of filmmaking, the camera work in *The General* is superb and the direction is flawless. One look at *The General* is all it takes to realize it is a masterpiece in filmmaking, yet one look is not enough. Every time you watch the film, you will see something you didn't see before: a gag, a camera shot, or a special effect

Buster said this about *The General*:

Now this is my own story, my own continuity. I directed it, I cut it, and I titled it. So actually it was my pet. Not my biggest money-maker though, that was *The Navigator*.

I went to the original location, from Atlanta, Georgia, up to Chattanooga, and the scenery didn't look very good.

Figure 4-2 – Buster Keaton as Johnny Gray in The General.

In fact, it looked terrible. The railroad tracks I couldn't use at all, because the Civil War trains weren't narrow-gauge. And the railroad beds of that time were pretty crude; they didn't have so much gravel to put between the ties, and you always saw the grass growing there.

I had to have narrow-gauge railroads, so I went to Oregon. And in Oregon, the whole state is honeycombed with narrow-gauge railroads for all the lumber mills. So I found trains going through valleys, mountains, by little lakes and mountain streams – anything I wanted. So we got rolling equipment, wheels and trucks, and we built our freight train and our passenger train, and we remodeled three locomotives. Luckily, the engines working these lumber camps were all so doggone old that it was an easy job. They even had burners. At that period they didn't have to pay much attention to numbers of engines – they named them all. That's why the main engine was called the *General* and the one I chased it with was the *Texas*. It was the *Texas* I threw through the burning bridge.

We built the bridge and dammed up the water underneath so the stream would look better. I planned the scene and we had a forge and a blacksmith's shop right on the lot.

Extras came from miles around to be in that picture. None of them were experienced – we had to train them.

Railroads are a great prop. You can do some awful wild things with railroads.

As opposed to other silent films, *The General* was one film which could have been filmed without any intertitles whatsoever, as these intertitles were basically used to breakup scenes. In most of the other silent films, the intertitles were an intricate part of the film, used as important guidelines so the audience would be able to follow the film and plot. This was not the case with *The General*. Judge for yourself. For the first time in print, each of the fifty-six intertitles is listed below in the same order they appeared in the original film. After reading these fifty-six intertitles, you will see that they do not tell a story at all.

THE GENERAL

CAST

Johnny Gray.. Buster Keaton
Annabelle Lee.. Marion Mack
Her Father.. Charles Smith
Her Brother.. Frank Barnes
Captain Anderson.. Glen Cavender
General Thatcher.. Jim Farley
Recruiting Officer.. Frank Hagney
Confederate Soldier..................................... Joseph Keaton

Directed By:
Buster Keaton
and
Clyde Bruckman

#1: The Western and Atlantic Flyer speeding in Marietta, Georgia, in the Spring of 1861.

#2: There were two lovers in his life, his engine and his . . .

#3: (Annabelle's brother to her father) "Fort Sumter has been fired upon."

#4: (Annabelle's father to her brother) "The war is here?"

#5: (Annabelle's brother to her father) "Yes, dad, and I'm going to be the first to enlist."

#6: (Annabelle to Johnny) "Aren't you going to enlist."

#7: (Recruiting Officer to Johnny) "Your name?"

#8: (Johnny to the Recruiting Officer at the recruiting office) "Johnny Gray."

#9: (Recruiting Officer to Johnny) "Occupation?"

#10: (Johnny to the Recruiting Officer) "Engineer on the Western and Atlantic Railroad."

#11: (Head Recruiter to the Recruiting Officer) "Don't enlist him. He is more valuable to the South as an engineer."

#12: (Recruiting Officer to Johnny) "We can't use you."

#13: (Recruiting Officer to Johnny, who is now attempting to enlist while disguised) "Name?"

#14: (disguised Johnny to the Recruiting Officer) "William Brown."

#15: (Recruiting Officer to the disguised Johnny) "Occupation?"

#16: (disguised Johnny to the Recruiting Officer) "Bartender."

#17: (Johnny to the Head Recruiter after his disguise fails) "If you lose the war, don't blame me!"

#18: (Annabelle to her brother) "Did Johnny enlist?"

#19: (brother to Annabelle) "He didn't even get in line."

#20: (father to Annabelle) "He's a disgrace to the South."

#21: (Annabelle to Johnny) "Why didn't you enlist?"

#22: (Johnny to Annabelle) "They wouldn't take me."

#23: (Annabelle to Johnny) "Please don't lie — I don't want you to speak to me again until you are in uniform."

#24: A year later. In the Union encampment just north of Chattanooga.

#25: General Thatcher, and his chief spy, Captain Anderson.

#26: (Captain Anderson to General Thatcher) "I know every foot of the railroad from Marietta to Chattanooga — and with ten men picked, I cannot fail."

#27: (General Thatcher to Captain Anderson) "Then the day we steal the train I will have General Parker advance to meet you."

#28: (Annabelle to her brother) "As soon as I arrive I will let you know how seriously father is wounded."

#29: (a train conductor to the train passengers) "Big Shanty. Twenty minutes for dinner."

#30: (Johnny to a soldier at an army camp) "Three men stole my General! I think they are all deserters!"

#31: (one Confederate soldier to another) "Why not stop and fight them?"

#32: (one Confederate soldier to another) "I'm afraid they have us greatly outnumbered."

#33: The Southern Army facing Chattanooga is ordered to retreat.

#34: General Parker's victorious Northern Army advancing.

#35: (one Confederate soldier to another as he sees Johnny in pursuit of them) "There is only one man on that engine."

#36: In the country — hopelessly lost, helplessly cold and horribly hungry.

#37: (General Thatcher to a group of his men) "At nine o'clock

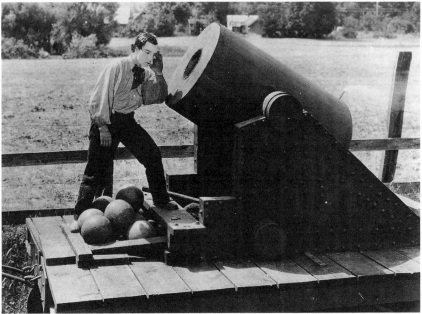

Figure 4-3 – Buster in a scene from The General *with the real Civil War cannon which almost proved fatal.*

tomorrow our supply trains will meet and unite with General Parker's army at Rock River Bridge."

#38: (General Thatcher to a group of his men) "Then the army, backed by our supply trains, will advance for a surprise attack on the rebels' left flank."

#39: (General Thatcher to some of his men) "Once our trains and troops cross that bridge, nothing on earth can stop us."

#40: (a Confederate soldier to General Thatcher regarding Annabelle) "This girl was in the baggage car when we stole the train, so I thought it best to hold her."

#41: (Johnny to Annabelle after rescuing her from the Confederate soldier) "We better stay here until daybreak to see where we are."

#42: (Annabelle to Johnny) "It was so brave of you to risk your life, coming into the enemy's country, just to save me."

#43: After a nice, quiet, refreshing nights rest.

#44: (Johnny to Annabelle) "We've got to get back to our lines somehow and warn them of this coming attack."

#45: (Johnny to Annabelle) "We must pick up more firewood."

#46: The Rock River Bridge.

#47: The Northern division nearing the bridge to meet the supply trains.

#48: (General Parker to his platoon of men) "That bridge is not burned enough to stop you, and my men will ford the river."

#49: Heroes of the day.

#50: (Union General to Johnny after he saved the day) "Is that your uniform?"

#51: (Johnny to the Union General) "I had to wear it to get through the lines."

#52: (Union General to Johnny) "Take it off!"

#53: (Union General to a Recruiting Officer referring to Johnny) "Enlist the Lieutenant."

#54: (Recruiting Officer to Johnny) "Occupation?"

#55: (Johnny to the Recruiting Officer) "Soldier."

#56: The End.

That is the entire original written script of *The General.*

Compared to most of the films of the silent era, this is what sets *The General* apart from the others. Buster could tell a story without a script of continuity, that is, a written script which, when read, makes no sense. With *The General*, Buster once again accomplished an artistic impossibility: he showed all doubters that what they said "couldn't be done," could be done, and done to utter perfection!

As was Buster's way of making films, *The General* was not filmed in Hollywood, but on location in the small, rural community of Cottage Grove in Oregon, using most all of the citizens as extras. Before filming even began, Buster and his crew built a Civil War city on the outskirts of Cottage Grove. This city was an exact duplicate of Marietta, Georgia, during the days of the Civil War, based, once again, on the photographs taken by Mathew Brady.

Along with the replicated town, Buster also had to have trains which were exact duplicates of the trains used during the Civil War. How they (Buster and his crew) made the somewhat modern trains into Civil War trains was actually quite simple. They had shipped a couple of train engines to Cottage Grove and the crew simply remodeled them to look exactly like the trains in the photographs taken by Brady during the Civil War. The cars for the trains were built using

Figure 4-4 – During the filming of The General, *this bar fell across Buster's neck, pinning him to the train and providing yet another in a long line of injuries.*

used cars from the lumber trains which were already in the area. The crew did not have to lay any railroad track because Cottage Grove was a lumber railroad town. As far as the costs for all this pre-production, Buster did not even give it a second thought and this he would regret, and regret dearly, in later years.

The story of the film *The General* is simple: Johnny Gray has his train, the *General*, stolen and he must get it back. In the course of recapturing his beloved train, he also saves the Southern Army from defeat and, in the end, wins the girl he lost as the film begins. It is a typical "happily ever after" film done with twists of fate and numerous sight gags.

In the beginning of the film, Johnny is visiting his girl, Annabelle, where he learns from her brother and father that Fort Sumter has been shot upon, thus the war has begun. Annabelle's father and brother decide to enlist and fight for the Southern Army and, with the urging of Annabelle, Johnny (Buster) decides to do the same. When Johnny goes to the recruitment center, he is dismayed to be turned down because it is felt he would be more important to the South as a train engineer (his occupation), yet they don't bother to tell him this, thus he feels like an incompetent, unqualified, and unwanted oaf. When he goes back to Annabelle and she inquires as to the outcome of his trip to the recruiter, he says that he was turned down, yet her brother had told her that he wasn't even there. Annabelle's takes her brother's word over her lover's and rejects Johnny saying, "I don't want you to speak to me again until you are in uniform."

As the war goes on, Johnny finds contentment in not being a Southern soldier but remaining a train engineer of the *General*. When Annabelle hears that her father is injured while in battle, she goes to check on his well-being, traveling on the *General*. On the train, she runs into Johnny and once again spurns him. In the course of this trip, they come to the small town of Big Shanty where the conductor announces they will be stopping for a twenty minute dinner stop. It is while at this stop that the *General* is hijacked by members of the Northern Army, with Annabelle still on board. This is the point in the film when *The General* becomes a *tour-de-force* of nonstop action.

As he sees his train rolling down the tracks without him at the helm, Johnny starts to run after it in a feeble attempt to catch it. Realizing that he won't be able to catch his *General* on foot, Johnny comes across a railroad handcar, hops upon it, and starts to pump, building up a head of steam. As he is in pursuit, the handcar comes across a break in the railroad tracks and both the handcar and Johnny go flying head first into a river.

Next, Johnny finds a two-wheel bicycle (not your common every day type of bicycle as this one has a large front wheel and a small back wheel) and he continues his chase of the *General* on this bicycle. While peddling along the railroad tracks, the front wheel falls apart sending Johnny crashing onto the tracks. He gets up and brushes himself off, once again taking off on foot. Johnny soon arrives at a Southern Army camp where he relays the stealing of the train by the Northern Army. Wanting to capture these scoundrels from the Northern Army, the Southern Army gives Johnny a train named the *Texas* to chase the *General*. In one of the freight cars, a platoon of Union soldiers gather to join Johnny, yet when Johnny takes off, the freight car is not coupled to the engine. Johnny is once again alone in his pursuit, much to the dismay of the Union soldiers who thought they were going to be in on the chase.

As he chases the *General* in the *Texas*, Johnny comes across many deterrents, most of which are the result of the Northern Army trying to keep Johnny off their tail. During the chase, Johnny has no idea that his girl, Annabelle, is still aboard the *General*. In the course of this chase, actually the first of two, Buster proves his mastery over trains as all of the gags, stunts, and engineering feats were performed by Buster without any trick photography, stunt doubles, or fake (stationary) mechanisms.

As the *General*, still under the engineering leadership of the Northern Army, reaches one of their encampments, they disembark for a night's rest and strategy meeting.

After hearing one of these strategy meetings, Buster sneaks onto his beloved *General*, knocks out a Northern soldier who is aboard acting as a sentry, and recaptures the train.

In the meantime, he has also rescued his ladylove, Annabelle. With Johnny and Annabelle behind the instruments of the *General*, Johnny takes off to warn his Southern comrades about the Northern Army's plan of attack which he overheard.

As soon as the *General* takes off from the Northern Army encampment, the Northern Army soldiers hop on the deserted *Texas* and pursue.

As Johnny heads into Southern Territory, he crosses a bridge in the *General* and stops. He douses the tracks of the bridge with kerosene from the *General's* lantern and sets the bridge on fire to stop the Northern Army. When Johnny, Annabelle, and the *General* pull into a divisional headquarters of the Southern Army, Johnny tells them about the advancing Northern Army. The Southern Army mounts their horses, groups into platoons, and starts off for a battle. Johnny follows , this time without Annabelle, in the *General*, to lend his *style* of support.

As the Southern Army is approaching, the Northern Army is at the burning bridge. Surveying the situation and the burning bridge, a Northern Army Captain tells the engineer of the *Texas* (a Northern Army soldier) that the "bridge is not burned enough to stop you, and my men will ford the river." Taking the Captain at his word, the engineer puts the *Texas* into gear and starts out across the Rock River

Bridge. Just as the train is about to the end of the bridge, the bridge collapses sending the *Texas* crashing into the mighty Rock River. A battle breaks out between the two armies as the train is destroyed by fire.

In the course of this battle (the only Keaton film which adheres to graphic violence in a very real form), one sees cannons of various sizes shooting cannonballs from one side of the Rock River to the other. Bodies are seen falling in heaps, flying through the air, and dying with great dramatic flair. As this battle between the North and South continues, Johnny Gray finds himself in various confrontations, winning them all . As the battle comes to an end, the Southern Army claims victory and heads back to their divisional headquarters where, once again, Johnny follows in the *General*.

As the *General* pulls into the Southern Army encampment, Johnny notices that on his train is a dazed Northern Army soldier whom Johnny takes into custody and turns over to the Southern Army General as a prisoner. For his bravery in the battle and for bringing the prisoner to justice, Johnny is granted his original wish: induction into the Southern Army as a Lieutenant.

As the film comes to a conclusion, we find our beguiled hero claiming his ladylove, yet not forgetting his *real* first love, the *General*. With Annabelle at his side and both sitting on the front wheel of the *General*, Johnny attempts to steal some kisses from her, yet each time he is interrupted by passing soldiers who are saluting him and, of course, he must return their salutes. Does Johnny get his long sought after kiss? Yes, right as "The End" falls into frame.

As mentioned previously, *The General* was based on a true story from the Civil War. It is interesting to compare this true story of the *General* with Buster's fictional account. Many would expect that Buster made changes from the true account to make the story more adaptable to the screen. But this is not true. The only things that Buster really added were gags. As to the story itself, for the most part, Buster kept it pretty much intact.

THE TRUE STORY OF THE *GENERAL*

In Atlanta, Georgia, on June 7, 1862, Captain James Andrews and several of his men were to be hanged for stealing a train. The accounts of this crime make it the most illustrious crime in the history of the American railroad. The train which was stolen was the *General*.

The main proponent of this crime was James J. Andrews, a spy and Union Army Captain under the direction of General Don Carlos Buell. To make himself a hero of the war, Andrews knew he must accomplish something that would be looked upon as valiant and heroic; an impossible task that people would marvel at once he proved to them that it was possible, but only for him.

Requesting the assistance of General Ormsby McKnight Mitchell and recruiting twenty soldiers, Andrews led them through the Confederate lines into Marietta, Georgia, one of the homes of the Western and Atlantic Railroads.

The plan, thought up by Andrews and Mitchell, was to steal a train, cut telegraph lines (the only form of long distance communication at the time), and run the train to Chattanooga, Tennessee, all the while burning the tracks behind them to avert being chased. This was all done by Andrews and half of the recruited men. Mitchell and the rest of the recruited men were to attack the Memphis and Charleston Railroad located in Huntsville, Alabama, and cut off all of their lines of communication as well. According to their plan, once they had accomplished these feats, Chattanooga would be just right for the Union to invade and take over. This was all to take place on Friday, April 11, 1862.

On April 11, 1862, at exactly six o'clock in the morning, Mitchell and his men accomplished their part of the plan and it went off without even the slightest bit of a problem. They had captured numerous freight cars and an unbelievable fifteen locomotives. This was easy, or so Mitchell thought at the time, and now he decided to throw caution to the wind and go beyond what was originally planned. Mitchell sent half of his men Eastward along the railroad tracks, having them destroy numerous bridges and ultimately taking an additional five locomotives. A mistake was made when they tried to destroy the Bridgeport Bridge. There, the Confederate Army had beaten them to the punch, forcing them to retreat and thus giving notice to the Confederate Army that the Union had invaded their territory. Because the telegraph lines were down, they could not contact their comrades along the line. This, of course, put Andrews and his men in great danger.

On April 12, in a small town near Atlanta, Georgia, called Big Shanty, Andrews and his men took over one of the mightiest trains in railroad history, the *General*, while the crew and passengers were eating breakfast. The train's engineer, Jeff Cain, thought his train was being stolen by Confederate deserters, as no one at the time had known of the Union insurgence into Confederate territory.

The trek of the *General* did not go as originally planned because Andrews had to wait a day before making his move. The train schedule he had studied was for April 11 and not April 12, the day he stole the *General*.

Because he was working with the wrong train schedule, Andrews met many obstacles in his attempt to take the *General* into Union territory. Among the most hazardous of these obstacles was the possibility of a head-on collision with another train, as in this area of the South there were not two sets of tracks. On more than one occasion, Andrews was forced to stop, yet, since all lines of communication had been destroyed, nobody who stopped him knew of his crime and thought, since he was not in uniform, that he was just running late. Often times his excuse for being on the tracks unscheduled was, "I'm hauling powder to General Beauregard," who was the top Confederate General.

Outside of the township of Kingston, where Andrews had stopped the *General* to cut more telegraph lines and attempt to destroy the tracks, he and his men heard a shrill whistle coming up on their rear. Ordering his men back onto the train, Andrews had the *General* put on full-throttle and headed toward the Oostenaula Bridge, a bridge that it was apparent they had to destroy. The train that was bearing down on them was the *Texas*, one of the fastest trains of its era, with Jeff Cain, the *General*'s real engineer, at the throttle.

As the *Texas* came closer to the *General*, Andrews realized his initial plan was not going to work. There was no way he would be able to destroy the Oostenaula Bridge, since both trains reached the bridge at the same time.

Defeat, something which was a stranger to the life and career of Andrews, was now something that was beginning to enter his mind. He had one more option left to him and that was to get to the bridge near Chickamauga and destroy it. With the *Texas* right on the tail of the *General*, Andrews did everything he could to derail the *Texas*, yet all of his efforts failed.

As the *General* steamed out of the town of Dalton, it built up a little lead over the *Texas*, enough of a lead that Andrews decided to set one of his cars on fire and leave it on a bridge to burn. Andrews thought that by the time the *Texas* got to the bridge, the bridge would collapse, thus enabling him, his men, and the General to go home safely.

By the time the *Texas* reached the bridge, the bridge was engulfed in flames. The car that Andrews had set ablaze was pushed off the tracks by the *Texas*, going full throttle. As soon as the *Texas* crossed the bridge, the bridge collapsed and fell, burning, into the rapidly flowing river below it.

As Andrews saw the *Texas* safely cross the bridge, he knew that he was a defeated man. The *General*, the greatest of all trains, was now out of fuel and water and was moving slower and slower. In a last ditch effort to escape, Andrews ordered his men to jump and run into the surrounding woods. What Andrews did not know was that the woods were teeming with Confederate soldiers and Andrews and all of his men were picked up and placed under arrest.

The saga of the *General* ended on June 7, 1862, in Atlanta, Georgia, when Andrews and his men were executed.

The film *The General* is a beautiful story, told in a hauntingly beautiful way, yet some of the real stories lay behind the scenes of this great classic of the American cinema.

As opposed to previous Buster Keaton films, *The General* did not rely solely on gags to bring audiences into the theaters, yet this film is loaded with sight gags, each one seeming to top the one which precedes it.

In *The General*, no one gag stands out above the others for one very simple reason: they come at such a rapid succession you can't really appreciate them after only one viewing. A few of the gags which should be noted when viewing *The General* are:

1) When Buster first starts chasing the stolen *General*, watch for the way he manipulates the railroad handcar and pay special attention to the magnificent pratfall he performs when the handcar runs out of track and goes flying, with Buster on board, into a river.

2) Buster chasing the *General* on a strange looking bicycle is a scene that is memorable. He takes off on the bicycle after being tossed from the handcar. In chasing the *General* on this bicycle, he rides it on the railroad tracks until the bicycle literally falls apart with him on it.

3) When Buster saves Annabelle, they spend the night hiding out in the woods. When morning comes and they get ready to make their escape, both Buster and Annabelle have a very humorous encounter with a bear trap that Annabelle inadvertently step on.

4) The *General*, being a steam engine, relies on wood for its power, and when Buster stops to gather some wood which is sitting along the tracks, nothing goes right for him in the loading of the wood onto the train. Attempting to toss the wood slat onto/into one of the freight cars, the wood either flies over the car, landing on the other side of the tracks, or it hits the side of the car and falls back to his feet. The look on Buster's face is that of pure frustration and, as we watch, we too can feel his vexation.

5) During the battle scenes between the North and the South, Buster is at his comedic-tragic best. Two scenes to watch for in this action-packed sequence are Buster attempting to wield his sabre and failing to the point where it falls apart in his hands, and the scene which has him attempting to use a cannon.

6) The last sequence of scenes from *The General* has Buster dealing with how to steal a kiss from his ladylove, Annabelle. Because he is given the rank of Lieutenant, all soldiers that pass him must salute, and as protocol demands, he must return a salute. He soon finds that it is impossible to salute the troops and kiss Annabelle at the same time. In order to rectify this problem, we see Johnny Gray (Buster) come up with the best idea he ever had and does get the kissed he'd longed for.

The General was without a doubt the most difficult film for Buster to direct in his career. Because of his desire for the film to be so realistic, Buster and his crew had to work harder on *The General* than on any of his previous films. Working in Oregon, they didn't have the conveniences of having a studio nearby to get props from or a casting company at hand where they could get extras. For the battle at Rock River, it looked as if Buster was going to be in trouble, as he needed two armies, a Northern Army and a Southern Army, to fight the climactic battle. This was a difficult task since there were not enough people in the area of Cottage Grove to fill all of these parts. It was then when Buster decided to call the Oregon State National Guard. With the National Guard, Buster figured he'd have all the bodies needed to fill the two armies. Buster figured wrong.

The Oregon State National Guard consisted of five hundred men and for his climactic battle scene, Buster needed one thousand men, five hundred for the North and five hundred for the South. Not wanting to scrap the battle scene from the film, Buster came up with an idea that was pure genius.

The idea was to use the same men to play the soldiers in both armies. This is the way that Buster figured it: "I'd put them in gray uniforms and have them going right to left, then take them out, put them in blue uniforms and have them go from left to right and this is how we fought the war."

In implementing this idea, Buster was well aware of the fact that it would slow down production, but the way he was looking at it, it would be worth it if he could accomplish the look he was after.

It was the filming of these battle scenes which caused a few injuries to the personnel involved and almost caused a forest fire which could have easily erased Cottage Grove off the face of the earth.

During the filming of the battle, nine of the National Guard soldiers were injured. These injuries were due to Buster's order, once again, that everything be realistic, and this meant using real gunpowder in both the cannons and the rifles. It was this reality which caused the injuries, though none was considered to be serious. It should also be pointed out that Buster, too, was injured, when one of the cannons he was near went off, sending him flying. When he landed, he was knocked-out cold. In talking with some of the men who were members of the Oregon State National Guard at this time, and extras in *The General*, they all stated that working with Buster on these battle scenes was just like "being in a war which was real."

With the use of real gunpowder, Buster took every precaution to guard against the threat of fire, as the terrain they were shooting on was rather dry and they were also filming during the summer season. Even with all of his precautions, there was a fire which erupted. The fire was started because of all the sparks from the explosions which were being detonated. When the fires started, it moved very rapidly.

The whole crew, including Buster, got involved in putting the fire out. At one point, according to those present, Buster even went so far as to take off his pants in an effort to beat out some of the flames and, because of the actions on his part, he received various burns on both his legs. Once the fire was extinguished, the next problem was the smoke. Because the area was so dry and still, the smoke lingered, thus making it impossible to continue filming. According to those at the scene, the smoke halted production for about a week, until some rain came through the area and cleared the air. This week of non-production time drove the budget of *The General* up considerably.

Film compilations of the "clowns of the golden age of film comedy," or of Buster Keaton alone, usually show the same two scenes from *The General*: Buster versus a cannon and Marion Mack (Annabelle) getting blind-sided by a water tower.

With the cannon on the *Texas* being an actual Civil War cannon, no one really knew how to use it. In order for Buster to make sure he was going to get the shot he wanted, he had to experiment with firing the cannon. The first time the cannon was loaded with gunpowder, he put in enough, or so he thought, to shoot the lead cannonball fifteen feet, just far enough to make it into the engines cab without doing any damage, as this was to be a sight gag, not an explosion. Buster put too much gunpowder in the cannon and, when it went off, there was a thunderous boom and the cannonball went soaring over everything. It was, as Buster put it, "the luck of God that we were turning on a curve at the time the cannonball flew right by the engine and ended up landing in some open space." If the cannonball would have hit the target Buster had planned, Buster surely would have been killed. Using this trial-and-error method of determining the right amount of gunpowder, Buster loaded the cannon again using half as much powder as at first. Again the cannonball went too far, once again overshooting its intended target. The next time, Buster literally counted the kernels of gunpowder, picking them out with a pair of tweezers. Using less than half of a handful, Buster finally got the shot he wanted.

Using the very same Civil War cannon, Buster used a whole tin of gunpowder to get the shot which ended up hitting the *General* and the explosion almost sent Buster flying from the *Texas*.

The other scene from *The General* which is always shown in film compilations deals with a water tower, Buster, and Marion Mack. In this scene, Buster and Marion, as Johnny and Annabelle, stop at a water tower to fill the *General* with water. In the course of getting this water, Marion Mack felt the consequences of Buster's lack of rehearsing.

"When I went out that morning," Mack recalled years later, "I was made up and all ready to work and I didn't know they were going to make a scene with the water spout aiming at me. When the train would stop, they would let me have it. But they didn't tell me that they were going to do this. So, the scene you see in the movie, that was quite a surprise. I was pretty angry about it and believe me, I let Buster know it!"

Buster finished this classic of classics in time to qualify for the first Academy Awards, but M-G-M controlled the newly found Academy and Louis B. Mayer saw no reason to nominate a film which was made by another production company (Buster was with United Artists for *The General*).

Because *The General* cost so much money to produce, the studio decided to artistically handcuff Buster and, to do this, they informed him that in future films he would have to work with a production supervisor. The man entrusted with this job was Harry Brandt. Restricting Keaton in this way, the studio took away his style, his persona, and, as it would later turn out, his livelihood.

5

A STAR BEGINS TO FALL

With *The General* being a miserable failure at the box office and one of the costliest films of its era, United Artists started to look at Buster with somewhat of an evil eye. Not wanting to waste any more money on losers, United Artists was saying to Buster a word with which he was not at all familiar: "NO." When Buster would have an idea for a film and take it to the studio moguls, if they felt it would cost more money than it would take in, in their opinion, they would respond tell him, "No." If Buster wanted to add a gag which took a great deal of technical knowledge and cost money, United Artists told him, "No." Understanding what was happening to him and not liking it at all, Buster did something which he had never done before: he buckled under the pressure. It was because of United Artists' concern for money and their demanding a box office hit that Buster came up with his next release, a film titled *College*.

During this time, the late 1920's, films about college life flooded the film market and most of them were comedies. Since United Artists wanted a hit and didn't really care about the artistry of the film, Buster decided to go with the flow of popularity and filmed *College*. *College* is so unlike Buster's previous films, which were all original in their ideas, that it almost seems as if there is a Buster Keaton look-alike on the screen and not the real man himself. Buster did not want to make this film and this is very evident when viewing it. To put it rather simply, *College* is a film which defines the cinematic term "lightweight."

Although *College* was an undisputed artistic bomb, it was a complete Buster Keaton film, as he wrote the script and directed the film (although United Artists gave directorial credit to James W. Horne), and engineered all the gags. Although Buster always took the credit for producing the film, he did not. *College* did make a minimal amount of money at the box office, so the moguls who ran United Artists did indeed have a slight smile which creased their otherwise sullen lips.

One positive point of the film is that Buster got a chance to show off his immense athletic prowess and ability, something which is truly a joy to watch. Being the fantastic clown that he was and an almost perfect mime with his physical movements, Buster's athletic ability has often been overlooked when people reflect on his career. Considering the fact that his physical stunts are still viewed in awe, it is strange that these stunts were never really looked upon as physically demanding.

As *College* begins, Buster portrays what today would be termed a "nerd" or, as he put it, a "bookworm." Because of his brainy and weakling ways, he loses his girlfriend, who decides she wants to be seen with an athlete instead of a man whose favorite sport is that of turning the pages of a book which he is reading or studying. As she leaves him, she makes it a point of telling him why she is "dumping" him. As this sinks in, he feels that she is putting down his manhood, something he will not stand for.

In an effort to win back his girl and gain some popularity in the fictional college he is attending, he decides to drop his books in favor of sports and becomes, as those around him didn't believe he was, a man. In the course of making this change, there are some vintage Keaton sight gags and some great physical stunts, but they are so few and far between that they almost lose their visual punch during the sixty-five minutes that this film runs.

To achieve the goal which he has set for himself, the winning back of his girlfriend, we see Buster tackling a football game on the gridiron, attempting to excel at track and field, trying to make the grade on the rowing team, and attempting to master the skills of baseball (which in reality was an obsession with Buster as his love of baseball was second only to his love of trains). In all of his sporting attempts, he fails and soon feels that his girl is lost to him for good.

As the film approaches its conclusion, Buster finds out that his girlfriend has been abducted by the college's top athlete and is being held against her will. Taking this unfortunate circumstance and turning it to his advantage, Buster decides that he now has a chance of winning her back by rescuing her. He uses all of the athletic abilities he learned while trying to master the sports previously mentioned and accomplishes the improbable; he out athletes the "top jock" and wins his girl as she realizes that he is everything she wants and more.

With *College* making the money it did, United Artists almost forgave Buster for making *The General . . .* almost. When Buster went to the studio moguls regarding his next film project, their favorite word, "no," was used less often than during the filming of *College*. This next film, *Steamboat Bill, Jr.*, was the last true Buster Keaton classic that he would ever make on his own.

When people who have studied the art of filmmaking, or for that matter Buster himself, consider *Steamboat Bill, Jr.*, the first thing which comes to mind is *the shot*. It has been over sixty years since Buster performed this stunt and it is still regarded as one of the greatest stunts ever filmed, as well as one of the most dangerous. This scene, however, was not an original scene engineered for *Steamboat Bill, Jr.* This scene is the one which has Buster standing in front of his house and the front of it comes crashing down on top of him, yet he is saved by an open window. The truth about this scene is that Buster performed it a few times before in some of his previous films, yet it was not until *Steamboat Bill, Jr.* that it became widely noticed. This is not to say *the shot* does not deserve its place in film history, since no matter how many times he performed it, it was, and still is, the most dangerous stunt in cinematic history, simply because there was absolutely no trick photography used.

What made the outcome of this stunt even more questionable was the suspicion by some that Buster was contemplating suicide. Buster had just received two stunning pieces of terrible news. First, Natalie, his wife, was leaving him and taking away their two sons. Second, and some in the business would argue most important, he had received the word that he had been handed over to Metro-Goldwyn-Mayer and thus would lose all of his creative freedoms. These two pieces of wretched news came to Buster's attention just minutes before he was to film this dangerous stunt.

According to those on the set at the time, when Buster received these two pieces of news, all signs of life drained from him. It is reported that Buster stated, "nothing matters anymore. It's all over. This is it. The end." What with the bad news he received and his reported statements, there were those, including Charles Riesner, a friend and co-worker of Buster's, who were of the firm belief that Buster was very seriously thinking of committing suicide and what better way to go than being smashed to the ground by the front of a house and having the whole thing captured on film for the whole world to view.

All of the personnel who were on the set that day to witness the stunt still love to talk about it. Dan Riesner, son of Charles Riesner, recalls:

> The famous scene where Buster is standing in the street and a whole front of a building crashes down and he's standing right under it. One of the most spectacular stunts ever done and of course it was very dangerous. The whole front of the building was on a base plate and on hinges. It must have weighed a thousand pounds, the damned thing, and if Buster was six inches out of place, one way or the other, it would have driven him into the ground like a little tent peg. He was a game little guy, that Buster.

There is just one correction which must be made to Dan Riesner's comments. There was not six inches of space between Buster and the falling house. According to blueprints of the scene, Buster had two inches on either side of him and when you watch this scene, you notice the force of the falling house almost knocks his trademark pork pie hat off his head, even though it was in fact glued on.

In Buster's original storyline for *Steamboat Bill, Jr.*, it called for the film to be based around the natural disaster of a flood. This idea received with a solid "no" from United Artists, as they were afraid of the backlash it would cause due to some "killer" floods which had occurred in the South during the previous couple of years. United Artists was thinking that some people would feel that Buster was making fun of them. Not having any choice in the matter, Buster changed the storyline but still kept it centered around a natural disaster; a cyclone.

Steamboat Bill, Jr. was shot on location in the state capital of California, Sacramento. Even though the story is supposed to be centered in the South (Mississippi), Buster felt that the area known as "Old Sacramento" would be a better setting for the film. Instead of using the Mississippi River for the water scenes, he used the Sacramento River.

The story for *Steamboat Bill, Jr.* takes place on what is supposed to be one of the last Mississippi River steamboats. Buster, in the persona of Steamboat Bill, Jr., returns to his small hometown from college to help his father, Steamboat Bill, Sr., as he is in a feud with another steamboat captain. Things really start to heat up when Steamboat Bill, Sr. finds out that Junior is involved with the daughter of his enemy, this being the other steamboat captain. It is from this point on that the gags come fast and furious.

In a rather poignant scene, we see Buster parody himself. This scene has Steamboat Bill, Sr. and Junior in a men's clothing store where Junior is trying on hats, awaiting his fathers approval for which one to purchase. As he is going through a series of hats, Buster picks out and tries on his trademark pork pie hat, then quickly removes it and puts it back on the hat rack before his father has a chance to look at it.

As with some of Buster's previous films, *Steamboat Bill, Jr.* has some underwater scenes and, also like the others, these scenes did not go at all as planned. The reason for these particular underwater scenes is so Steamboat Bill, Jr., could save his girl from drowning. Before the actual shooting began, Buster had no idea just how strong the currents were in the Sacramento River. He found out when he was almost swept away the first time he dove in. These underwater scenes required more retakes than any of his previous films because, as was always the case with Buster, these shots had to be perfect.

Buster's girlfriend in this film was portrayed by Marion Byron, who was only sixteen years old during production. Byron was chosen for this role because of her great looks. No one ever thought to ask her if she could swim, which was obviously an important aspect of her role. As it turned out, Marion Byron could barely swim well enough to save her life. When Buster heard about Byron's lack of aquatic moveability, he simply shrugged his shoulders and walked over to a set telephone and called his sister Louise. Louise Keaton was an excellent swimmer and doubled for Byron in all of the swimming scenes. The change of women is not noticeable in the film since Louise Keaton and Marion Byron were identical in both weight and height. The difference of how their faces looked proved to be no problem as Buster just changed some of the underwater scenes to the point where the girl's face would not be shown.

One of the greatest sequences of scenes in film history is also included in *Steamboat Bill, Jr.*, Buster's last great classic. This sequence highlights Buster's battle with a cyclone.

In this sequence, Buster gets hit on the head by a falling piece of wood and is taken to the hospital. While in the hospital, the cyclone hits the town with all of its deadly force. The strength of the winds caused by this storm rips the hospital apart, hurling Buster onto the street, still in the hospital bed. As he is being flown about, various parts of the town are flying by him, some just missing him and others making crashing contact. As another big gust of wind comes by, Buster is wept into a demolished theater, much like the type he performed in during his vaudeville days. While in this theater, one gets the feeling that Buster is in a trancelike state because of the way the various sight gags appear. There is an ominous jack-in-the-box which seems as if it is real and a wooden dummy that just glares at him with a stare that is nothing short of pure evil.

The most enduring sequence of scenes from the cyclone are really the most obvious ones, those of Buster literally fighting the force of the wind. At one point, we see him standing at a forty-five degree angle in a vain attempt to take a step into the gusting winds. Realizing that this is impossible, he tries something different; he decides to jump into the wind in an effort to gain some headway and escape the apparent eye of the cyclone. This backfires as the wind picks him up and tosses him backward through the air.

Buster never did divulge how he came up with the idea for the cyclone scenes after his original idea of a flood was turned down by the people at United Artists, but one can come to the conclusion that he used his own life as the basis of these scenes. When Buster was three years old, he was literally swept away into the eye of a cyclone.

Steamboat Bill, Jr., of course, was not the first film of Buster's where his life imitated his art.

Since this was the last true Keaton classic that he would make (though obviously this was not known at the time), perhaps it was only proper that the spectacular nature of his slapstick situations and heroic resilience, resourcefulness, and perseverance were so regally brought to life.

For whatever reasons, *Steamboat Bill, Jr.* bombed miserably at the box office, once again causing United Artists to see blood red just at the mention of the name "Buster Keaton."

In 1928, there was not a bigger or better studio in Hollywood than Metro-Goldwyn-Mayer. Even as early as 1924, M-G-M was known as the "House of Hits." The studio motto then, as it is now, "Make it good . . . Make it big . . . Give it class."

In 1928, Metro-Goldwyn-Mayer was flying high with the release of such classics as *The Patsy* starring Marion Davis and Marie Dressler; *Alias Jimmy Valentine* starring William Haines and Lionel Barrymore; *Show People* starring Douglas Fairbanks, Sr. and Norma Talmadge; *Bringing Up Father* starring Marie Dressler and Polly Moran; *The Wind* starring the first lady of the American cinema, Lillian Gish, and *The Viking* starring Donald Crisp and Pauline Starke.

Of all the stars which were under contract with M-G-M in 1928, Buster Keaton was the only one who was not there of his own accord. Whereas Buster's first venture with M-G-M was of his own choice, this second trip really was not.

Of all the stories surrounding the legend of Buster Keaton, the stories regarding his second stint with M-G-M are some of the most interesting. There are those who believe that Buster and Joseph Schenck had a fight and that, in an effort to hurt Schenck, Buster left him and went to M-G-M out of spite. This story is untrue.

Another famous story is that, behind Buster's back, Joseph Schenck sold Buster's contract to his brother, Nicholas Schenck, who was heading a portion of M-G-M during that time. This story is also untrue, even though Nicholas Schenck was a mogul at M-G-M.

The true story of Buster's involuntary move to M-G-M is not really as dramatic as Hollywood might have us believe. Buster's own words provide the facts: "In 1928, I made the worse mistake of my career. Against my better judgment, I let Joseph Schenck talk me into giving up my own studio to make pictures at the booming M-G-M lot in Culver City."

In fairness to the memory of Joseph Schenck, it should be pointed out that he did not hold a gun to Buster's head and force him to sign the contract. Buster had full trust in the way Schenck was handling his career and it was this undying trust which entered Buster's mind when he signed the M-G-M contract. It should also be pointed out that after his last couple of box office failures, M-G-M was the only studio willing to open its pocketbook for Buster's services.

The deal Buster made with M-G-M was not a bad one at all. Included in this ten page contract, which was to run for two years, was a salary of one hundred and fifty thousand dollars per year with a stipulation that he must make two films each year. For each additional film over the stipulated two, he was to be paid fifty thousand dollars per film. All of this was definitely to Buster's advantage. One clause in the contract, though, was not at all advantageous to Buster and this was the paragraph which stated that he "shall be controlled as to story and direction, but the decision of the producer shall be final." In signing this contract, as he did, Buster Keaton essentially committed artistic suicide.

Once Buster signed, M-G-M had their first *real* comedian within their ironclad grasp. Even though such comedic stars as Wallace Beery and Marie Dressler were under contract with M-G-M, Buster was the first critically acclaimed and hailed comedian to sign with them.

Upon hearing of Buster's mulling over of the M-G-M contract, both Charlie Chaplin and Harold Lloyd tried to talk Buster out of signing. Charlie Chaplin told him, "Don't let them do it to you Buster. It's not that they haven't smart showmen there, they have some of the best, but there are too many of them and they'll all try to tell you how to make your comedies. It will simply be one more case of too many cooks."

Buster did not take Chaplin's advise to heart, yet he did try to shop around before he signed the contract. At one point, he went to Adolph Zukor and inquired about signing with his studio, but Zukor had just signed Harold Lloyd and he thought it was unwise to have two big name comics under contract. Other studios gave Buster the same type of responses, though none of the studios was really being truthful to Buster. The truth was, United Artists had been very vocal about Buster's spendthrift ways and the fact that he had started to drink rather heavily. United Artists was not lying on either count, but the way in which they spread the news was nothing short of malicious. Buster was essentially blackballed. Even in his later years, whenever Buster talked about his move to M-G-M, there was sadness in his voice.

From the very start, I was against making the switch to M-G-M. It seemed to me I would be lost making pictures in such a big studio. When Joe [Schenck] continued to argue for it, I asked Chaplin what he thought.

Joe Schenck never steered me wrong in his life until then. I do not think he meant to that time, either. But letting him override my own instinctive judgment was stupid. As I have said, it turned out to be the worst move I ever made.

When I went over to M-G-M, I was again assured that every effort was made to let me continue working with my team whenever possible. It turned out to be possible very seldom. The worst shock was discovering I could not work up stories the way I'd been doing, starting only with the germ of an idea. I learned that when I brought Irving Thalberg my first idea for a Buster Keaton comedy.

Thalberg, as well as being a fine judge of light comedy and farce, also appreciated good slapstick whenever he saw it on the screen. No truck driver ever guffawed louder at my better sight gags than did that fragile, intellectual boy genius. Nevertheless, he lacked the true low-comedy mind. Like any man who must concern himself with mass production, he was seeking a pattern, a format. Slapstick comedy has a format, but it is hard to detect in its early stages unless you are one of those who can create it. The unexpected was our staple product, the unusual our project, and the unique was the ideal we were always hoping to achieve.

Brilliant as he was, Irving Thalberg could not accept the way a comedian like me build his stories. Though it seems an odd thing to say, I believe that he would have been lost working in my little studio. His mind was too orderly for our harum-scarum, catch-as-catch-can, gag-grabbing method. Our way of operating would have seemed hopelessly mad to him. But, believe me, it was the only way. Somehow some of the frenzy and hysteria of our breathless, impromptu comedy building got into our movies and made them exciting.

In the late 1920's and on through the 1930's, the most beloved man by the people in front of the cameras in Hollywood was Irving Thalberg. This feeling by actors and actresses toward a studio executive was very rare indeed, but Irving Thalberg was a very rare man.

Irving Thalberg was born on May 30, 1899, in Brooklyn, New York. He was a frail and sickly child and shuddered from rheumatic heart conditions. Because of these conditions, his doctors, when he was a child, told him that the chances that he would not likely live to see his thirtieth birthday. Taking heed to what his doctor had said, Thalberg balked at going to college and instead took up the common secretarial trades upon his graduation from high school.

Thalberg's first job was with the Universal Film Manufacturing Company, where he was a secretary to the head of the company, Carl Laemmle. After only a few years, Laemmle appointed Thalberg to be his Head of Production.

When he was barely past his twentieth birthday, the slight and innocent Thalberg had made quite a name for himself in the blossoming Hollywood community. It was at this point that he gained the nickname of "the boy wonder."

For fans of F. Scott Fitzgerald, it should be pointed out that in his novel *The Last Tycoon*, the hero is based on Irving Thalberg.

In 1923, Thalberg left Laemmle and joined what was at the time a small production company headed by a man named Louis B. Mayer. This company was soon to become Metro-Goldwyn-Mayer. With M-G-M, Thalberg assumed the position of vice-president and supervisor of production.

As 1927 rolled along, Thalberg married Hollywood's and MGM's number one starlet, Norma Shearer. Even though his health was deteriorating, he personally made it a point to supervise most of the studio's top productions from beginning to end.

During his career at M-G-M, Thalberg supervised such great film classics as *The Merry Widow* (1925), *Ben Hur* (1926), *Anna Christie* (1930), *Private Lives* (1931), *Strange Interlude* (1932), *Mutiny On The Bounty* (1935), *A Night At The Opera* (1935), *Romeo and Juliet* (1936), and *The Good Earth* (1937).

Whereas Irving Thalberg was universally loved and respected by the actors and actresses under him, the same cannot be said of Louis B. Mayer. Mayer was respected by most in the film community, but loved he was not. If there were any emotions toward Mayer, and there certainly were, hate and despise were often the words mentioned. Buster should have known this and perhaps he did, yet his trust in Joseph Schenck was stronger than the winds of warning he had received from Chaplin, Lloyd and countless others.

Louis B. Mayer was the type of man who could not be talked to. If he said the world was flat, there was not a person on the face of the earth who would be able to convince him otherwise. When a film was being shot by M-G-M, it had to be done Mayer's way or it would not be done at all. As far as comedians were concerned, Mayer loved to laugh and appreciated nothing more than a great comedic film, however, that film had to be his, with his ideas, his workings, his stories, his everything. If you worked at M-G-M during the tyrannical reign of Louis B. Mayer and you had a mind of your own, chances are you wouldn't make it.

Louis B. Mayer started life in Minsk, Russia, where he was born on July 4, 1885. His real name was Eliezer Mayer, but was changed to Louis when, with his family, he immigrated to New York.

Mayer's first job as a young adult was not in the film business since there was no film business. In 1907, while running a junk business, Mayer responded to a newspaper ad which showed a dilapidated movie theater for sale in Haverhill, Massachusetts. Borrowing money from whoever would lend it to him, he bought and refurbished the theater and started to book first-run, top-quality films. Within a couple of years of this initial purchase, he bought more theaters and, by 1921, he owned the largest theater chain in all of New England. In 1914, wanting to get into the film business in a bigger way, he entered the world of film distributing and, in 1915, he made a bundle when he distributed D.W. Griffith's epic *The Birth of a Nation*.

By 1917, Mayer was heading his own production company in Los Angeles. He had under contract only one star, Anita Stewart, who started in his first production, the forgettable film, *Virtuous Wives*.

In 1924, Marcus Loew, who owned Metro Pictures, purchased Goldwyn Pictures and Louis B. Mayer Productions, combining all three in Metro-Goldwyn-Mayer. Loew made Mayer the Vice President and General Manager. Mayer held these positions until 1951, when he lost a power struggle to his aide, Dory Schary.

Under Mayer, M-G-M was known as "the studio with more stars than there are in heaven." In the 1930's and 40's, Mayer was the most powerful man in Hollywood and the highest paid person in America. Mayer had a way about him which was very vengeful. When he lost his position in 1951, he was very bitter and spent most of his last years trying to start a rebellion of the stockholders against the management of Loew Inc., the parent company of M-G-M. He was unsuccessful in his attempts. Louis B. Mayer died in 1957.

Louis B. Mayer was one of the founding fathers of the major motion picture industry, but to get to the position he achieved, he ruined many careers and lives, with Buster Keaton being the most prominent.

As Buster was preparing for his first M-G-M film, *The Cameraman*, Irving Thalberg stepped in and, due to Buster's reputation of being a spendthrift where his films were concerned, Thalberg assigned Laurence Weingarten to supervise the production. Laurence Weingarten had no comedy experience when it came to making films; his specialty was biblical films, a mainstay for M-G-M at the time. Keaton and Weingarten clashed immediately, neither man wanting to give into the other's whims.

Buster felt deceived by Thalberg. During the initial contract talks between Buster, Thalberg, and Nicholas Schenck, Thalberg had said that he would personally supervise Buster's films. Buster approved of this since he and Thalberg were friends, often playing bridge together. Because of his huge work load, Thalberg reneged and gave these supervisory duties to Weingarten. As the clashes between Buster and Laurence Weingarten became more intense, Buster stormed into Thalberg's office and demanded that something be done. Thalberg, being the cool-headed businessman which he was, calmed Buster down, but did not give into his wishes of replacing Weingarten.

With no other choice, Buster did indeed give in, yet he did not do so lightly.

Even though Buster's feud with Laurence Weingarten was major, his initial contractual work with M-G-M was not really that bad. Buster's first film, *The Cameraman*, was his first film as a "star" without his handpicked production staff. (It should be noted that when Buster went to M-G-M, so did his production staff. But once they got there, they were separated and sent to various producers and directors and were no longer working solely with Keaton.)

The Cameraman was released by M-G-M on September 15, 1928. In Buster's earlier films, as previously mentioned, he never worked with a script, just outlines. With *The Cameraman*, M-G-M insisted that there be a script and also insisted that Buster follow it to the letter.

In *The Cameraman*, Buster once again does a parody, this time poking a little good-hearted fun at William Randolph Hearst and the way he ran the Hearst International Newsreel Company (Buster was still upset at the way the Hearst newspapers handled the Roscoe "Fatty" Arbuckle incident). Another point that Buster wanted to project with *The Cameraman* was his respect for cameramen and his love for this tool of reproduction.

As far as plot goes, *The Cameraman* is not unlike some of Buster's other films, in which he does all he can do to win the heart of a girl. The character portrayed by Buster in this film is that of a lonely tintype photographer who meets a secretary for the Hearst Company (portrayed by Marceline Day). Knowing the pretty woman would have nothing to do with the type of photographer which he was, he decides to become a free-lance newsreel photographer and, in the course of this career move, he goes out and purchases a moving picture camera. In getting some newsreel footage, he fouls up in his shooting. He comes up with scenes such as a naval battleship cruising up New York's famed Great White Way (Broadway), as well as some action sequences with everyone moving in a reverse. When he submits this film to the Hearst people, they watch it and come to the conclusion that this man (Buster) just may be the next Albert Einstein type of genius. Never once does it enter their minds that he got these scenes because he did not now how to operate his new moving picture camera.

There are a couple of segments in *The Cameraman* which show that Buster, even though he was artistically handcuffed by M-G-M, could still sneak in a few of his trademark sight gags. One of these scenes centers around Buster and his love for baseball. These scenes were shot in New York's Yankee Stadium and show a baseball game in progress. The interesting and eerie thing here is that Buster plays all of the positions, both offensively and defensively.

Another of these segments has Buster and another character in a locker room. While both of these men are getting dressed, they get their clothes mixed-up and both men are proportionally different when it comes to their sizes. In watching the series of events in this sequence, it is obvious that Buster ignored M-G-M's order of working strictly by the script. This segment is obviously ad-libbed all the way through and because of this, the comic genius of Buster Keaton shines through.

There seems to be some question as to where this film was actually produced. Some have stated that the crew was in New York to film on location, but had to leave because wherever they went to shoot, Buster was mobbed by throngs of people. So, except for the Yankee Stadium sequence, they moved production to Hollywood. It is understandable how this story came to be as when they originally started to shoot, huge mobs did in fact gather around Buster. To get around this problem, Buster and the crew just changed filming schedules. What they did to finally get their street scenes was to start shooting on Sunday mornings at five o'clock. After the Yankee Stadium sequence and the various street scenes, the company packed up and headed for Hollywood to complete shooting.

The Cameraman was not a huge success for Buster or M-G-M, yet, in 1948, M-G-M remade the film as *Watch The Birdie* starring Red Skelton in Buster's role. For this remake, Buster was the uncredited gag supervisor.

In 1929, the silent era for films was reaching its end. More and more studios were making films with sound or, as they were being called at the time, "talkies." Buster wanted to get involved with this new phenomenon within his industry, but M-G-M had other ideas. Even though M-G-M was releasing some "talkies" at this time, they did not want to use Buster in this way and thus his second film for M-G-M, *Spite Marriage*, was yet another silent film.

It was with *Spite Marriage* that Buster Keaton really felt the confinement of working for Metro-Goldwyn-Mayer. With *Spite Marriage*, Buster had no input; he was not involved in the writing, directing, or stunt coordination. This was also the last Keaton film where dangerous stunts were performed since M-G-M, like most of the other major studios, prohibited their stars from performing such feats. As far as the studios were concerned, this was why they had stunt people on their payrolls.

Spite Marriage teamed Buster with an actress who was by far the most talented of all his leading ladies, Dorothy Sebastian, who was an M-G-M contract player. Throughout the filming of *Spite Marriage*, and even after it was released into the theaters, people in and out of the industry remarked on the chemistry between Buster and Sebastian. There were two reasons for this apparent chemistry. Sebastian was the first of Buster's leading ladies who actually had a major role, unlike his usual female leads who were just there for story continuity; he always needed to have a woman to be after or to fight for. Also, unknown to most people, Buster and Dorothy Sebastian were in the throes of a rather steamy, yet private, affair.

Apparently the executives at M-G-M had a phobia about the name "Elmer," so Buster used this name in just about all of his films for M-G-M. In *Spite Marriage*, Elmer (Buster) plays an assistant to a tailor who is in love with Trilby Drew (Sebastian), but she does not feel the same way toward him (this is the stereotypical relationship in Buster's films). Elmer is aware that Trilby doesn't want to have anything to do with him, but this does not stop him from continuing to woo her. Before long, she does say "yes" to his numerous proposals of marriage and he thinks he has finally won her heart. He is wrong! She agree's to marry him out of spite, this after she and her boyfriend have a big fight.

Spite Marriage contains one sequence of scenes that since has been copied by every slapstick comedian in one form or another. This sequence involves Buster's attempt to get his drunken, unconscious wife into bed on their honeymoon night. This sequence really belongs to Dorothy Sebastian. During this entire sequence, her body movements had to be perfect to match those of Buster. This is the only original scene in *Spite Marriage*; the rest are basically reproduced from some of Buster's earlier films. Points-in-fact:

1) The scenes from *Spite Marriage* with Buster and Dorothy on a

yacht are copied from the scenes in *The Navigator* which Buster performed with Katheryn McGuire.

2) The fight scene with between Buster (as Elmer), and a rum-running pirate are the same as his fight scene in *Battling Butler*, which pitted Buster and Snitz Edwards.

3) The scenes in *Spite Marriage* which have Buster and Dorothy on a Broadway stage were a recreation of the scenes he performed in his classic film *The Playhouse*.

Buster entered the "talkie" revolution in a big way. As opposed to popular belief, Buster did not star in his first talking picture. It was a big, splashy M-G-M musical production called *The Hollywood Revue of 1929*. It was in this musical where the world first heard the voice behind the "great stone face."

In this film, everyone who was on the payroll of Metro-Goldwyn-Mayer was featured. This list of Hollywood heavyweights included Jack Benny, John Gilbert, Norma Shearer, Joan Crawford, Laurel & Hardy, Lionel Barrymore, Marion Davis, Marie Dressler, and Conrad Nagel, just to name a few. The way that it was put at the time, anyone at M-G-M who could sing, dance, talk, whistle, mumble, or groan to music was told that they had to be in this film. As it turned out, *The Hollywood Revue of 1929* was one of M-G-M's biggest money-makers of that year. In this film, which was really a group of various skits set to music, Buster performed in two sequences. The first was a skit where he did an Oriental dance routine titled "Dance of the Sea." He then appeared in the films finale where the entire cast joined in on a rollicking version of "Singing in the Rain" (this was years before the movie of the same title was released).

Although many of the great silent screen stars were afraid of the "talkie" revolution and hesitant about entering films with sound, Buster Keaton was not. M-G-M finally gave into his wish when they allowed him his first "talkie," a film titled *Free and Easy*.

Free and Easy was put together by the M-G-M story department with no input from Buster. Trying to put Buster in a "talkie" was not as simple a task as most would think, since Buster's voice was quite low and gruff; this did not fit the persona of Buster — that of being a smallish, impish, shy, and quiet man. M-G-M did not know how Buster would be received by the film-going public once they heard his voice. M-G-M was not the only studio who was worrying about how their silent film stars would be received once they opened their mouths. As it turned out, when sound became a staple of the film industry, many silent film stars became unemployed. Film fans were stunned to hear the high and somewhat squeaky voice of John Gilbert, the romantic leading man of his time. Because of sound, Gilbert's popularity dropped and never again regained its stardom. The great Norma Talmadge, the silent screen's true *femme fatale*, had her career ruined because her voice was not at all what the public had imagined; her voice and characterizations were a definite contradiction to one another.

When people talk about the change in films from silent to sound, it is often referred to as the "sound revolution." With the big stars who had become overnight "has-beens," the word "revolution" could actually have been an understatement. In 1952, M-G-M produced a film which dealt with this "revolution" and how it affected the stars. The film in question is the classic Gene Kelly vehicle, *Singing In the Rain*.

There are not many good things to say about the 1930 release of *Free and Easy*. It had a terribly written script with dialogue often of elementary school level. The gags are there, but the usual Buster Keaton belly-laughs are not. Where M-G-M came across the title for this film, *Free and Easy*, is unknown, but they did not get the title from the films contents. Without a doubt, the strangest part of this film is the scene where we witness Buster performing a song-and-dance routine. Even though Buster Keaton was the greatest film comedian who ever lived, he was not a singer or a dancer – not by any stretch of the imagination.

There are many who believe that M-G-M came up with *Free and Easy* in an attempt to change Buster's screen image. This may very well be true but their plan backfired in a monumental way, even though the film was a big money maker. Why did such a terrible film do so well at the box office? As director Edward Sedgwick once said, "It was solely due to the name Buster Keaton illuminated in neon on the theater's marquee."

In *Free and Easy*, Buster once again plays a character named Elmer. This time, Elmer is a lowly auto mechanic, almost the same type of character which he portrayed in his 1922 classic release, *The Black-*

smith.   This time, Elmer goes to Hollywood with his girlfriend (portrayed by Anita Page) who has just won a beauty contest and was crowned Miss Gopher Prairie from Indiana.   While in Hollywood, Elmer takes her to a movie studio, which incidentally happens to be M-G-M, in the hope of getting her a move contract. His efforts go for naught, but in trying, Elmer creates havoc on the numerous sets, much to the chagrin of the actors, actresses, and directors. During the course of *Free and Easy*, Buster loses his girl to a young up-and-coming actor (portrayed by a real up-and-coming actor, Robert Montgomery), though this is not a surprise.

The final scene in *Free and Easy* has Buster in full clown makeup. This makeup is not of a happy clown, but a sad one; a clown appealing for sympathy and pity; Pagliacci come to life!

It is rather apparent that M-G-M thought *Free and Easy* was a great project for Buster.   They invested just under a million dollars to produce it, but they rewarded Buster with a ten thousand dollar bonus and a three month vacation with full pay.

For Buster's April 28, 1930, release of *Voice of Hollywood #101*, he was loaned out by M-G-M to a small independent studio named Tiffany Films. *Voice of Hollywood #101* was a compilation of skits and was the type of film which was shown in theaters between the two feature-length films. In *Voice of Hollywood #101*, Buster, with Lew Cody and Cliff Edwards, does some hamming in front of a lion cage.

The practice of studios lending their talent to other studios was a common one. When things were slow at one studio, most actors and actresses, under various contracts with their own studios, could be loaned to another studio. In this lending of talent, the studio doing the lending, acting as an agent, received a percentage of the star's salary, usually about ten percent.

As the 1930's were beginning, Buster was not working nearly as much as he had been when the century had begun. From 1917, when he first entered the world of film, until he signed his M-G-M contract in 1928, Buster had made forty-eight films, not including the compilations to which he had lent his talents. The main reason he was not working much now was because his M-G-M films were taking much more time to produce.

Buster's only other film for M-G-M in 1930 was one Buster

always considered to be very personal. This film was titled *Dough-boys* and was released on August 30, 1930.

It is unknown how much of an artistic input Buster had regarding this film, but according to what was stated about the film, he must have at least been a co-writer, for he often mentioned that *Dough-boys* was autobiographical. This is rather hard to believe since the film did have some very funny moments and, as we all know, war is never funny. Also, Buster's Army days were so few they could not have provided enough material for a full length film.

When Buster was in the Army and stationed in France, his main duty was to entertain the troops and keep the soldiers' morale high (much like Elvis a few decades later). In *Doughboys*, his character's main chore is the same and this is just about where the similarities to Buster's real days in the Army end.

Buster's character in *Doughboys* is the same type of character as in all of his M-G-M films: an inept bungler. But this time he is a wealthy "Elmer" and gets drafted into the Army by mistake. As mentioned, *Doughboys* does have its funny moments, mostly due to the tremendous way in which Buster uses his body as a tool for comedy, but, on the whole, this film was, as one reviewer put it, "a real yawner."

Even though Buster was anxious to be a part of the sound revolution, there was one thing he missed about the silent film era and that was the old cameras used to make the silent films. The old cameras were noisy and had staccato rhythm as they worked and this rhythm created a beat for the actors and actresses, especially the comedians who used this beat for their comedic timing. The cameras used for making sound films, rather obviously, were quite silent.

As the filming of *Doughboys* was wrapping up, Buster's drinking was becoming more and more apparent in his personality. On more than one occasion, filming of *Doughboys* had to be held up because of Buster not showing up on the set, something which until this time in his career was unheard of for him. He was also, more times than not, a very argumentative man, picking verbal fights with anyone who was close to him. Once the M-G-M bosses got wind of Buster's activity, they started to watch him like a hawk, not because they were concerned about his health, but because they were concerned about their checkbook – time delayed, for whatever reasons, was money wasted. Regardless of M-G-M's eagle eyes, Buster's drinking was getting progressively worse.

For Buster's only compilation film of 1931, M-G-M once again lent him out, but this time it was a little different than before. The studio they loaned him to was not a small independent; it was M-G-M's main competitor, the up-and-coming Paramount Pictures. This film, *Stolen Jools* (pronounced jewels) was almost like a who's who of Hollywood. Aside from Buster, this film included the likes of Edward G. Robinson, the comedy kids from Our Gang, Hedda Hopper, Joan Crawford, Victor McLaglen, Irene Dunne, Buddy Rogers, Maurice Chevalier, Barbara Stanwych, Fay Wray, Joe E. Brown, and Gabby Hayes, and others.

This film was presented by the National Variety Artists to raise funds for a tuberculosis sanatorium. It concerns a stolen pearl necklace belonging to the character portrayed by Norma Shearer. Buster plays one of the four Keystone Cops who appear at the very beginning. This film was also released on the British Isles under the title *The Slippery Pearls*. Apparently Buster, for whatever reasons, could not see that he was no longer wanted for his talents, it was just his name on the marquee that the studios and producers wanted.

Whether it was coincidence or not, planned or not planned, on the day *Stolen Jools* was released, Buster's next M-G-M film, *Parlor, Bedroom and Bath*, was also released.

When M-G-M handed Buster the script for *Parlor, Bedroom and Bath*, he laughed. This laughter was not because the script was funny; it was because it was so bad. Buster tried to talk Irving Thalberg into trashing the script, but Thalberg would hear nothing of it. Realizing that M-G-M would not back down regarding the making of this film, Buster then pleaded to be given the chance to rework the script. Once again he was denied. Realizing that all of his efforts were going for naught, he took the stance of, "then let's do it and get it over with!" They did and it certainly shows.

Parlor, Bedroom and Bath is another film which totally takes Buster out of character. M-G-M actually tried to make Buster into a comedic romantic lead. The basic story line for this film is, as one reviewer put it, "a total waste of celluloid." The Don Juan character which Buster portrays is Reginald Irving, yet for all intents and purposes, it is nothing more than another "Elmer." As Reginald,

Buster frolics with all of the females in the cast, this being done in either a parlor or a bedroom. Where the word "bath" enters is unknown, unless M-G-M concluded that those who paid to see this were flushing their money down the toilet.

One historical point to *Parlor, Bedroom and Bath* is that the opening scenes of the film were shot at Buster's sprawling mansion which he called his "Italian Villa." Next to Pickfaire, the legendary home of Mary Pickford and Douglas Fairbanks, Sr. (unfortunately torn down a few years ago), Buster's Italian Villa was one of the most beautiful pieces of real estate in Southern California. Buster was very proud of his home and this was his way of showing it to the entire world. Little did he know that, within a few short years, he would lose his mansion.

Also in this flop of a film, for the first time since *The General*, Buster has a scene with a train playing a pivotal role. This scene, which runs about seven minutes, was filmed with no sound, bringing back Buster's silent film days. There is nothing original about this scene, as it is basically the exact same scene as played in *One Week*, yet this time it is a car which gets hit by the train and not a house. As was M-G-M's way of writing scripts for Buster, they could not match his talents in writing, so they simply bastardized his career. This fact is plainly obvious in all of his M-G-M films.

When M-G-M handed Buster the script for his next film, *Sidewalks of New York*, he couldn't believe what he was looking at it. As soon as he read the script, he once again marched directly to the office of Irving Thalberg and told the "boy wonder" that there was "no way this film is going to work." Thalberg did not disagree with Buster, yet he did tell him that he would have to make the film. When Buster again attempted to protest, Thalberg informed him that if he did not make the film, he would be suspended without pay and may very well face legal actions for breach of contract. Against his better judgment, yet having no other choice in the matter, Buster went ahead with the filming. What Buster did not know at this time was that Irving Thalberg was not being difficult on his own; he was under the direct orders of Louis B. Mayer, who wanted *Sidewalks of New York* made and he wanted Buster to star in it. As previously noted, whatever Mayer wanted, Mayer always got.

In *Sidewalks of New York*, Buster plays a character who is the playboy owner of an apartment house who falls in love with a beautiful, yet tough, female tenant (played by Anita Page). Once again, this film reuses material from other Buster Keaton films, most notably *Battling Butler*. *Sidewalks of New York* has only one somewhat amusing scene that centers on the sport of boxing. The conclusion of this film once again has Buster doing something in which he had no talent: dancing. In spite of this film being a "dog" with no redeeming value or artistic touches, *Sidewalks of New York* made M-G-M nine hundred thousand dollars at the box office and this profit created more than one smile on the thin lips of Louis B. Mayer along with a few "I-told-you-so's."

The year 1932 was not a one for Buster either professionally or personally. Professionally, M-G-M took it upon themselves to make Buster part of a comedy team and the partner they chose for him was Jimmy Durante. A worse choice they could not have made.

Buster's personal life in 1932 was a nightmare. His personal problems started one day in February when, as Buster put it, "all hell broke loose."

Buster reflected:

> An actress invaded my dressing room at M-G-M and announced that she made up her mind that I should support her. When I refused, she ripped off my shirt and started to scratch and claw away at me. Ukulele Ike Edwards and Clarence Locan, an M-G-M publicity man, were there when this tigress walked in. But both men ran for their lives when she steamed into action. Meanwhile, this gentlewoman was breaking my dressing room windows and screaming like some crazy old witch. I had been too stunned by her daffy behavior to move. But when the lady picked up a pair of long shears and lunged at me with them, I belted her in the jaw in self-defense.
>
> At this point, a couple of Culver City policemen arrived. They turned out to be unlucky cops. When they tried to drag her away, she kicked one in the genitals and took a backhanded swipe at the other, giving him a black-eye.
>
> The next day I was summoned to Irving Thalberg's office. Eddie Mannix was with him. They showed me a

report from the woman's doctor stating that when I hit her, I broke her jaw.

"Now she wants ten thousand dollars from you," Mannix said. "If she doesn't get it, she'll bring the whole mess into court."

"The hell with her," I said. "I didn't hit her hard enough to break her jaw. And no one with a fractured jaw was ever able to yell as loud as she did at those two cops."

"If you guys are so worried about this," I added, "let the company fork over the ten thousand dollars that will shut her up!"

"No," said Mannix, "you'll have to pay her. The name M-G-M must not be on the check."

But he seemed to think it was all right for the name of Buster Keaton to be on the check. We continued to argue, and, in the end, I made out the ten thousand dollar check and handed it over.

This confrontation with the wild woman was just the beginning of Buster's personal problems. Shortly after this incident in his dressing room, Buster received word that Natalie had finally started divorce procedures against him. Even though they had been separated and Natalie had disappeared with their two boys, this was the first time that divorce proceedings had been initiated.

Buster decided not to fight the divorce and made an unfortunate decision: he would not retain a lawyer. Because of this decision, Natalie received everything she asked for, including their home, the Italian Villa; two of their cars; thirty thousand dollars worth of property; all of the money in their joint bank accounts; sole custody of their children; eighty thousand dollars in insurance policies; and, of course, alimony and child support.

The hardest part of this was that once she finally had legal custody of their two boys, she changed their name from Keaton to Talmadge. To say this broke Buster's heart would be a gross understatement, as his two sons were his pride and joy, his greatest thrill, and, as some have said, his reason for living. With all of this personal trauma coming at him at such a furious pace, Buster and the bottle became even closer friends than they were before.

In working with Jimmy Durante, Buster felt rather ill at ease. Buster liked Durante personally, saying he was a "very good man," but one thing which Buster found unnerving about Durante was that he "could not keep quiet, he talked nonstop." The team of Buster Keaton and Jimmy Durante lasted for three pictures, all of which were directed by Edward Sedgwick.

Of all the "professional experiments" M-G-M tried with Buster Keaton, their teaming of him and Durante was the worse. To put these two totally different comedians together was like mixing oil and water; there was absolutely no combining of their talents.

When Buster and Durante started their first film, *The Passionate Plumber*, Buster became aware of what was going on. There was no doubt in his mind that M-G-M and Louis B. Mayer, in particular, were attempting to get rid of him; to sweep him under the cinematic carpet. This became evident to everyone when, in their last two films, *Speak Easily* and *What! No Beer?*, Jimmy Durante received top billing and was given all the best lines.

The forced teaming with Durante made Buster feel that, in addition to his personal life, his professional life was coming to a crashing end, as well. He had faced personal problems before and, for the most part, came out unscathed. Professionally, though, he had never faced any bad luck or bad conditions and there were many who thought that this was something which Buster could not handle. As it finally turned out, he did handle it, but just barely.

The Passionate Plumber, the first of the Buster Keaton/Jimmy Durante joint projects, was released on February 6, 1932. The script for this film was written by Lawrence Johnson and Ralph Spence, two writers of immense talent, yet with this script their talents did not shine. One of the main reasons for this may have been the lurking eyes and ego of Louis B. Mayer.

One thing positive to be said about *The Passionate Plumber* is that M-G-M enlisted some of its better known contract players in the supporting roles, including Polly Moran, Mona Maris, Gilbert Roland, and the great character actor, Henry Armetta.

By now, Buster Keaton was a full-fledged alcoholic, yet he would not admit it. Even though his alcoholism was evident to everyone on the set, amazing as it may seem, it did not really affect his performance in *The Passionate Plumber*. In this film, Buster's moves are fluid and graceful, his timing is, at it always was, impeccable. Buster's perfect timing is quite evident in the scene where Gilbert Roland challenges him to a duel. The sight gags in this sequence of scenes are marvelous and Jimmy Durante, as Buster's idiotic sidekick, is quite amusing.

One sequence of scenes which separates *The Passionate Plumber* from other Keaton/Durante films takes place in a Monte Carlo casino. These scenes are reminiscent of the Buster Keaton of old; the Buster Keaton who was revered and admired by all in the cinematic community. In these scenes, Buster's movements are quite simply unbelievable. Not only does Buster prove that timing is the main element of film comedy, but he also proves, without a shadow of a doubt, that physical comedy is a true art form. On the few times this film has been viewed at film festivals or revivals, this sequence of scenes very often receives a standing ovation.

Speak Easily, the second of the three Keaton/Durante films, was released on August 13, 1932. *Speak Easily* was the first time since Buster had left the Comique Film Corporation and Rosco "Fatty" Arbuckle that he did not receive top-star billing. Playing the "second banana" to Jimmy Durante did bother Buster, but not as much as most people would have thought. At this point, Buster had lost his drive and really didn't care. This morose feeling was caused by his personal problems, his professional problems and the thought of becoming a "Hollywood has-been," and his drinking which was making him numb to any feelings other than those related to melancholy.

When M-G-M was putting the cast together for *Speak Easily*, they made some interesting decisions concerning the supporting cast. This cast included Thelma Todd (whose infamous murder in 1934 has yet to be solved), Hedda Hopper (who would later go on to become queen of the Hollywood gossip mongers), and Sidney Tolar (known to all as one of the actors to play the Oriental sleuth Charlie Chan). Even though M-G-M put together this excellent supporting cast, it still did not help the film.

The basic story line for *Speak Easily* has Buster playing a college professor who inherits a large sum of money, leaves his academic profession, and pursues the bright lights of Broadway. He pursues investing in a traveling vaudeville-type show and comes across the character portrayed by Jimmy Durante, the show's director. As with all of Buster's films, there is a woman in his sights played by Thelma Todd.

As one follows the career of Buster Keaton, marveling at his early works, following the way his genius matured, and standing in awe of the pure artistry of his films, it is sad to watch these Buster Keaton/ Jimmy Durante films and see the destruction of his genius. *Speak Easily* was a sad excuse for a comedy film, but looks like a classic when compared to *What! No Beer?*.

What! No Beer? was, as it would turn out, Buster's swansong with Metro-Goldwyn-Mayer and a worse lasting impression he could not have made.

According to Buster himself, *What! No Beer?* was "a one hundred percent turkey!" It was during the filming of *What! No Beer?* that Buster's drinking started to affect his comic ability noticeably. Often he would report to the set and be so "out of it" that director Edward Sedgwick would have to stop filming until Buster was sober enough to resume his character. On some occasions, this break in filming would last an entire day or so. Of course when this would happen, M-G-M still had to pay everyone who showed up to film and this made Louis B. Mayer climb his office walls. Buster did not feel as if setting back production was any big matter since M-G-M's number one actress, Greta Garbo, was known to walk off sets for a multitude of personal reasons, costing M-G-M more money in delays than they were putting into the entire production budgets of Buster's films with Jimmy Durante.

What! No Beer? is basically Jimmy Durante's film with Buster thrown in as a backdrop of sorts. Unfortunately, there is very little comedy in this film. The premise of the film was good and, if it had been properly written, it could have been one of the funniest films to come out of M-G-M up to that point.

In this film, Buster sleepwalks through his role of a taxidermist who joins forces with a nonstop talking con man (Jimmy Durante) in making illegal beer. There is one scene from this film which stirs memories of Buster's golden days of silent comedy and, interestingly enough, this scene was filmed without sound. In this scene, we see Buster near a truck which is loaded with barrels of beer. Soon, one of the barrels falls from the truck and, as one might expect, the rest soon follow. As they fall, Buster does a dance to keep from getting hit and then takes off running down a hill as the barrels roll after him. This scene is reminiscent of the boulder chase scene in his 1925 film, *Seven Chances*. It is a wonder that Buster was able to perform this scene at all, as he later admitted that he was drunk everyday he was being filmed and it took six weeks to make this picture.

After the release of *What! No Beer?*, Buster Keaton and Jimmy Durante went their separate ways. This was the decision M-G-M and Louis B. Mayer who had had enough of Buster's drunken ways and fired him. In later years, when Buster would talk of his teaming with Durante, Buster often complained about the physical abuse he took from Durante, which was just a part of Durante's nature. On and off the set, whenever Jimmy Durante would be talking to Buster, he would hit him on his arms and torso; this was not done out of spite, malice, or dislike, it was done in a jocular manner, much like teenage boys when they get together. Since Durante was a much stronger man than he looked, this punching was turning Buster into a walking bruise. Buster thought about hitting Jimmy Durante back but this was just not Buster's way of dealing with people, so instead he took the barrage of "fun punches" for the duration of their short time together.

Much to the credit of Louis B. Mayer, as he was watching Buster drown his talents, career, and, possibly, his life in bottles of whiskey, he decided he must do something. Since Mayer did have a lot of money invested in Buster, he decided to send Keaton to a clinic to "dry out." Buster, not wanting to admit that he was suffering from the disease of alcoholism, balked at this move by Mayer. While Buster was trying to convince Mayer that his drinking was not a problem and something he could handle on his own, Mayer just leaned back in his chair with his eyes closed. When Buster was finished with his pleading speech, Mayer opened his eyes and told Buster, "It will be a four day stay. You are a drunk and you need help!" As usual, Buster lost out to Mayer whose final word was always just that . . . final.

M-G-M sent Buster to a clinic and spa known as Arrowhead Springs. It was at Arrowhead Springs where most of the *high class* people in Hollywood and the film community went to rid themselves of their drinking and drug problems. Buster stayed his prescribed four days and was not at all surprised when he found out that the entire bill for his stay and medical needs was paid by Louis B. Mayer and M-G-M.

Upon his release from Arrowhead Springs, Buster was sober, but this lasted for only a short period of time. When he started up his drinking again, it became even worse than before. He was now disappearing for weeks at a time, traveling around on horrendous drinking binges and sprees. He would often suffer from mental blackouts; times when he could remember nothing whatsoever. It was these blackout which are the reason for his second marriage. His second wife, Mae Scribbins, was a nurse who Buster met while he was drying out at Arrowhead Springs. From what is known, Buster married Mae Scribbins in Mexico, where he had taken her on a vacation from Los Angeles. While he was in the throes of a complete drunken stupor, he married Scribbins and, amazingly enough, never knew about the marriage until weeks later when he finally sobered up and found her in bed next to him. His drunken blackouts had reached this intensity.

On another occasion where he was drunk, Buster had his only recorded scrape with the law. This incident happened while he was in Arizona on a vacation of sorts. Buster staggered into a bar in a little desert town and ordered himself a couple of drinks. He was refused by the bartender because it was closing time. Refusing to take the bartenders "no" as an answer, Buster started to tear the place apart. The police soon arrived, placed Buster under arrest, and took him off to jail. As expected, word of these happenings were getting back to Louis B. Mayer at M-G-M. This was not at all the kind of publicity M-G-M wanted, and Mayer, thinking he'd done his best in trying to help Buster, made the final decision to fire him.

The story of Buster's firing from M-G-M has been retold so many times in the Hollywood film community that the facts are difficult to separate from the fictional accounts. To set the record straight, one must first understand that M-G-M knew everything that was going on in Buster's personal life since he was living on the studio's backlot in his dressing room. This living arrangement came about because, as a result of his divorce from Natalie, he lost his house and didn't have enough money to buy another one. When one thinks of a dressing room, the thought of a little cubicle with a lighted mirror comes to mind. In the case of Buster's dressing room, this image could not be farther from the truth.

Buster's dressing room on the M-G-M back lot was a large mobile home (Buster called it his "land yacht"). This dressing room had everything he needed to live comfortably. There was a large bedroom area where he could frolic with as many "showgirls" as he desired, a large kitchen area where bridge, poker, and other card games were played on a nightly basis and, most important, a well-stocked bar. If a guess was to be made regarding where the most popular employee hangout on the M-G-M lot in Culver City was, the winning guess would have been the dressing room/home of Buster Keaton. There was always a party going on. Comedy writers came to entertain visiting girls who then remained to entertain the writers. Rumors of debauchery spread throughout the studio and soon reached the ears of Eddie Mannix, one of the M-G-M general managers. Being a skirt-chaser himself and an occasional party-sharer with Buster, Mannix was in no position to seriously protest to Buster about his life-style.

However, when Louis B. Mayer heard of these parties, they were described to him as "orgies." When Mayer went to see Buster about these "orgies," he was met by a group of raucous men and women who were drinking. Mayer ordered the trailer cleared. Buster ordered Mayer out of his dressing room, to which Mayer ordered Buster off his studio lot. Both men complied with the others wishes, although only Mayer had a choice in the matter.

Irving Thalberg liked Buster and was not happy to hear the news that he had been fired. He told Eddie Mannix that Buster should have been handled differently. "I can't make stars as fast as L.B. can fire them," Thalberg once said.

Thalberg told Mayer that he wanted to give Buster another chance. "Go ahead, argue with me," Mayer yelled at Thalberg. "Show me where I was wrong!" Thalberg reminded Mayer of the personal problems facing Buster, and Mayer said he would not object to Buster's return. This shocked everyone at M-G-M. Buster refused the offer to come back and told Irving Thalberg, "you studio people warp my character!"

Being fired in the way he was and for the reasons involved, virtually blackballed Buster as far as other major studios were concerned. Hollywood's film community, being the clique community it was (and for that matter still is), looked upon Buster as being "bad news." As Buster approached the other major studios, they all slammed their casting doors in his face. He was turned down by Paramount, Columbia, Warner Brothers, Universal, Twentieth Century-Fox and RKO. Buster Keaton, who had been Hollywood's shiniest star, was now nothing more than a rapidly fading glimmer. The king of film comedy was now a court jester. Whereas once Buster Keaton had been the most sought after comedian (even more so than Charlie Chaplin), he was now on his way to begging for work; taking anything which any studio would throw his way.

At thirty-seven years of age, Buster Keaton was now a "Hollywood has-been."

6

FADE TO BLACK

The fall of Buster Keaton from superstardom signalled the end of the golden age of screen comedy. Charlie Chaplin and Harold Lloyd were still making pictures which were still making their studios money, but soon they, too, would feel their glory begin to fade, albeit for different reasons than Buster.

It was at this point in Buster's life when more and more people were starting to compare him to Charlie Chaplin, Harold Lloyd, and even Harry Langdon, and in these comparisons, they always referred to Buster in the past-tense, as if he were dead (which he was approaching in a professional sense). It was also during this time of comparisons when everyone took notice that Buster was more than just a mere comedian; more than just a funny little fellow who could fall in many different ways and positions. Now, Buster was being looked back upon as a very special talent and some in the film industry were feeling that Buster's genius may have been noticed too late. In some ways they were correct, yet in others they were not.

When it came to screen comedy at this time in Hollywood's history, two names were always brought up: Buster Keaton and Charlie Chaplin, in that order. Chaplin was still working and a major star. Keaton was having problems just walking a straight line. As far as the downfall of Buster Keaton, make no mistake about it; Buster had no one to blame but himself for the decline of his once great and legendary career.

Undoubtedly the biggest mistake Buster made during this point in his career, as well as in his earlier days, was that, unlike Chaplin and Harold Lloyd, Buster did not keep contractual control and ownership of his films. It was this business mistake which almost put Buster in the "poorhouse" and kept him from starting over again with his own studio.

When talking about his lifelong career in show business, Buster often stated that the worse part of his life was from 1933 to 1934. During this time, Buster was virtually out of work (there were some independent films, but they paid next to nothing) and his drinking was now to the point where he was on a collision course with death. His marriage to Mae Scribbins was nothing more than a sick practical joke he had played on himself, while Scribbins was spending what little money he had and then belittling him when there wasn't enough to keep her happy. Even though Buster never really talked about his marriage to Mae Scribbins (possibly because he couldn't remember much of it), one can only surmise that it must have been a nightmare come to true. The facts indicate that Mae Scribbins was really nothing more than a gold-digger; a gold-digger who found that her motherlode had run dry before she could ever really stake her claim.

When Doctor Harry Martin, the husband of gossip columnist *extraordinaire* Louella Parson, saw Buster literally running around Hollywood one day in 1933, he could not believe what he was seeing. The Buster whom he knew and considered to be a good friend, was now nothing more than a shell of a man. Being the type of friend to Buster that he was, Doctor Martin grabbed Buster and, using his immense powers of persuasion, got Buster to once again check into Arrowhead Springs for another try at drying-out. As with his first attempt at Arrowhead Springs, Buster failed in his attempts to become sober. It was then when Doctor Martin tried to rid Buster of his disease with mild drugs; this plan too failed miserably.

Even though Buster's drinking problems were legendary in Hollywood, for unknown reasons, word of his problems never really made the tinsel-town tabloids. This is indeed strange when celebrity problems like Buster's were what the tabloids lived for (and still do). Unlike any celebrity of his time, the legend of Buster Keaton was being protected. To prove this point, take note of the following story from the Rueter's News Service which appeared on the front page of a New York newspaper:

> Buster Keaton, the famous film comedian, who is lying seriously ill in Los Angeles, has been transferred to the psychopathic ward of a hospital.
> In addition to his pneumonia, the actor is now reported to be suffering from a nervous breakdown.

As you will note, nowhere in this front page "blurb" does it mention the taboo subject of the day: alcoholism. Buster was in a hospital, but he was not suffering from pneumonia. This was perhaps the first time in medical history when pneumonia and alcoholism were mistaken for one another, at least by the press.

During the time of his constant drinking, Buster did find some work. Due to his immense popularity overseas, he was contracted by several independent producers to perform in their films. These films were *Le Fiesta de Santa Barbara* (Mexico), *Le Roi des Champs-Elysees* (France), and *The Invader* (England). When *The Invader* was released in the United States, the title was changed to *An Old Spanish Custom*. With the exception of *Le Roi des Champs-Elysees*, these were all released a couple of years after they were filmed; *Le Fiesta de Santa Barbara* on December 7, 1935 and *The Invader* on January 2, 1936. Interestingly enough, both *Le Fiesta de Santa Barbara* and *The Invader* were released by Metro-Goldwyn-Mayer, even though they had nothing to do with the production.

With the film *Le Roi des Champs-Elysees*, Buster was paid a total of fifteen thousand dollars, though this amount did not include his traveling expenses or his living expenses while he was residing in Paris for the filming. As it would later turn out, Buster actually lost money in making this film.

Contrary to popular belief, *Le Roi des Champs-Elysees* was released in the United States, though its theater life here was brief. The one truly amazing thing about this film is that, even though Buster was drinking heavily during its entire production, he delivered a good performance and was quite convincing in his character portrayal. He was not even close to his old self, but, considering the shape he had put himself in, he was incredible just the same. When viewing this film, it is impossible to believe that Buster was only thirty-nine years old at the time. His addiction to alcohol had aged him far beyond his years.

In *Le Roi des Champs-Elysees*, Buster plays a dual role, yet both characters are essentially from the same mold. One is a bogus millionaire who goes around Paris passing counterfeit French banknotes which are valued at one thousand francs each. The other character is a European version of the stereotypical American gangster who is the spitting-image of the bogus millionaire. As the film unfolds, these two look-alike characters cross paths without knowing it, creating some rather brilliant slapstick routines. One thing about *Le Roi des Champs-Elysees* which directly parallels Buster's earlier classic films is that, once again, the female lead proves to be the reason for his problems, causing one to question whether this is another incident of art imitating life.

Le Roi des Champs-Elysees was well received in Europe and met with a much critical acclaim. The reason for this high acclaim is clear: Europe was in love with Buster, much as they are presently with Jerry Lewis, and felt that he could do no wrong. The fact that this film did have the Keaton touch regarding all of the sight gags certainly did not hurt matters any.

Le Fiesta de Santa Barbara, produced in Mexico and released in the United States by M-G-M, was actually a compilation which had an all-star cast. Aside from Buster, *Le Fiesta de Santa Barbara* also starred the talents of Gary Cooper, Harpo Marx, Warner Baxter, Leo Carillo, Robert Taylor, and Ida Lupino.

The story line for *Le Fiesta de Santa Barbara* is nearly invisible. The whole film is essentially a boating party that is sailing to a Mexican carnival. All of the stars in the film are seen quite briefly either on the boat or at the carnival. If there is a plot to this film, the writers (unknown) did a fantastic job of hiding it.

The film which was produced in England, *The Invader*, was the first "real" Buster Keaton film since the days when he worked out of his own studio. This was "real" in the sense that Buster wrote and directed the film (though he received no screen credits for either in accordance with his contractual agreement).

The basic plot for *The Invader* deals with a woman who has two men in her life. In order to get these two men into jealous rages so they will do anything to please her, she takes the hapless character (portrayed by Buster) and uses him as her pawn in what can only be termed her "macabre chess game of love."

Even though Buster is the uncredited writer and director of this film, there is very little of the Buster Keaton magic. When watching *The Invader*, it is evident that Buster has become a shell of a man who has lost his spirit. Regardless of how bad these foreign films were, they did help Buster get back into the American film market.

The return of Buster Keaton to an American film studio took place around the beginning of 1934, when he signed a multiple year contract with a low budget studio called Educational Pictures. The Educational Pictures films Buster made were all two-reelers and were produced using as little money as possible, with shooting times rarely exceeding one week per film. Two things remained a constant in Buster's Educational Pictures films: they were all terrible and they were all directed by veteran film director, Charles Lamont.

Charles Lamont, a longtime friend of Buster's, was born on May 5, 1898, in San Francisco, California. Lamont was a fourth generation actor and had appeared on the stage and screen from 1919 until 1921, when he turned his talents to directing and began producing a great number of comedy films for Mack Sennett and others. In the mid-thirties, he began directing feature films which starred, among other comedy teams, Abbott & Costello and Ma & Pa Kettle (Percy Kilbride and Margorie Maine).

After trying his hand at comedy, Lamont moved toward the mainstream and directed a few westerns and exotic adventure films, a few of which have gone on to acquire cult status, including *Salame, Where She Danced* and *Frontier Girl* (both of which were released in 1945).

Educational Pictures, as a studio, was actually the laughing stock of all the major film studios. Educational Pictures established itself in 1919, initially for the purpose of making educational films for schools. Instead, the company became a virtual factory for comedy shorts in the twenties and featured such stars as Lloyd Hamilton and Lupino Lane.

Educational Pictures continued to prosper in the early thirties despite the generally poor quality of its tight budget short films, but went out of business at the end of the decade. Operating out of studios located in Astoria, Queens, New York, it mostly used actors who were appearing in Broadway shows or in the area on the vaudeville circuit. Among the "name" stars who were employed by Educational Pictures at one time or another, aside from Buster, were Harry Langdon, Edward Everett Horton, Bert Lahr, Irene Ryan (Granny on the *Beverley Hillbillies*), Milton Berle, the Ritz Brothers, and Danny Kaye (who in later years would portray Buster Keaton in the film-flop, *The Buster Keaton Story*).

The slogan for Educational Pictures was "The Spice of the Program." Unfortunately for Buster and Educational Pictures, the "spice" was not as potent as the seemingly dead air their films were shot in and around.

Buster was well aware of the fact that his films for Educational Pictures were disasters, artistically and in every other way. As a matter-of-fact, he one time admitted that, "I hated them!" The only reason Buster made sixteen films for Educational Pictures was because he needed the money. At the time, they were his sole source of income.

During his days with Educational Pictures, Buster and his dependency on alcohol did not get any better, though he now realized he had a drinking problem. During this time, Buster would often go on drinking binges which lasted for days on end. This, rather obviously, affected his natural athletic abilities as evidenced when watching these films.

When Buster realized his drinking was a problem, he did in fact seek some help on his own, receiving the Keeley Treatment in a hospital and under a doctors observations. The Keeley Treatment, which is no longer being practiced, was a forced feeding of alcohol. The idea behind this method was that it would get the patient so sick of alcohol that he would find alcohol to be totally repulsive. In practice, every thirty minutes, one of the doctors would come into the patients room and administer a drink which was always straight, never diluted or mixed. These half-hourly drinks were never the same; always something different: vodka, scotch, whiskey, and so on. This treatment would go on for four days, twenty four hours a day, without a break. If the patient was asleep at four in the morning, the patient was awakened and forced to drink a glass of whatever was next on the liquor list.

As one may very well expect, Buster always remembered his days of going through the Keeley Treatment (which, it should be pointed out, he did twice). Buster recalled:

Needless to say, you are revolted and rebellious long before your four day round-the-clock drinking marathon is over. When you plead, "Oh no! Take it away please!" all you get from your bartender and barmaids in white coats is a friendly smile.

"Please take it away," you repeat, "it hurts my stomach."

"Just one more," they say, for the purpose is to make the hurt in your stomach grow until it becomes uncomfortable. And being a weakling, you take that one more just as you did in a thousand barrooms.

The Keeley Treatment cure may have worked wonders for some alcoholics, but it did nothing for me the first time. When I got out I could think of too many excuses for drinking; the grandson of my grocer was having a birthday, or I had to celebrate good ol' Saint Swithin's Day, the inauguration of Rutherford B. Hayes, or some other important occasion.

After taking the Keeley Treatment a second time, I was taken home and immediately went for a walk on the golf course. I walked over the entire eighteen holes, and on reaching the clubhouse, I walked to the bar and ordered two manhattans. I drank them one right after the other. They not only tasted great, they stayed down.

After proving to myself that I could drink if I felt like it, stop it if I felt like it, I did not touch a drop of whiskey or any other alcoholic drink for five years.

While he was under contract with Educational Pictures, Buster made a total of sixteen pictures, including *The Gold Ghost, Allez Oop, Palooka From Paducah, One Run Elmer, Hayseed Romance, Tars and Stripes, The E-Flat Man, The Timid Young Man, Three on a Limb,*

Grand Slam Opera, Blue Blazes, The Chemist, Mixed Marriage, Jail Bait, Ditto, and *Love Nest on Wheels.*

In *Palooka From Paducah,* released on January 11, 1935, Buster brought his father, Joseph Keaton, his mother, Myra, and his sister, Louise, back into the business. They also joined him in a couple of other Educational Pictures productions. These were the last times the Keaton family would ever appear together in any type of show business act.

During the course of his contract with Educational Pictures, Buster's second marriage ended in divorce in 1935. As with his divorce from Natalie Talmadge, when Mae Scribbins divorced Buster, she took from him what little he had saved. So once again, Buster Keaton was in desperate financial straits. After his divorce from Mae Scribbins, Buster was legally declared bankrupt.

As his contract with Educational Pictures came to an end, Buster signed a deal with one of the major studios, Columbia Pictures, which was second behind Metro-Goldwyn-Mayer. Buster's contract with Columbia was a multi-year deal which was to pay him a little over three thousand dollars per film. This was a slight raise from the pittance he was making at Educational Pictures.

Columbia Pictures, an American motion picture production and distribution company incorporated in 1924, was an outgrowth of the CBC-Film Sales Company, founded in 1920 by brothers Harry and Jack Cohn, and Joe Brandt, all former employee's of Carl Laemmle. From a fly-by-night little company on Hollywood's Poverty Row, Columbia developed into a major motion studio in the thirties, thanks largely to the dynamic leadership of Harry Cohn and the creative talents of.

In the forties, still trailing in both prestige and size behind M-G-M, Columbia concentrated its efforts on the production of many slick and profitable commercial blockbusters starring Rita Hayworth, most notably *Gilda.* Also very successful at the box office were *The Al Jolson Story* and its sequel, *Jolson Sings Again.* Between 1940 and 1946, the company's gross income doubled and its net profit was up six-and-a-half times.

The two-pronged crises which rocked Hollywood in the late forties had only a mild effect on Columbia. Since the company owned no motion picture theaters, it was spared the upheaval shared by other major studios that had to divest themselves of their theater chains, a result of new antitrust laws. The threat from television that all but ruined some companies was met realistically early in the fifties when Columbia became the first major studio to learn to live with the new medium through its television subsidiary, Screen Gems. Profits from sales of old films to television were channeled into new film production, and, before long, the company was solidly entrenched at the top.

Among the films that contributed to the growth of Columbia Pictures in both box office returns and prestige since the late forties include *All The King's Men*, *Born Yesterday*, *From Here To Eternity*, *The Cain Mutiny*, *On The Waterfront*, *The Bridge Over The River Kwai*, *Dr. Strangelove*, *Lawrence of Arabia*, *Easy Rider*, and *Oliver*. In 1968, the company reorganized, changing its corporate title from Columbia Pictures Corporation to Columbia Pictures Industries, with Columbia Pictures and Screen Gems as its major divisions.

In 1939, when Columbia signed Buster Keaton to a multi-year contract, they were signing him just for his name and not for his talents. Regardless of his past couple of films and his now tarnished reputation, the name Buster Keaton was still being associated with the premiere clown in the business, and this is exactly what Columbia was thinking when they offered him a contract. Once the Columbia contract was signed and Buster started to make films, it became obvious that he was just not the same old Buster and most of this was the fault of Columbia Pictures. In the films Buster was featured in for Columbia, they wanted him to do nothing more than imitate the "big name" comedians of the time. These Columbia roles had him mimicking the likes of Harold Lloyd (who, interestingly enough was mimicking early Buster Keaton) and Charlie Chaplin, which Buster really could not do. If Buster Keaton could not be himself, he was just not funny and in the ten films he starred in for Columbia Pictures, the laughs were missing.

Of his ten Columbia films, eight were directed by the same director, Jules White, who would later become famous as the director for The Three Stooges. Buster's eight films under Jules White were *Mooching Through Georgia*, *Nothing But Pleasure*, *Pardon My Birth Marks*, *The Taming of the Snood*, *The Spook Speaks*, *His Ex Marks the Spot*, *General Nuisance*, and *She's Oil Mine*. Buster's other two Columbia films were *Pest from the West* and *So You Won't Squawk*.

The Columbia films which Buster made were all two-reelers, known in the business as shorts (which were the types that Buster gained critical success with early in his career). Columbia did not spend large sums of money on these films. They were produced as "fillers," which were films shown in between the two major feature-length films which made up a theater's double-feature.

On more than one occasion, Buster went to the executive office of Harry Cohn, head of Columbia Pictures, and pleaded with him to be given cinematic properties with substance and humor, but each time, in a somewhat gentle way, Buster was turned down. Harry Cohn was a brilliant man when it came to dealing with Hollywood egos (read as actors and actresses) and he was well aware of the main reason Buster wanted better projects: to make more money. In an effort to aide Buster with his rather large financial burdens, Cohn and Columbia Pictures agreed to lend Buster out to other studios, so he could work more and make more money.

Because of the release dates of Buster's Columbia films, a new era of film-going audiences were being introduced to the "great stone face." This new introduction, however, was not showing the true talents of Joseph Francis "Buster" Keaton.

The only fragments of the Buster of old in these Columbia films was his legendary "stone face," as his contract with Columbia Pictures, like all of his previous contracts, prohibited him from smiling on film. Audiences thought Buster was just another old man who never smiled and tried to act funny. His genius had been buried.

Even though this new era of film audiences was seeing a Buster Keaton who was not at the top of his craft, the studios were seeing someone quite different. As Buster was starting to sober up, his genius for gags was once again beginning to blossom.

On one of the occasions when Columbia lent Buster out to another studio, Buster was lucky enough to latch on to a Darryl Zanuck production of a Twentieth-Century-Fox production titled *Hollywood Cavalcade*, which was directed by Irving Cummings. It was this film where the other major film studios noticed that the Buster of old was showing a glimmer of his former self. The two major stars of *Hollywood Cavalcade* were Don Ameche and Alice

Faye, two of the biggest stars of the late thirties and early forties; yet it was the supporting cast of Buster Keaton, Ben Turpin, Al Jolson, Mack Sennett, and the Keystone Cops, the "golden oldies," who really shined in this film.

One of the rumors regarding this film was that Buster once again donned his director's hat in addition to acting. This rumor was not true. Buster was not a co-director of *Hollywood Cavalcade*, however he was one of the comedy consultants. *Hollywood Cavalcade* was also a "first" in the world of film as it was the first feature length film to actually be two films in one. Part one is comedy in its purest and most simple form, while part two is much more serious, almost melodramatic. Rather obviously, Buster is only in the first half.

Hollywood Cavalcade starts as a semi-documentary detailing how the advent of film comedy achieved its roots (the silent comedy shorts). Even though the credited director of *Hollywood Cavalcade* is Irving Cummings, this section of the film was mostly directed by Mack Sennett and Mal St. Clair (St. Clair being one of Buster's co-directors in some of Buster's films shot at the old Keaton Studios, including the classics *The Goat* and *The Blacksmith*). When Buster was cast for this film, his role was one which only he could play: Buster Keaton.

Buster recalled:

> My deal called for me to act in this film and not surprisingly, there were some pie-throwing episodes in the picture. I had not thrown even a custard pie in years and lost no time in getting in some practice when not busy on the set.
>
> I had the studio bakers make pies according to our original 1917 recipe. Two crusts were cooked, one inside the other, until brittle. The double crust prevents crumbling when you slide across the bottom in delivering the confectionery. Tin plates are never used because of the danger of cutting the recipients eye, something that could happen when the plate slides sideways at the crucial moment of impact. The shortest throw, across a distance of three to six feet, is called a short putt, and this was the custard pie surprise I was to heave at sweet-faced Alice Faye.

I was worried about her flinching. Besides spoiling the shot, this would mean hours of delay while Alice took a shower, got a whole new makeup, a hairdo, and was fitted for a duplicate clothes outfit.

I decided not to warn her when the great moment approached. I placed George Givot, who was playing the villain, between Alice and me. Givot faced me, but Alice, standing right behind him, was facing in the opposite direction.

When we made the shot, Givot turned Alice around too quickly, which forced me to speed up my throw. Consequently the pie hit her harder in the face than should have been necessary.

You never saw a more stunned looking girl in your life than Alice Faye that day. We required no retake, but Alice did not thank me for that.

When 1940 rolled around, it was not only the start of a new decade, it also signaled the start of a brand new Buster Keaton. In 1940, two events in the life of Buster Keaton proved things were beginning to look up for him.

On the professional front, Buster was lent out from Columbia to RKO Pictures and made a film which some consider to be a minor classic and others considered a cinematic joke: *Li'l Abner*.

It is interesting to note that Buster's role in *Li'l Abner* was not a large one. Even to this day, when the film is shown on television, audiences remember Buster as the little, unsmiling man who always seems to be running around the set.

Li'l 8 was one of the most loved comic strips of its time and, for this reason alone, the film was a financial success for the studio. The whole story of *Li'l Abner* takes place in a small town called Dogpatch, a hillbilly haven in the Ozarks which is known as "the most useless community in America." If *Li'l Abner* were to be filmed today with the same story line, it would probably be considered somewhat controversial since Dogpatch was a "test town" for the atomic bomb.

Originally, *Li'l Abner* was a Broadway musical and the transfer over to film was accomplished exceptionally well. Joseph Lilley and the late, great Nelson Riddle were nominated for their musical work on this film.

On the personal level, the greatest thing to ever happen to Buster occurred when he married his third wife, an M-G-M dancer named Eleanor Norris. Even though there was a considerable age difference between the two (Buster was forty-four and Eleanor was twenty-one) a more loving couple could not be found. It has often been said by those in the know that Buster arose again within the Hollywood film community due to the love and nurturing he received from Eleanor (although his talent certainly contributed, as well). As far as marriages go, for Buster Keaton, the third time was, without a doubt, the charm. The marriage of Joseph Francis "Buster" Keaton and Eleanor Norris Keaton lasted until Buster's death in 1966.

As 1940 approached, Buster did something he swore he would never again do . . . go back to work for Metro-Goldwyn-Mayer.

Buster's return to M-G-M was not as regal as his first two stints with the number one film production studio in the world, but it was a return nonetheless. This move occurred while Buster was still under contract with Columbia Pictures, but Harry Cohn did not protest.

When Buster signed on for his third hitch with M-G-M, many people in the entertainment industry were quite stunned. What with the way he was treated by M-G-M the last time he was under contract with them, to hear of him re-signing was something many people could not understand.

The reason Buster opted to go back to M-G-M was two-fold. First, M-G-M was still the top studio in the business and to say you were under contract with M-G-M was an incredible ego booster, something which Buster desperately needed at this point in his professional life. Second, Buster was just plain sick and tired of being associated with films which were laughed at not because of their comedy content, but because they were so awful. On this third turn with M-G-M, Buster was not signed on as an actor; he was hired as a "gag consultant." Still, he did make his way into films.

The money which Buster was being paid by M-G-M has often been mistakenly reported. Some accounts were that he was being paid three hundred dollars a month; other accounts mention two hundred dollars a week. Buster himself reported that the figure was one hundred dollars a week. It is sad to think that in just a matter of a few short years, Buster went from being one of the highest paid performers in Hollywood to that of being paid "slave wages," at least by Hollywood standards.

The idea of going back to M-G-M was initiated by Buster himself. Wanting to share his wealth of talent in whatever way he could, Buster had a meeting with Eddie Mannix at the M-G-M corporate offices. During this meeting, Buster told Mannix about various ideas he had regarding some sight gags and films. As soon as Mannix saw that Buster had a clear head and that old, mischievous sparkle in his eyes, Mannix signed Buster. The small amount of money offered to him was not really a concern to Buster. "If I'm worth it," Buster mentioned regarding his small salary, "they'll pay me more." Later on, M-G-M did just that.

With his new job at M-G-M, Buster worked with everyone who was under contract with "the studio of the stars." Among the most notable of these stars were Mickey Rooney, Lana Turner, Van Johnson, Judy Garland, Gene Kelly, and Clark Gable. Then there were the comedians: Red Skelton, Danny Kaye, Groucho, Harpo and Chico Marx and Bud Abbott and Lou Costello.

Buster coached Clark Gable, otherwise known to his still admiring fans as "The King," on the sight gags he performed in the film *Too Hot To Handle*. This film was one which brought back a lot of memories for Buster as it was very reminiscent of his classic *The Cameraman*. In recounting the time he worked with Buster, Gable stated, "the man's mind was a comedy machine, he literally thinked funny. If ever there was a genius in comedy, it most definitely is Buster Keaton."

Buster never really had any problems or personality clashes when he worked with so-called serious actors and actresses, but when it came time to work with his fellow comedians, it was a different story altogether.

The most famous comedians who worked with Buster during this stint at M-G-M were Abbott and Costello and the uproarious Marx Brothers.

In working with the team of Abbott and Costello, Buster found himself literally pulling out his hair. According to Buster, Bud Abbott and Lou Costello were two of the most "unprofessional" show business performers he ever had the "misfortune" to encounter.

Whereas most film actors were always prepared for their day on the set, Abbott and Costello never were. On days when they were to film, they would always call before going into the studio to find out what it was they were working on, what time they had to be there, and, believe it or not, what script they were to read their lines from. To a consummate performance professional such as Buster, he found their lack of dedication to their art to be inexcusable. On each set where Buster worked with Abbott and Costello there were heated arguments and, in some cases, these arguments almost resulted in fist fights.

In working with the Marx Brothers, things were a little different. The main problem with the Marx Brothers was getting all three of them on the set at the same time. This got to be such a problem that it is reported that each brother had an assistant director assigned to him so the director would know where each brother was at any particular time.

Of the four performing Marx Brothers (there were five brothers altogether: Groucho, Harpo, Chico, Zeppo, and Gummo), Groucho was the spokesman. When dealing with the brothers on professional matters, Groucho spoke for Chico, Harpo, and Zeppo. The working relationship between Grouch and Buster was strained, to put it mildly. Neither man respected the other's sense of humor, to a point where Buster once walked off one of the sets screaming that Groucho was impossible to deal with.

What was actually going on between these two great screen comedians was a clash of professional respect, admiration, and jealousy. Buster saw many characteristics of himself in Groucho and wanted to mold him in "his own likeness and image." Groucho was in awe of Buster's past and didn't want to show it, thus he let down an armor he had toiled long to build. It is interesting to point out that the Marx Brothers made their films much like Buster had made his classics — they ad-libbed everything.

Regardless of his stormy and often warlike dealings with Groucho and his brothers, Buster is responsible for two of the most famous scenes in two of the Marx Brothers most popular films, *A Night at the Opera* and *A Day at the Circus*.

One of the most famous scenes in the history of film comedy takes place in the Marx Brothers film, *A Night at the Opera*, which was released in 1935. This scene, which still garners uncontrollable laughter, is one in which Groucho, Harpo, and Chico are joined in their stateroom by a myriad of guests and steamliner workers. With so many people in this little stateroom, there is hardly room to breath and Harpo is just about walking on the ceiling. Then, up to the outside door walks the character portrayed by the eternal matriarch, Margaret Dumont. When she opens the door to the stateroom, everyone comes tumbling out in a heap. This scene was created by Buster in his role as M-G-M's gag consultant, however, he had used a similar scene in *The Cameraman*.

The other famous Marx Brother's scene was from the film *A Day at the Circus*, and it, too, was a Buster Keaton created sight gag and one which he was extremely proud of. This scene revolves around Harpo (who was actually a gifted actor and harpist) who is an employee in a circus sideshow and his co-worker who is a midget. Harpo's job is selling helium-filled balloons to the circus-goers. As one of these circus-goers buys a balloon from Harpo, paying for it with a large bill. Harpo hands the customer his balloon and gives the rest of the helium-filled balloons to his midget partner while he gets change from his pocket for the customer. As the midget is holding the balloons, he starts to rise off the ground and float away. Just in the nick-of-time, Harpo grabs the midget by his floating ankles and brings the little guy back down to earth. This sight gag is pure Buster Keaton.

While at M-G-M as a gag consultant, Buster also had a hand in molding comedians he had never met, the result of the indoctrination program at Metro-Goldwyn-Mayer which included a screening of *The Cameraman*. This film had gained the official status of the "M-G-M comedy training film."

The exact number of films or artists that Buster worked with as a gag consultant is unknown and cannot be traced through either films or film credits, as Buster was what was commonly referred to at the time as "uncredited." For Buster Keaton fans and film historians alike, this is truly unfortunate as one can never really know just how many classic scenes Buster was responsible for; we can only make educated guesses.

Even though there were many personality conflicts, Buster did take one young comedian under his wing; a comedian who to this very day is loved and admired as one of the worlds greatest clowns, a true American treasure . . . Red Skelton.

Those who were present on the day when Buster met Red Skelton have all commented that there appeared to be immediate rapture between the two men. At this point in his career, Red Skelton was an up-and-coming star who had left the world of stage and burlesque and was trying to make it into the world of films. As all of these passing years have proved, not only did Red Skelton make it in films, he also ruled the world of television for many years. As some will point out, whereas Uncle Miltie (Milton Berle) was the all-time King of Television, Red Skelton was indeed the High Prince. Red Skelton was the only celebrity to ever appear on *The Tonight Show Starring Johnny Carson* as a sole guess – Red Skelton and Johnny for sixty of the best minutes in television history (Johnny Carson was a writer for Red's television show).

Red Skelton became a superstar because of his God-given talents. If it were not for Buster Keaton, though, those talents may very well have gone unnoticed.

When talking about Red Skelton, Buster would often glow with pride. Buster took to Red the way he did because, as Buster put it many times, "he reminded me of me at a younger age." The initial relationship between these two men was like that of a teacher and his star pupil. Buster even went so far as to go to the executives at M-G-M and asked to be given Red so that he could mold him in the fine art of screen comedy. M-G-M rejected Buster's tutorial services, telling him that his contract was with the studio at large and not with any contracted player in particular. Rejection was also the word used by the M-G-M staff when Buster offered to set up a special development course in comedy for all M-G-M contracted players.

The two films in which Buster worked closely with Red Skelton are two of Skelton's most remembered films. These two films were the 1944 release of *Bathing Beauties* and the 1948 release of *A Southern Yankee*.

The film *Bathing Beauties*, was simultaneously blessed with a great cast and cursed with a lousy script. The cast included Esther Williams, in the first of her many starring roles, Red Skelton, Basil Rathbone, Xavier Cougat, and the great character actor, Keenan Wynn. Midway through the filming of *Bathing Beauties*, director

George Sidney came to the artistic conclusion that his film was going nowhere but directly down drain. After hearing this, the M-G-M brass brought Buster Keaton, their comedy troubleshooter, onto the set and told him to go to work on the script. After reviewing the script and the direction of the film, Buster met with Sidney and told him what he should do to make the film noticeable. Taking Buster's advice to heart, Sidney resumed filming and came up with a film which is, at the most, halfway decent. The director's appraisal of Buster in his role of gag consultant was short and to the point: "He was magic!" And that he truly was.

Bathing Beauties, as one might expect with Esther Williams as the star, was a film which was centered around water, or what was known in the business as an "aquamusical."

The second film Buster worked on with Red Skelton, *A Southern Yankee*, was, interestingly enough, a remake of *The General*.

The writers who penned this remake (Buster was not one of them) changed the story just to the point where those familiar with original would not think that *A Southern Yankee* was a cinematic "rip-off."

In addition to Red Skelton, *A Southern Yankee* starred the character actors Brian Donlevy and John Ireland, as well as actress Arlene Dahl. As with *The General*, *A Southern Yankee* takes place during the Civil War, yet instead of Skelton playing what was originally Buster's role of Johnny Gray, he plays a Southern hotel bellhop who acts the part of an armed forces spy. This film is worth watching, not for its story content or acting, but for the various assortment of sight gags, all of which were written, diagrammed, and choreographed by Buster. There are some resurrected, yet modernized, gags Buster made famous in his own classic films.

It would not be a misnomer nor an overstatement to say that M-G-M comedies of the late thirties and early forties owe most, if not all, of their success to the brilliant comedic mind of their genius gag consultant . . . Buster Keaton.

Some of the better known films which Buster worked on (and did a little acting in as well) are *New Moon*, *The Villain Still Pursued Her*, and *In the Good Old Summertime*.

The release of *New Moon* on July 18, 1940, was met with a lot of Hollywood fanfare due mainly to the film's two stars: Nelson Eddy and Jeanette MacDonald. This version of *New Moon* was actually a remake of the operetta of the same name which was released on film and starred Lawrence Tibbett and Grace Moore.

Buster was not just the gag consultant on *New Moon*, he also did some acting in the film. This is relatively unknown to most film fans because, before the film was released, his part was left on the cutting room floor. This is the way in which Nelson Eddy explained Buster being edited out:

> When the film was screened for the stars and studio bigwigs, it was discovered that Keaton stole too many scenes and the featured stars would have suffered by comparison; hence the film was re-edited to cut out Keaton's part. However the editing was not perfect and he can be glimpsed in a few scenes left in the final version.

Another film which Buster acted in as well as consulted on was the Judy Garland and Van Heflin musical, *In the Good Old Summertime*. This film was the type which was called a "goodtime" film, one filled with smiles and uplifting songs. The gags throughout this film are all from the mind of Buster Keaton and are quite amusing, yet his acting is entirely forgettable.

Regardless of his acting abilities during these times, the foreign film market was still offering Buster starring roles. One of these was a Mexican film which was being directed by Jamie Salvador and released on August 2, 1946, in Mexico. As opposed to popular belief, this film, the very forgettable *El Moderno Barba Azul* (*The Modern Blue Beard*), was never theatrically released in the United States. In this film, Buster plays a prisoner who is held hostage by some Mexican's who, when they don't get what they're asking for, strap him onto a rocket and send him to the moon. After seeing this disaster of a film, some might say that if there were any justice in the film world, when Buster was sent to the moon, he would have taken all the copies of this film with him.

Even though in the United States Buster was a "lowly" gag consultant, in Europe he was still considered to be a "superstar" and a living legend. Because of this cult following he has amassed in

European countries, Buster was often asked to make personal appearances there. The one place where he loved to perform live and always did so to standing room only crowds was the Cirque Medrano in Paris, France. His performances at the Cirque Medrano consisted of him doing routines with Eleanor and a couple of skits with the resident clowns. Each one of these trips to the Cirque Medrano was hailed by critics as an artistic triumph, thus the world, via Europe, was once again beginning to take notice of the "great stone face."

With European crowds starting the "new" Buster Keaton revival, Buster soon invaded England (home of Charlie Chaplin) and toured the various music halls which were scattered throughout the British Isles. This tour of Great Britain was a revue of sorts, as on the playbill besides Buster were some of the giants of British comedy, such as George Robey and Hetty King. It was during one of these performances that Charlie Chaplin, who was in the audience, took notice of Buster's renewed comic vitality. A few years later, Chaplin would cast him in his last truly classic film, *Limelight*.

During one of his European treks, Buster went before the cameras and made a film which was released only in Europe on September 7, 1950. This film, directed by Pierce Bondy, was produced in France and was titled *Un Duel A Mort* (*A Duel to Death*). This film captures some of the skits which Buster performed at the Cirque Medrano and is quite amusing.

When Buster returned to the United States after one of his 1949 European jaunts, he was pleasantly surprised to see that *Life Magazine*, in an extended article on the greats of the silent cinema, had paid a special tribute to him and his career. This article was written by author and film critic James Agee, a man who was well respected within the Hollywood film community. Many will attest to the fact that it was this article, in part, that brought Buster's non-smiling face back into the United States and forced the "new blood" which was running Hollywood to realize that Buster Keaton had returned.

One of the people to take notice of Buster was legendary film director, Billy Wilder. While Wilder was getting his preproduction chores in order for his classic film *Sunset Boulevard*, he called Buster and inquired if he would like to be in the film. Without even the slightest bit of hesitation, Buster accepted Wilder's invitation. Wilder's timing could not have been more perfect, as a few days before

Figure 6-1 — Buster Keaton and Charlie Chaplin (foreground) in the dressing room scene from Limelight. *This was the first time these two great comedians worked together. Most of Buster's scenes were cut from the film because he got more laughs than Chaplin (who produced, wrote, directed, starred in, and scored the film).*

Wilder's call, Buster had left M-G-M. Leaving M-G-M this time was Buster's decision.

The part which Buster played in *Sunset Boulevard* was one with which he was quite familiar. Once again, Buster Keaton was asked to portray Buster Keaton. By no stretch of the imagination was this a major role; it was a cameo appearance, but a stronger cameo has never been made. The scene called for Buster to be playing in a bridge game with the character portrayed by Gloria Swanson (Nora Desmon), as well as Anna Q. Nilsson and H.B. Warner who were also playing themselves. As all the players were sitting around the card table, the camera panned to Buster and, with his ever somber "puss" is a quasi-close-up, he says "pass." The word "pass" is his only line in this film, but it may very well have been the most important word he ever muttered in any film because an entire world heard it and, more importantly, noticed what was his trademark . . . his incredible "stone face."

If ever there was an "angel of actors," that angel was without a doubt watching over Buster during his scene in *Sunset Boulevard*, as it was this scene, small as it was, which had Hollywood and the film community once again opening their arms to Buster Keaton, the onetime King of Comedy.

During the time when Buster was re-emerging on the Hollywood entertainment scene, a new entertainment medium was finding its niche. This new medium was television. Whereas Buster Keaton helped to make the film industry what it was, he was now ready to do the same with this new swaddling child in vacuum tubes.

Buster's first venture into this miraculous new medium of television was in the ever present world of the television commercial. With most of the commercials in which he was involved, Buster was allowed to contribute his own ideas, which he did with great joy and pride. It is a shame that these commercials are no longer available (even though some of the products still are) because if they were shown on the air today, they would be so much more humorous and imaginative than most of the regular programs.

Buster's first guest appearance was on the *Ed Wynn Show* in 1949. Ed Wynn, like most of the people who were in on the advent of television, was enlisted from the world of film. One year after being named by his fellow comedians as "the greatest visual comedian of our time," and more than forty years after he began his career in vaudeville, Ed Wynn became a regular television performer with his own variety show. Buster enjoyed working with Wynn because they were both from the "old school" of comedy. Buster's appearance on the *Ed Wynn Show* as a guest star led him to being a guest on this top-ranked show more than anyone else, except Ed Wynn.

Even when Buster was not on a television show, his genius was still represented. A perfect example of this was on the *Abbott and Costello Television Show*, which aired from 1951 to 1953. On most of these shows, Bud Abbott and Lou Costello borrowed most of their material from the old silent comedy films, including a virtual re-enactment of Buster's 1920 classic, *One Week*, in which a jealous suitor (Bud Abbott) sabotages the house Lou Costello has built for his fiance.

Another type of programming which was popular during the early days of television were shows which featured compilations of silent comedies. One of the first shows of this genre was *Comedy Circus* (1951). *Comedy Circus* showed quite a few of Buster's early shorts and aided in strengthening his comeback.

In 1949, with all of his television guest appearances helping him on the comeback trail, Buster Keaton received his own television show on KHJ Television in Los Angeles. The fact that Buster had his own show is not common knowledge because the show was locally produced and not nationally televised. If you were going to have a program broadcasted in only one town, Los Angeles was the best town to do it in. On this show, Buster performed many of his old gags and stunts without using stunt men or stunt doubles. The show was a big hit, but lasted only about six months due to production costs being too high. Buster loved doing this show because it was produced before a live audience and this brought back many great memories from his vaudeville days. When Buster talked about the Buster Keaton Show, he said, "it was a thrill, a lot of fun. If we could have gone on for two more years, who knows, we may have gone national and things would have been different."

Whereas Buster took to television as if it were made for his talents, Charlie Chaplin, the Little Tramp, found television to be a slap-in-the-face of a film performer, degrading, and a fad which would never last. With regard to the film industry, Keaton and Chaplin hardly ever disagreed. However, when it came to the subject of television, well . . . there was not a meeting of the minds.

Buster once recalled:

Charlie Chaplin's mind is so frisky and intuitive that it is difficult to surprise him. Yet I have caught him off guard at least twice.

The first time was on a night way back in 1920 when Charlie and I were drinking beer in my kitchen. He was going on at a great rate about something new called communism, which he had just heard about. He said that communism was going to change everything, abolish poverty. The well would help the sick, the rich would help the poor.

"What I want," he said, banging on the table, "is that

every child should have enough to eat, shoes on his feet, and a roof over his head."

Naturally, this amazed me, and I asked, "but Charlie, do you know anyone who doesn't want that?"

Charlie look startled. Then his face broke into that wonderful smile of his, and he began to laugh at himself. I, myself, have gone through life almost unaware of politics, and I only wish my dear old friend had done the same thing. He must know by now that communism, wherever it has been practiced, bears not the slightest resemblance to the benign system he described to me forty years ago.

Nobody made so many people laugh as did Charlie Chaplin with his Little Tramp. And there was never a time in history when more people needed something like Charlie's Tramp to help them forget their fears and troubles.

The second time I took Charlie unaware was one day in 1951 when he sent for me to discuss doing a scene with him in *Limelight*, the last picture he made in this country.

He seemed astonished at my appearance. Apparently he had expected to see a physical and mental wreck. But I was in fine fiddle. I'd just been in New York for four months doing an average of two guest shots a week. So I was prosperous and looked it.

"What have you been doing Buster?" he asked. "You look in such fine shape."

"Do you look at television, Charlie," I asked.

"'Good heavens, no!" he exclaimed. "I hate it! I will not permit it in my house. The idea of actors letting themselves shown on that lousy, stinking little screen!"

"Don't you even have it in the kid's room, Charlie?"

"There least of all. Oona [Charlie's wife and the daughter of Eugene O'Neil] has enough trouble with the lively little bouncers. They are darlings, but mischievous. There would be no controlling them at all if we let them see all that tripe on television. Should be done away with! It is ruining the whole country!" Then he said again, "But Buster, tell me, how do you manage to stay in such great shape? What makes you so spry?"

"Television," I said.

He gasped, choked, got red, and then said, "Now about the sequence we're going to do together!"

The subject of television was not mentioned again during the three days we did the sequence in *Limelight*, in which I play the near-blind pianist and he the fiddler.

The film *Limelight* was not just another film to roll out of Hollywood on a spool, it was, and still is, a true historical event. For it is *Limelight* which brought together, on film for the first and only time, the two men who perfected the fine art of screen comedy; two men who gave the world unlimited laughs . . . Buster Keaton and Charlie Chaplin. *Limelight* was released everywhere except the United States on October 22, 1952.

Some of the people who welcomed an elderly Charlie Chaplin back to Hollywood in 1971 to receive a belated Academy Award for his contribution to their industry, were the same who drove him out of the United States during the McCarthy witch hunt, the same time he was making *Limelight*. During that time, only two American stars, Buster Keaton and Claire Bloom, had remained grateful for the chance to work with Chaplin.

Chaplin began writing the script for *Limelight*, originally titled *Footlights*, in 1948. He employed many of his large family in bit parts; his eldest son, Sidney (as composer Neville) and Charlie, Jr. (as a clown); his younger children Geraldine (in her screen debut), Michael, and Josephine as street urchins; and his half-brother, Wheeler Dryden, as a doctor. Chaplin's method of directing was to act out each nuance of each role for his performers to imitate exactly – thus his cast became extensions of himself in a way which few other directors would desire, or for that matter, even attempt. One exception to his rule, to whom Charlie Chaplin gave free reign, was Buster Keaton. Buster's admiration for Chaplin was so great that, on many occasions, he had said that he would have worked on the film for free (though he did accept his check gratefully).

Because of Charlie Chaplin's liberal politics, RKO Pictures chairman, Howard Hughes, tried to get *Limelight* banned; Los Angeles theater owners cancelled showings when the American Legion threatened to picket their theaters; and F.B.I. Chief, J. Edgar Hoover, terrified of the Little Tramp's worldwide popularity, went after him with all of the government resources he could muster. Banished from the United States as an "undesirable alien" after he had gone to London for the premiere of *Limelight*, Charlie Chaplin met a huge, adoring public in his native country. *Limelight* won an Academy Award for Chaplin's musical score in 1972 when the film was finally commercially released in Los Angeles, twenty years after it was produced.

In his 1983 book titled *Tales From the Hollywood Raj*, author Sheridan Morley commented on how it was on the set of *Limelight*.

> The arrival on the set of Buster Keaton was greatly anticipated by us all. He hadn't been in a film for many years and was to appear with Chaplin in the final theater sequence. Keaton was fifty-six years old when he made *Limelight*, but gave the impression of suffering through a life twice that long. From his lined face and grave expression, one would have thought that he had neither known a lighthearted moment nor was able to instigate one. His reserve was extreme, as was his isolation. He remained to himself on the set until one day, to my astonishment, he took from his pocket a color postcard of a large Hollywood mansion and showed it to me. It was the sort of postcard that tourists pick up in Hollywood drugstores. In the friendliest, most intimate way, he explained to me that it had once been his home. That was it. He retreated back into his silence and never addressed a word to me again. In his scene with Chaplin, however, he was brilliantly alive with invention. Some of his gags may have been a little too incandescent for Chaplin, because, laugh as he did at the rushes in the screening room, Chaplin did not see fit to allow them all into the final version of the film.

There are many stories surrounding the reasons that Charlie Chaplin cut out most of Buster's part. Some say it was nothing short of petty jealousy, that Chaplin had thought Buster was trying to upstage him. The real reason that Buster's scenes were cut down was because, since they were at the conclusion of the film, Chaplin knew that Buster's performance would be the one everyone would have remembered when leaving the theater. In this case, Charlie Chaplin was not wrong. For those at the original screening of *Limelight*, the conclusion was unanimous. Buster Keaton stole the show. Chaplin, being one of the biggest egomaniacs in the history of the cinema, could not take this, and thus edited out of most of Buster's scenes.

Limelight was the last great film which Charlie Chaplin ever made and, interestingly enough, it was somewhat autobiographical. In *Limelight*, Chaplin plays an English vaudeville performer who has seen many better days. As he goes day-by-day reliving his past in his memories, he comes across a young ballerina who has attempted suicide. Finding her before she succumbs to death, he takes her in and becomes her mentor of sorts. With his pushing and urging, she becomes a big star and he, too, gets one last chance on the stage.

His final appearance on a music hall stage is met with great critical acclaim and, as the old show business adage goes, "he died doing what he loved best, performing on the stage." At the end of his final performance, Chaplin falls into the orchestra pit, landing in a bass drum (a shot which was made famous by Buster and the Three Keaton's during their heyday on the vaudeville circuit), and says his final words: "Ladies and gentlemen, I would like to say something, but I am stuck." *Limelight* was indeed a one hundred percent Charlie Chaplin film as he produced, directed, wrote, scored, and starred in it.

Limelight is truly a work of cinematic art and it is a total joy to watch. There are many memorable scenes in this film, but one of the most haunting is when Buster and Charlie are sitting in a dressing room and Buster, looking into his makeup mirror, says, "I never thought I'd come to this."

Limelight proved to everyone in Hollywood that Buster Keaton was still a master of timing, the greatest comedic talent who ever lived, and a complete poet with his body language.

Shortly after Buster filmed *Limelight*, he received one of the highest awards to be given to him as a film performer, the coveted George Eastman Award. This award, presented to Buster and nine other performers, was handed to him at the first George Eastman Festival of Film Arts Gala. The other nine legendary performers were Mary Pickford, Lillian Gish, Mae Marsh, Harold Lloyd, Richard Barthelmes, Norma Talmadge, Gloria Swanson, Ronald Coleman, and Charlie Chaplin. Since Buster had as yet not received an Academy Award (he later did in 1955), this was the first major award ever to be bestowed upon him. With his critically acclaimed television credits, his memorable part in *Limelight*, and the George Eastman award, Buster was once again the "king of the hill." Then, as was often the case throughout his life, tragedy struck. Buster Keaton almost died.

It was on an afternoon in December, 1951, shortly after Buster had completed his portion in the filming of *Limelight*, when he was rushed to a hospital suffering from acute hemorrhaging.

For nearly thirty hours, doctors had Keaton hooked up to blood transfusion machines. It has always been reported that Buster's condition during this time was "serious but stable." The truth of the matter is, the doctors advised Eleanor to call the family to the hospital since they were not at all sure how long Buster would survive. At one point, it was reported that one of the doctors told Eleanor that, if Buster could make it past a couple of days, he just might pull through; but at the same time, this same doctor was not optimistic, not in the least.

As was Buster's nature, he was not to be kept down and out for long. To the utter astonishment of everyone, including the doctors at the hospital, Buster pulled through and did so to the point where he was up and about within a couple of weeks. After a couple of more weeks, Buster was home and feeling great, even though his doctors had put him on a very strict diet and Buster did not take kindly to restrictions. What caused the hemorrhaging was never divulged, however, it can now be deducted that this was, in all probability, the beginnings of the cancer which would eventually take his life.

Upon leaving the hospital, Buster was told by his doctor, "Buster, you're not a young man any longer. You have the constitution of an ox, but even an ox must slow down or it will burn itself out." Buster could not heed this advise simply because it was against his nature. Buster had been a workaholic since he was three years old and as the old adage goes, "you can't teach an old dog new tricks."

Actually, Buster did not even wait until he left the hospital to continue working. While he was recuperating, he had made a deal with Paramount Pictures for the film *The Buster Keaton Story*, a film which would star Donald O'Conner as Buster. In the deal that Buster

Figure 6-2 – Donald O'Connor and Ann Blyth from The Buster Keaton Story. *The film, a box office bomb, centered on Buster's rough times.*

worked out, he was to receive fifty thousand dollars for the rights and would also be the creative consultant, receiving an undetermined amount of money for this role.

The Buster Keaton Story, which was actually more fiction than fact, was written by Robert Shaw and Sidney Sheldon (the same Sidney Sheldon who is now one of the worlds best-selling novelists). Probably the worst thing about *The Buster Keaton Story* is that it deals with his downfall years and not the years of his greatest artistic achievements.

Even though Buster was the creative consultant on this film, everything he was telling Paramount was landing on deaf ears; they were paying no attention to anything he was saying. In *Halliwell's Film Companion, Fourth Edition*, noted film historian and critic, Leslie Halliwell, commented on *The Buster Keaton Story*: ". . . an interesting recreation of Hollywood in the twenties and thirties is the main asset of this otherwise dismal tribute to a man whose greatness the star [O'Conner] is unable to suggest apart from a few acrobatic moments."

While filming *The Buster Keaton Story*, Donald O'Conner, who was in good shape and one of Hollywood's premiere dancers, found it almost impossible to accomplish some of the stunts which Buster had performed during his heyday. A couple of scenes which were originally written into the script had to be scrapped because they included some of Buster's stunts which neither O'Conner nor any of the stunt men could pull off. By the time shooting was completed, O'Conner was in awe of the talents which had made Buster Keaton a legend in laughter.

With the release of *The Buster Keaton Story*, Buster found himself on the road to promote the film. Everywhere he traveled, he was met by throngs of adoring fans, autograph seekers, and people who were just curious and wanted to see the man who was now being referred to as a "living legend" in America and overseas.

The term "living legend" was a reference Buster did not care for. Whereas the great Charlie Chaplin possessed the largest ego in the history of Hollywood, Buster was as modest as is humanly possible. In talking about this promotional tour for the film, Buster had always commented that "Paramount worked me like a town pump," yet if the truth be known, he did love every minute of it.

With the money he received from *The Buster Keaton Story*, Buster bought a home and some land just outside of Los Angeles in the San Fernando Valley, and resided there for the rest of his life. It was this home, which he called his ranch, that Buster felt was the only true home he ever had. Living there with the love of his life (Eleanor) and his Saint Bernard, Buster was actually living out the title of one of his films, *Love Nest*.

After *Limelight* was released in 1952, Buster spent the next four years concentrating on television, even though he did have film scripts being sent to him. One exception was the Italian film (never released in the United States), *L'Incatevole Nemica*. The reason Buster was in this film is unknown as his role was small, consisting of one very brief sketch.

Buster was being seen quite often on television. While on the *Eddie Cantor Comedy Hour*, Buster played in a skit which was written especially to showcase his many talents. The skit was called "The

World of Alonzo Pennyworth," with Buster playing the title role: a bashful travel agent who had never been anywhere and who was doing badly in romance, as well.

On the television show, *Best of Broadway*, Buster had a ball. This television show, which was s produced live in New York City, presented Broadway plays and musicals using a vast variety of guest stars. On the show on which Buster performed, they did a version of the Kaufman and Hart play, *The Man Who Came To Dinner*. Buster played the role of Doctor Bradley and was greeted on stage with resounding applause.

One of the most interesting television shows on which Buster lent his talents for a fee was *Douglas Fairbanks, Jr. Presents*. Fairbanks was a good friend of Buster's and, since the inception of his show in 1952, he had tried to book Buster. In 1954, he finally succeeded.

Douglas Fairbanks, Jr., who had been a major Hollywood star since the early twenties, hosted this show, one of televisions classiest and most successful anthology series. He also served as executive producer and starred in approximately one-fourth of the episodes. The scripts were first-rate and usually wide ranging, from psychological studies to light farce, with an occasional murder yarn thrown in to keep the television audience interested. The series was produced in England, with an eye to authenticity; if they needed a castle, they went out and got one. The episode in which Buster starred was titled "The Awakening" and was based on Gogol's *The Overcoat*. Buster portrayed a timid individual who was beset by nothing but trouble.

Another television show which was similar to *Douglas Fairbanks, Jr. Presents* was the 1955 series, *Screen Directors' Playhouse*. As with the Fairbanks show, this too was an anthology series with a ranging scope of story lines. What made this show different was that each episode was directed by a great director of major Hollywood motion pictures. The episode which starred Buster was titled "Silent Partners." The story line for this episode had Buster playing a show business has-been. While watching the Academy Awards on television in a bar, he sees Bob Hope give a special medal to a producer who used to be Buster's old partner. The emotion and seriousness which Buster puts into his character took a lot of people by surprise; people who thought of the "great stone face" as just another comedian and not the true consummate actor which he truly was.

Buster also appeared on *Producer's Showcase*, a top-rated television show which ran from 1954 to 1957. *Producer's Showcase* was a live ninety-minute show which was known to throw limits out the window when it came to their production costs. The episode on which Buster appeared was "The Lord Don't Play Favorites," and it was a musical comedy about a traveling circus that got stranded in a Kansas town around 1905.

On March 6, 1956, everyone who loved comedy was awaiting Buster's appearance on *The Martha Raye Show*. If there ever was a comedy performer who could be considered the female counterpart of Buster Keaton, it was indeed Martha Raye. Raye, who was a loudmouthed comedienne and singer, could take a pie in the face or perform a pratfall with the best of them. Raye's gift for comedy and timing have never been truly recognized, but the fact is that Martha Raye is the undisputed queen of slapstick comedy. *The Martha Raye Show* had a different story line each week, with each story being performed in a musical-variety vein. The only constant of this show was Raye's boyfriend, who was always portrayed by boxing immortal, Rocky Graziano. On the night Buster was on the show, he and Raye performed an uproariously hilarious parody of the scene originally made famous by Buster and Charlie Chaplin. This scene between these two naturally physical comics is truly one of the greatest gems of televisions golden era.

While performing on the numerous television shows, Buster caught the eye of film producer Michael Todd (who was one of Elizabeth Taylor's husbands). As he was casting his Academy Award winning feature film, *Around the World In 80 Days*, Todd had many cameo appearances to fill. Being a lover of old and classic films, Todd decided to fill these cameo appearances with actors and actresses he grew up watching; this being his personal way of paying tribute to these stars and giving them a personal "thank you" for the memories they had bestowed upon him. In these cameo appearances he had included Joe E. Brown, Charles Coburn, Ronald Coleman, Noel Coward, Andy Devine, Marlene Dietrich, Hermione Gingold, Trevor Howard, Beatrice Lillie, Victor McLaglen, John Mills, and George Raft. When Todd signed Buster, he wanted him to have a little more than just a typical cameo, so he gave Buster the role of a train conductor who was aboard a train going between San Francisco and

Fort Kearney, a role Buster loved as it once again had him playing on a train.

It is clear from Buster's credits that, since the advent of television, he was actually more in demand than during his heyday in films. For what was probably the first time in his life, Buster was finding it difficult to keep up with his ever-increasing work schedule, a work schedule which had him traveling across the Atlantic more often than most steamships.

In 1958, before going to England to make a few personal appearances, Buster managed to find time to appear on two of the highest rated television programs of all-time: *Playhouse 90* and *The Donna Reed Show*.

Most television critics and historians agree that *Playhouse 90* was one of the best dramatic-anthology shows ever to air on television. *Playhouse 90* was a high-budget series which aired once a week for ninety minutes, with each show being performed live. With the budget of *Playhouse 90* the largest in television at the time, they always had the best personnel both in front of and behind the cameras. This produced one of the highest rated television dramas of all-time, the classic "Requiem For A Heavyweight."

The *Playhouse 90* episode on which Buster starred was "The Innocent Slap." In this episode, Buster played a citizen of a fictional town who was struck deaf and dumb at a trial in which he was accused of killing his father. Buster's moving portrayal in this television vehicle proved once and for all that, when called upon, he could act in a serious mode as fabulously as he could in a comedic mode. This is something for which he never received credit. Keaton was, in fact, a complete actor, something that cannot be said about many actors of either yesteryear or today.

The Donna Reed Show was, without a doubt, one of the most valuable parts of television history. *The Donna Reed Show* ran for eight years and was the number one show on television for most of that time. During the reign of this show, it won many awards including those from such diverse groups as the National P.T.A., various youth and woman's groups, and even the American Medical Society (Carl Betz, the television father portrayed a doctor on the show).

Buster's appearance on *The Donna Reed Show* was for the Christmas telecast shown on December 24, 1958. This episode was titled "A Very Merry Christmas" and had Buster portraying a philanthropist who provided the money for the annual party at the children's ward in a local hospital and who was talked into playing Santa Claus by Donna Reed. For the entire 1958 television season of *The Donna Reed Show*, this was the episode which received the highest ratings.

In 1959, Hollywood finally paid homage to the man who made film comedy an accepted art form, for it was in 1959 when the Academy of Motion Picture Arts and Sciences presented Buster with a special Academy Award. As Buster was introduced to the audience of his peers, he was given a thunderous standing ovation, unseen at the Academy before or since. Moving to the microphone to make his acceptance speech, Buster was emotionally moved. This was the moment he had been waiting for his entire career, which in Buster's case, was his life, as well. The engraving on his Academy Award reads as follows:

> To Buster Keaton for his
> unique talent which brought
> immortal comedies to the screen.

One of Buster's forgotten television appearances occurred on February 7, 1960, when he performed on the short-lived program *Sunday Showcase*. The episode of this show on which Buster appeared was titled "After Hours." *Sunday Showcase* was actually a series of specials which were considered a weekly series. Subjects covered were drama, music, comedy, and history. "After Hours" was a comedy involving a mistaken identity crisis in which Buster once again played Santa Claus.

Whereas Buster's appearance on *Sunday Showcase* was a forgotten one, his appearance on *Candid Camera* was without a doubt one of the funniest moments in the history of television.

No one knew what Buster was going to do on *Candid Camera* once the infamous hidden camera started to roll, not even the host, producer, and creator, Alan Funt. All anyone knew was that Buster was going to go into a "greasy spoon" diner and have breakfast. There were going to be no tools, props, or special effects; Buster was just going to improvise and use his comedic mind. There will never be a comic who could do this better than Buster Keaton.

While Buster was sitting at the counter and eating breakfast, all sorts of mishaps befell him. At one point, the toupee which he was wearing fell into his oatmeal. The looks on the people who were seated next to him were memorable. Throughout all of these mishaps, Buster kept eating away and always kept his "stone face" as stoic as ever. The entire Buster Keaton segment was accomplished in one take, a fact which amazed everyone involved with the production of *Candid Camera*, including Alan Funt, who commented afterwards, "the man is a genius."

Buster loved performing on *Candid Camera* since it gave him a chance to relive his days with Roscoe "Fatty" Arbuckle and the way the two of them pulled practical jokes on people who were totally unsuspecting.

On December 15, 1961, Buster starred in an episode of *The Twilight Zone*, a very strange television show. At the time this series was on, it was only a marginal hit, receiving neither critical acclaim or high ratings. Now, however, it is considered to be a classic, a ground-breaker in television history. One television station in San Francisco (Channel 20) even runs *Twilight Zone* marathons every Halloween and receives high ratings. There has recently been a syndicated television show called *The New Twilight Zone*, which is precisely where it ended up shortly after its debut . . . in the twilight zone.

Buster's appearance on *The Twilight Zone* was in an episode titled "Once Upon A Time." In this episode, considered by many fans and television historians as a classic of the series, Buster portrayed a character by the name of Woodrow Mulligan.

Disgruntled over the clamor and high prices of 1890, janitor Woodrow Mulligan uses a time helmet invented by his employer, Professor Gilbert, to travel to 1962, expecting to find Utopia. Once there, he realizes the error in his assumption and is eager to get back to 1890, but the helmet has been damaged – and in only fifteen minutes he will be unable to return. He meets Rollo, an electronics scientist, who takes the helmet to a repair shop. Once the helmet is fixed, Rollo's motives become clear: he intends to use the helmet himself. Mulligan grabs hold of him and the two materialize in 1890.

Mulligan is overjoyed, but Rollo soon becomes dissatisfied; to him, 1980 is hopelessly backward. Mulligan then plops the helmet onto Rollo's head and ships him back to 1962.

Richard Matheson, writer of the script for "Once Upon A Time" said:

> I met Buster Keaton through Bill Cox, a writer friend of mine, and I thought, "Gee, that would be wonderful if we could get Buster Keaton into a *Twilight Zone*."
>
> To oversee this episode, Buck Houghton, the producer, turned to Norman McLeod, an old time director who was in semi-retirement. McLeod's credits read like a history of film comedy: *Monkey Business, Horse Feathers, It's A Gift, Topper, The Secret Life of Walter Mitty,* and *The Paleface.* "He wasn't working a lot, he didn't want to," said Buck Houghton, 'but he thought, my God, work with Buster Keaton? Lead me to it!"
>
> "The experience of working with Keaton was absolutely wonderful," said Houghton. "Here's a legend in his own time, for goodness sake, and he was exactly as reported. He was very sober about comedy. He'd take me out to the street and say, 'Buck, you can't do it that way. If I start here, then the gag works, but if I start there you can never make it work.' Such things as walking behind a policeman in step and disappearing down a manhole just before the bird comes, you know, these Rube Goldberg devices that the picture was full of. He knew right down to the jot what made it work. It was fascinating, too, to be walking around the backlot and having the art director say, 'you know, this section of the street was built for a Buster Keaton comedy in 1921.'
>
> Sad to relate the humor in "Once Upon A Time" is not very funny. The sequence in 1890 at the beginning and end are silent, with cards replacing dialogue. A typical gag shows Keaton walking past chickens and pigs on the street. A card appears which reads 'oink, oink . . . cluck, cluck.' Robert Benchley it ain't.

Some of the shows problems were apparent from the first. "This thing sat in the cutting room for weeks and weeks while Jason Bernie (the film editor) and I wondered how to get the goddamned thing to work better," says Houghton, "because it seemed to go kind of slowly, as if there's one apple . . . and two apples . . . and three apples – and by then you're bored to hear me talk about a fourth apple. So it needed a goose."

The solution which Houghton and Bernie arrived at was to print only two out of ever three frames in the silent sequence. This sped everything up and gave a jerky look to every movement, similar to early, hand-cranked films.

"Having done that and found that it was a good notion," says Houghton, "the episode needed an added sequence, and that sequence in the repair shop was directed by someone else [Les Goodwins] months later."

Richard Matheson was not pleased with the final results. "I had so much more going on, it was funnier, what I had written. Obviously because of cost reasons, the second act became this interminable scene in this repair shop, but I had in it a chase from beginning to end, with him going through a car wash and a supermarket on a bike. It never stopped for a moment. After he meets Stanley Adams (Rollo), though, it just stagnates.

"When all is said and done, Keaton's presence alone makes 'Once Upon A Time' worth watching. For all its faults, it is a warm reunion with a man who, long ago, made us laugh long and hard and well!"

After his classic and well-received appearance on *The Twilight Zone*, Buster once again went before the motion picture cameras. This time, like many times before, it was outside of the United States. As was the fad of the sixties, this was a teenage rock-and-roll film, although unlike other teen films of this era, it did not take place on a beach. The film was titled *Ten Girls Ago* and starred rock-and-roll legend Dion (of the Belmonts). For whatever reasons, the director of this film, Harold Daniels, decided to add some "golden oldies" to the cast , including Buster Keaton, Bert Lahr, and Eddie Foy, Jr.

If you have never seen *Ten Girls Ago*, there is a very good reason; it was never released. Apparently, the studio which produced this film had the very good sense not to torture the film-going public with this utter waste of celluloid. According to all reports, this film was produced in such an amateurish way that it was an embarrassment not only to the industry, but to the performers and studio as well. The real sad point of *Ten Girls Ago* is, it was the last film Bert Lahr would performed in, a disastrous end to a career which had been, at one point, one of the most illustrious in show business.

Back in the United States, Buster once again headed to his new haven, television. In 1962, one of the most popular television shows on the air was *Route 66*. There isn't a member of the "baby-boomer" generation who does not remember this show which ran, very successfully, for four years. Buster's appearance on *Route 66*, titled "Journey To Nineveh," had him playing a small-town jinx who brings bad luck to all those who come into contact with him. Of the four years during which *Route 66* aired, it was this episode that garnered the largest share of the ratings.

With the renewed interest in Buster Keaton from within the entertainment industry, there were more and more compilation films being released which spotlighted Buster during his days as the "King of Comedy." Some of these included *When Comedy Was King*, *Days of Thrills and Laughter*, and *30 Years of Fun*.

Some might consider that the November 7, 1963, United Artists' release of *It's A Mad, Mad, Mad, Mad World* was a film compilation of sorts. Strictly speaking, this may very well be true when you consider the fact that Stanley Kramer, the producer and director of the film, put together a cast which consisted of virtually every major comedian, past and present, who was in the business. Among the stars of yesteryear who performed in this film, in addition to Buster Keaton, were Eddie "Rochester" Anderson, Leo Gorcey, Edward Everett Horton, The Three Stooges (Moe, Larry, and Joe DeRita), Joe E. Brown, Andy Devine, Zasu Pitts, Ben Blue, Jimmy Durante (in his last film appearance), and Jack Benny.

It's A Mad, Mad, Mad, Mad World is the story of a frustrated police detective who gives in to temptation while pursuing a group of bumbling, inept, money-hungry tourists who are searching for a hidden cache of money. This film is three hours of nonstop laughter and it is fun to try and catch all of the great stars in their cameo appearances. Buster's cameo in this film is quick and to the point. He plays a burglar who runs across the set in a striped prison suit. If you blink, you'll miss him. For anyone who is studying the art of comedy or who just wants to sit back and enjoy three solid hours of belly-laughs, this is the film. *It's A Mad, Mad, Mad, Mad World* does revert back to Buster Keaton's forte, the comedy art form of slapstick, for most of its gags.

On November 11, 1964, one of the first "beach party" films was released: *Pajama Party*. Whereas most of the beach party films starred Annette Funicello and Frankie Avelon, this one did not. This time it was Annette Funicello and Tommy Kirk, a newcomer who never really made it in film. *Pajama Party* was a beach film which relied not just on girls in bathing suits and rock-and-roll, but also on a science-fiction plot. In *Pajama Party*, Buster plays an Indian chief who is the villain. Because of the intended audience for this film, Buster was once again being introduced to yet another generation of film-goers.

Apparently, Buster was a big hit with the producer's of *Pajama Party*, because on April 15, 1965, he was in yet another beach party movie. This date, one which will live in infamy for baby-boomers the world over, was the day *Beach Blanket Bingo* was released. In this "sand-crusted" film, Buster plays himself and does it awfully quickly, as the films producer's just wanted to get his name in the credits. It is not known why Buster took roles such as these, as he never talked about them. Some might assume it was the money, even though, at this point in his life, his financial state was much improved. The most plausible reason is that Buster Keaton always found it very hard to say "no" when it came to plying his craft.

Quite possibly, the most interesting film in which Buster participated was the June 5, 1965, release of Samuel Beckett's *Film*. In *Film*, Buster once again brings comedy back to the true art form which it was originally meant to be. It was a one-man *tour-de-force* for Buster and leaves an impact on the viewer which cannot be described.

Film was, for all intents and purposes, a silent film and Buster performed in pantomime. Make no mistake about it, *Film* is considered to be a "black comedy," yet it does have its serious side, as it is a psychological look at a man who is a prisoner within himself. The direction in which *Film* takes us is somewhat disturbing. All through this film, until the conclusion, we never see Buster's face.

Film was never meant to be a theatrical release. It was intended to be an experimental film. Throughout the film, the camera only catches Buster from behind as he tramples through the streets of New York on the way to his apartment. Since we only see the action from behind Keaton, we see the people as they pass Buster on the various streets he travels and we see that on each of their faces is a look of fright when they glimpse his face. When he finally enters his apartment, he keeps his pets, a dog and a cat, from seeing him by slapping at them so they will run off. He then covers up the fishbowl so that even his goldfish cannot see his face. After dealing with his pets, the camera pans to a family portrait which Buster grabs and destroys. Now is when the camera finally catches his face. The look on his face tells the whole story of the film. When he looks into the camera, his face is contorted into a horrifying expression. *Film* is a masterpiece in filmmaking; Samuel Beckett's shining hour and one of Buster's greatest pure acting roles.

Buster Keaton was seventy years old when he made *Film* and it was a very physical part. According to those on the set, the film was produced during the heat of summer. It was reported that, at the foot of the Brooklyn Bridge where the movie was being shot, it was an unbelievable one hundred and ten degrees (partly due to the heat reflecting off the concrete and the heat from the lights being used for the production). For his portrayal of this character, Buster had to be dressed in layers of clothing and a couple of overcoats. Clad in this garb and with the unbearable heat, Buster had to be continuously on the move; often actually jogging. Buster's health at the time was starting to take its deadly toll on him, yet at no time did he ever complain. Buster was from the old school and the old school taught, "the show must go on." Buster was a trooper, something that is unknown in Hollywood today.

Gerald Patterson, who was a member of the directional team of *Film* was awed by Buster. Patterson, who was a fan of Buster's, talked about working with him: "I loved Keaton. It was fantastic to find out that someone who was a God to you was in fact a God!"

After *Film* had a couple of private showings and began to receive critical acclaim, both for its originality and Buster's acting, the film was invited to the Venice Film Festival. Accompanying *Film* to the festival were Buster and Raymond Rohauer, and it was at this film festival where Buster, in the last year of his life, realized how much he was loved, cherished, idolized, and admired.

In September of 1965, the Venice Film Festival not only gave a viewing of *Film*, they also showed some of Buster's early classic films as a retrospective of his career and as a salute to him. On the day of this salute, often referred to by Buster as one of the high points of his life, when he was introduced to the audience and walked down the center aisle to the stage, he received the loudest and longest standing ovation ever accorded any artist in the history of the festival. As he walked, the movie screen on the stage was showing his face as it appeared at the conclusion of *Film*. Making his way toward the microphone, Buster was a tiny solemn figure and his character, as always, was emotionless.

Gloria Swanson, who was also at the Venice Film Festival, responded to the ovation Buster received this way:

> It was unbelievable. In all my life, I have never seen a performer greeted with so much aplomb and this, mind you, was from film critics and the press. As Buster was walking to the stage, he stopped in front of me and took my hand. Looking into those sad dog-eyes, I could see there was a tear which he would not let escape. His lips, those lips which never parted into a smile, were quivering. I truly believe this was the first time in his life where he felt his art was being appreciated and for any performer, I don't care who the performer may be, to get this type of accolade while you're alive, is unheard of in this sometimes rancid world we call Hollywood.

For the first time in his life, Buster had been able to witness part of the restoration of his true status in film history. That process has continued due to the efforts of the late Raymond Rohauer and, currently, because of Alan Twyman and his outstanding company, Alan Twyman Presents the Rohauer Collection. Beginning in the early sixties, Rohauer cataloged all of Buster's copyrights, resurrected his classic films, and licensed their commercial re-releases. Without the work of Raymond Rohauer, and, more recently, Alan Twyman, the art of Buster Keaton could have very easily been lost for ever, which would have truly been an artistic crime of the first degree.

After his triumphant appearance at the Venice Film Festival, Buster headed back to the United States and appeared in three rather forgettable films. These were *How To Stuff A Wild Bikini*, *Sergeant Deadhead*, and *The Railrodder* (the latter being a Canadian produced film).

In October 1965, Buster performed in his last film. This film, *A Funny Thing Happened On The Way To The Forum*, was released on October 16, 1966. It was in this film that, for the very first time in his career, Buster used a stuntman for his stunts. This is understandable when you consider the fact that at this time Buster was very frail, very sick, and seventy years old. The man who had the dubious honor of being the only man to ever stunt for Buster was an Englishman named Mick Dillion.

A Funny Thing Happened On The Way To The Forum is a film which takes place in ancient Rome and centers around a conniving slave (Zero Mostel) who is scheming to win his freedom. The original production of this work was actually a Broadway musical, inspired by Plautus, yet written in a farcical manner with a touch of New York Jewish humor tossed in. In this film, Buster portrays a character aptly named Erronus.

The director of *A Funny Thing Happened On The Way To The Forum*, Richard Lester, had been a Buster Keaton fan since as far back as he could remember and when he had the chance to cast Buster in this film, he didn't think twice. To Richard Lester, Buster was the greatest film comedian of all time. To this very day, whenever Lester talks about Buster, he refers to him as "the master."

In John Eastman's fascinating book titled *Retakes*, he recalls an interesting story from the set of *A Funny Thing Happened On The Way To The Forum*, which centers around the famed comedian, Phil (Sergeant Bilko) Silvers.

Phil Silvers went through the film blind in his left eye because of a cataract, causing him to miss his chalk mark, bump into furniture, and seethe with frustration. Lester had persuaded him to play Lycus the Producer without his trademark glasses, which didn't help matters. At one point,

Figure 6-3 — Buster's last film, A Funny Thing Happened on the Way to the Forum, *was the only one in which he used a stuntman. Keaton died a few months after this photo was taken.*

paralyzed with fear, Silvers had to be physically rescued from the high parapet of which, in a bit of trick photography, he jumps.

It was on a dreary February morning in 1966 when the life of Joseph Francis "Buster" Keaton came to an end. A man who had to fight more than his share of battles (movie studios, Hollywood moguls, wives, alcohol, finances) lost his fight against lung cancer.

"We never told him what was wrong with him," says Eleanor Keaton regarding Buster's fatal illness. "He thought he had chronic bronchitis. Outside of having really bad coughing spells where he'd be almost totally out of breath, he just kept getting progressively weaker. When he was ready to be buried, he had a rosary in one pocket and a deck of cards in the other, so he was set for whichever direction that he was going."

Looking back, it's clear that the "great stone face" was the greatest and purest of all film comedians, projecting skills with a delicate, dignified subtlety. The movies have never offered a sight more entertaining than Buster Keaton coping with adversity and calamity.

Reflecting upon his life and career, Buster said:

I think I have had the happiest and luckiest of lives. Maybe this is because I have never expected as much as I got. What I expected was hard knocks. I always expected to have to work hard. Maybe harder than other people because of my lack of education. And when the knocks came, I felt it was no surprise. I had always known life was like that, full of uppercuts for the deserving and undeserving alike.

But it would be ridiculous for me to complain. I find it impossible to feel sorry for myself. I count the years of defeat and grief and disappointments, and their percentage is so minute that it continually surprises and delights me.

Not long ago, a friend asked me what was the greatest pleasure I got from spending my whole life as an actor. There had been so many that I had to think about that for a moment. Then I said, "Like everyone else, I like to be with a happy crowd."

And that's a comedian's greatest pleasure and privilege,

I think; to have been with so many happy crowds who he has made laugh with his pratfalls and other clowning antics.

. . . AND THE LEGEND WILL LIVE ON!!!

FILMOGRAPHY

This filmography is published with the permission of The Rohauer Collection under the direction of Alan Twyman Presents, who owns the copyright.

This filmography does not include credits for Buster as a screenwriter, contributor to comedy sketches, or director for some M-G-M shorts made during the 1930's.

The Buster Keaton films from the silent era, as well as some of the later films and compilations, are distributed by Alan Twyman Presents: The Rohauer Collection, 592 South Grant Avenue, Columbus, Ohio, 43206-1250.

1) 04-23-17
   The Butcher Boy
   Comique Film Corporation/Paramount
   Director: Roscoe Arbuckle
   Cast: Fatty Arbuckle, Buster Keaton, Al St. John, Josephine Stevens, Arthur Earl, Agness Neilson, Joe Bordeau.

2) 05-21-17
   A Reckless Romeo
   Comique Film Corporation/Paramount
   Director: Roscoe Arbuckle
   Cast: Fatty Arbuckle, Buster Keaton, Al St. John, Alice Lake, Corrine Pacquet, Agnes Neilson.

3) 06-25-17
   The Rough House
   Comique Film Corporation/Paramount
   Director: Roscoe Arbuckle
   Cast: Fatty Arbuckle, Buster Keaton, Al St. John, Alice Lake.

4) 08-20-17
His Wedding Night
Comique Film Corporation/Paramount
Director: Roscoe Arbuckle
Cast: Fatty Arbuckle, Buster Keaton, Al St. John, Alice Mann, Arthur Earle.

5) 09-20-17
Oh, Doctor
Comique Film Corporation/Paramount
Director: Roscoe Arbuckle
Cast: Fatty Arbuckle, Buster Keaton, Al St. John, Alice Mann.

6) 10-29-17
Fatty at Coney Island
Comique Film Corporation/Paramount
Director: Roscoe Arbuckle
Cast: Fatty Arbuckle, Buster Keaton, Al St. John, Alice Mann, Agness Neilson, James Bryant, Joe Bordeau.

7) 12-10-17
A Country Hero
Comique Film Corporation/Paramount
Director: Roscoe Arbuckle
Cast: Fatty Arbuckle, Buster Keaton, Al St. John, Alice Lake

8) 01-20-18
Out West
Comique Film Corporation/Paramount
Director: Roscoe Arbuckle
Cast: Fatty Arbuckle, Buster Keaton, Al St. John, Alice Lake.

9) 03-18-18
The Bell Boy
Comique Film Corporation/Paramount
Director: Roscoe Arbuckle
Cast: Fatty Arbuckle, Buster Keaton, Al St. John, Alice Lake, Charles Dudley, Joseph Keaton.

10) 05-13-18
   Moonshine
   Comique Film Corporation/Paramount
   Director: Roscoe Arbuckle
       Cast: Fatty Arbuckle, Buster Keaton, Al St. John, Alice Lake, Charles Dudley, Joe Bordeau.

11) 07-08-18
   Good Night, Nurse
   Comique Film Corporation/Paramount
   Director: Roscoe Arbuckle
   Cast: Fatty Arbuckle, Buster Keaton, Al St. John, Alice Lake, Kate Price, Joe Bordeau, Joseph Keaton.

12) 09-15-18
   The Crook
   Comique Film Corporation/Paramount
   Director: Roscoe Arbuckle
   Cast: Fatty Arbuckle, Buster Keaton, Al St. John, Alice Lake, Glan Cavender.

13) 06-10-19
   A Desert Hero
   Comique Film Corporation/Paramount
   Director: Roscoe Arbuckle
   Cast: Fatty Arbuckle, Buster Keaton, Al St. John, Alice Lake.
   This is probably a re-issue title and was released at this time because Buster was just returning from the Army and no new film of his was available.

14) 09-07-19
   Back Stage
   Comique Film Corporation/Paramount
   Director: Roscoe Arbuckle
   Cast: Fatty Arbuckle, Buster Keaton, Al St. John, Molly Malone, John Coogan, Alice Lake.

15) 10-26-19
   The Hayseed
   Comique Film Corporation/Paramount
   Director: Roscoe Arbuckle
   Cast: Fatty Arbuckle, Buster Keaton, Molly Malone.

16) 01-11-20
  The Garage
  Comique Film Corporation/Paramount
  Director: Roscoe Arbuckle
  Cast: Fatty Arbuckle, Buster Keaton, Molly Malone, Harry McCoy,
Daniel Crimmins.

17) 08-01-20
  The Round-Up
  Famous Players-Lasky/Paramount
  Director: George Melford
  Cast: Fatty Arbuckle, Tom Forman.
  Buster Keaton appeared as an Indian extra in this Western.

18) 09-07-20
  One Week
  Buster Keaton Production/Metro
  Director: Buster Keaton & Eddie Cline
  Cast: Buster Keaton, Sybil Seeley, Joe Roberts.

19) 10-18-20
  The Saphead
  John L. Golden & William Smith/Metro
  Director: Herbert Blache
  Cast: Buster Keaton, William R. Crane, Beulah Booker, Edward
Connelly, Odette Tyler, Irving Cummings, Carol Holloway.

20) 10-27-20
  Convict 13
  Buster Keaton Productions/Metro
  Director: Buster Keaton & Eddie Cline
  Cast: Buster Keaton, Sybil Seeley, Joe Roberts, Eddie Cline, Joseph
Keaton.

21) 11-17-20
  The Scarecrow
  Buster Keaton Productions/Metro
  Director: Buster Keaton & Eddie Cline
  Cast: Buster Keaton, Joe Roberts, Sybil Seeley, Joseph Keaton.

22) 12-22-20
   Neighbors
   Buster Keaton Productions/Metro
   Director: Buster Keaton & Eddie Cline
   Cast: Buster Keaton, Virginia Fox, Joe Roberts, Joseph Keaton, Eddie Cline.

23) 02-10-21
   The Haunted House
   Buster Keaton Productions/Metro
   Director: Buster Keaton & Eddie Cline
   Cast: Buster Keaton, Virgina Fox, Joe Roberts, Eddie Cline.

24) 03-11-21
   Hard Luck
   Buster Keaton Productions/Metro
   Director: Buster Keaton & Eddie Cline
   Cast: Buster Keaton, Virginia Fox, Joe Roberts.

25) 04-12-21
   The High Sign
   Buster Keaton Productions/Metro
   Director: Buster Keaton & Eddie Cline
   Cast: Buster Keaton, Virginia Fox, Joe Roberts.

26) 05-18-21
   The Goat
   Buster Keaton Productions/Metro
   Director: Buster Keaton & Mal St. Clair
   Cast: Buster Keaton, Joe Roberts, Virgina Fox, Mal St. Clair.

27) 10-06-21
   The Play House
   Joseph M. Schenck/First National
   Director: Buster Keaton & Eddie Cline
   Cast: Buster Keaton, Virginia Fox, Joe Roberts.

28) 11-10-21
   The Boat
   Comique Film Corporation/First National
   Director: Buster Keaton & Eddie Cline
   Cast: Buster Keaton, Sybil Seeley, Eddie Cline.

29) 12-17-21
   The Paleface
   Comique Film Corporation/ First National
   Director: Buster Keaton & Eddie Cline
   Cast: Buster Keaton, Joe Roberts.

30) 02-15-22
   Cops
   Comique Film Corporation/First National
   Director: Buster Keaton & Eddie Cline
   Cast: Buster Keaton, Virgina Fox, Joe Roberts, Eddie Cline.

31) 06-12-22
   My Wife's Relations
   Comique Film Corporation/First National
   Director: Buster Keaton & Eddie Cline
   Cast: Buster Keaton, Kate Price, Monty Collins, Wheezer Dell, Tom
Wilson.

32) 06-26-22
   Screen Snapshots #3
   Producer: Jack and Louis Lewyn
   Buster is one of several stars shown in newsreel fashion in informal
settings.

33) 07-21-22
   The Blacksmith
   Comique Film Corporation/First National
   Director: Buster Keaton & Mal St. Clair
   Cast: Buster Keaton, Virginia Fox, Joe Roberts.

34) 08-03-22
   The Frozen North
   Buster Keaton Productions/First National
   Director: Buster Keaton & Eddie Cline
   Cast: Buster Keaton, Bunny Hill, Freeman Wood, Joe Roberts.

35) 09-28-22
   Day Dreams
   Buster Keaton Productions/First National
   Director: Buster Keaton & Eddie Cline
   Cast: Buster Keaton, Renee Adoree, Joe Roberts.

36) 10-19-22
The Electric House
Buster Keaton Productions/First National
Director: Buster Keaton
Cast: Buster Keaton, Virginia Fox, Joe Roberts, Joseph Keaton, Myra Keaton, Louis Keaton.

37) 12-21-22
The Balloonatic
Buster Keaton Productions/First National
Director: Buster Keaton & Eddie Cline
Cast: Buster Keaton, Phyllis Haver.

38) 03-06-23
The Love Nest
Buster Keaton Productions/First National
Director: Buster Keaton
Cast: Buster Keaton, Joe Roberts, Virginia Fox.

39) 11-19-23
Our Hospitality
Buster Keaton Productions/Metro
Director: Buster Keaton & Jack Blystone
Cast: Buster Keaton, Natalie Talmadge, Joe Roberts, Leonard Clapham, Craig Ward, Joseph Keaton, Buster Keaton, Jr.

40) 04-21-24
Sherlock, Jr.
Buster Keaton Productions/Metro
Director: Buster Keaton
Cast: Buster Keaton, Kathryn McGuire, Ward Crane, Joseph Keaton, Horace Morgan.

41) 10-13-24
The Navigator
Buster Keaton Productions/M-G-M
Director: Buster Keaton & Donald Crisp
Cast: Buster Keaton, Kathryn McGuire, Frederick Vroom, Noble Johnson, Clarence Burton.

42) 03-16-25
Seven Chances
Buster Keaton Productions/M-G-M
Director: Buster Keaton
Cast: Buster Keaton, Ruth Dwyer, Snitz Edwards, T. Roy Barnes,
Frankie Raymond, Jules Cowles, Ewin Connelly-

43) 11-01-25
Go West
Buster Keaton Productions/M-G-M
Director: Buster Keaton
Cast: Buster Keaton, Kathleen Myers, Howard Truesdale, Ray Thompson.

44) 08-30-26
Battling Butler
Buster Keaton Productions/M-G-M
Director: Buster Keaton
Cast: Buster Keaton, Sally O'Neil, Snitz Edwards, Francis
McDonald.

45) 12-31-26
The General
Buster Keaton Productions/United Artists
Director: Buster Keaton & Clyde Bruckman
Cast: Buster Keaton, Marion Mack, Glen Cavender, Jim Farley,
Frederick Vroom, Charles Smith, Frank Barnes, Joseph Keaton.

46) 09-10-27
College
Buster Keaton Productions/United Artists
Director: James W. Horne
Cast: Buster Keaton, Ann Cornwall, Flora Bramely, Harold
Goodwin, Buddy Mason, Grant Withers, Snitz Edwards, Florence
Turner, Carl Harbaugh.

47) 05-12-28
Steamboat Bill, Jr.
Buster Keaton Productions/United Artists
Director: Charles F. Reisner
Cast: Buster Keaton, Ernest Torrence, Tom Lewis, Marion Byron,
Tom McGuire.

48) 09-15-28
The Cameraman
M-G-M
Director: Edward Sedgwick
Cast: Buster Keaton, Marceline Day, Harold Goodwin, Sidney Bracy, Edward Brophy.

49) 04-06-29
Spite Marriage
Edward Sedgwick/M-G-M
Director: Edward Sedgwick
Cast: Buster Keaton, Dorothy Sebastian, Edward Earle, Lelia Hyams, William Bechtel, John Byron, Hank Mann, Pat Harmon.
Originally filmed silent; partial sound added later.

50) 09-23-29
The Hollywood Revue of 1929
Harry Rapf/M-G-M
Director: Charles Reigner
Cast: Jack Benny, Conrad Nagel, John Gilbert, Norma Shearer, Joan Crawford, Bessie Love, Cliff Edwards, The Bronx Sisters, Laurel & Hardy, Lionel Barrymore, Anita Page, Nils Astor, Marion Davis, William Haines, Buster Keaton, Marie Dressler, Polly Moran, Charles King, Gus Edwards, Paul Dane, George K. Arthur, Ann Dvorak, Gwen Lee.
In this revue of many acts, Buster does an Oriental dance routine in "Dance of the Sea" and appears briefly in the finale, "Singing in the Rain."

51) 03-22-30
Free and Easy
Edwards Sedgwick/M-G-M
Director: Edward Sedgwick
Cast: Buster Keaton, Anita Page, Trixie Friganza, Robert Montgomery, Fred Niblo, Edgar Dearling, David Burton, Edward Brophy, Gwen Lee, John Milijan, Lionel Barrymore, William Collier, Sr., William Haines, Dorothy Sabastion, Karl Dane, Jackie Coogan, Cecil B. DeMille, Arthur Lang, Joe Fernham.

52) 03-22-30
Estrellados
(Spanish version of *Free and Easy*)
Director: Unknown (probably Sedgwick)
Cast: Buster Keaton, Raquel Torres, Don Alvarado, Maria Calvo, Emil Chautard.

53) 04-28-30
Voice of Hollywood #101
Louis Lewyn/Tiffany Films
Director: Louis Lewyn
Cast: Robert Woolsey, Al St. John, Nancy Wilbur, Johnny Walker, Lew Cody, Cliff Edwards, Buster Keaton, the Meglin Sisters.
In this sound compilation of acts, Lew Cody, Cliff Edwards and Buster do short takes in front of a lions cage.

54) 08-30-30
Doughboys
Buster Keaton Productions/M-G-M
Director: Edward Sedgwick
Cast: Buster Keaton, Sally Eilers, Cliff Edwards, Edward Brophy, Victor Potel, Arnold Korff, Frank Mayo, Pitzy Katz, William Steele.

55) 08-30-30
De Fronte, Marchen
(Spanish version of *Doughboys*)
Director: Unknown
Cast: Buster Keaton, Conchita Montenegro, Juan De Landa, Romualdo Tirado.

56) 03-27-31
Wir Schalten Urn Auf Hollywood
(German version of *Hollywood Revue of 1928*)
Director: Frank Reicher
Made in Germany, with some speaking parts and sketches re-enacted with German actors (Heinrich George, Nita Parlo), but big musical and production numbers taken from the American original. Since Buster's slot was a non-speaking one, it was used as is.

57) 04-03-31
Stolen Jools
Pat Casey/Paramount & National Screen Services
Director: William McGann
Cast: Wallace Beery, Buster Keaton, Jack Hill, Allen Jenkins, J. Farrell McDonald, Edward G. Robinson, George E. Stone, Eddie Kane, Laurel & Hardy, Our Gang, Polly Moran, Norma Shearer, Hedda Hopper, Joan Crawford, William Haines, Dorothy Lee, Edmund Lowe, Victor McLaglen, El Brendel, Charlie Murray, George Sidney, Winnie Lightner, Fife D'Orsay, Warner Baxter, Irene Dunne, Wheeler & Woolsey, Richard Dix, Claudia Dell, Lowell Sherman, Eugene Pallette, Stu Erwin, Skeets

Gallagher, Gary Cooper, Wynn Gibson, Buddy Rogers, Maurice Chevalier, Douglas Fairbanks, Jr., Loretta Young, Richard Barthelmess, Charles Butterworth, Bebe Daniels, Ben Lyon, Barbara Stanwych, Frank Fay, Jackie Oakie, Fay Wray, Joe E. Brown, Gabby Hayes, Little Billy, Mitzie Green.

This short, presented by the National Variety Artists to raise funds for a tuberculosis sanatorium, concerns a stolen pearl necklace belonging to Norma Shearer. Buster plays one of the four Keystone Cops who appear at the very beginning. Released in England in 1932 as *The Slippery Pearls.*

58) 04-03-31
  Parlor, Bedroom and Bath
  M-G-M
  Director: Edward Sedgwick
  Cast: Buster Keaton, Charlotte Greenwood, Reginald Denny, Cliff Edwards, Dorothy Christy, Joan Peers, Eilers, Natalie Moorehead, Edward Brophy.

59) 04-03-31
  Boster Se Marie
  (French version of *Parlor, Bedroom and Bath*)
  Director: Claude Autant-Lara
  Cast: Buster Keaton, Mona Goya, Andre Luquet, Mireille, Francoise Rosay, Georgette Rhodes, Jean Halbing, Lya Lys, Rolla Norman.

60) 04-03-31
  Casanova Wider Willen
  (German version of *Parlor, Bedroom and Bath*)
  Director: Edward Brophy
  Cast: Buster Keaton, Paul Morgan, Marion Lessing, Egon von Jordan, Francoise Rosay, Leni Stengel, Gerda Mann, George Davis, Wolfgang Zilzer.

61) 09-26-31
  Sidewalks of New York
  Buster Keaton Productions/M-G-M
  Director: Jules White & Zion Meyers
  Cast: Buster Keaton, Anita Page, Cliff Edwards, Frank Rowan, Norman Phillips, Jr., Frank La Rue, Oscar Apfel, Syd Saylor, Clark Marshall.

62) 02-06-32
The Passionate Plumber
Buster Keaton Productions/M-G-M
Director: Edward Sedgwick
Cast: Buster Keaton, Jimmy Durante, Irene Purcell, Polly Moran, Gilbert Roland, Mona Maris, Maude Eburne, Henry Armetta, Paul Porcasi.

63) 02-06-32
Le Plombier Amoureux
(French version of *The Passionate Plumber*)
Director: Claude Autant-Lara
Cast: Buster Keaton, Jimmy Durante, Irene Purcell, Polly Moran, Mona Maris, Jeannette Ferney, Barbara Leonard, Maude Eburne, Del Val, George Davis.

64) 08-13-32
Speak Easy
M-G-M
Director: Edward Sedgwick
Cast: Buster Keaton, Jimmy Durante, Ruth Selwyn, Thelma Todd, Hedda Hopper, William Pawley, Sidney Tolar, Lawrence Grant, Henry Armetta, Edward Brophy.

65) 01-08-33
Hollywood on Parade #A-6
Louis Lewyn/Paramount
Director: Louis Lewyn
Cast: Richard Arlen, Frances Dee, Clark Gable, Tallulah Bankhead, Buster Keaton, Lew Cody.
In this compilation of walk-ons and minor acts, Buster plays host to Lew Cody on his big band cruise.

66) 02-10-33
What! No Beer?
M-G-M
Director: Edward Sedgwick
Cast: Buster Keaton, Jimmy Durante, Roscoe Yates, Phyllis Barry, John Milijan, Henry Armetta, Edward Brophy, Charles Dunbar.

67) 01-05-34
Le Roi Des Champs-Elysees
Nero Films/Paramount
Cast: Buster Keaton, Paulette Dubost, Collette Darfevil, Madeline
Guilty, Jaques Dumesnil, Pierre Piezade, Gaston Dupray, Paul Clerget,
Frank Maurice, Pitouto, Lucien Callamand.

68) 03-16-34
The Gold Ghost
Educational/20th Century-Fox
Director: Charles Lamont
Cast: Buster Keaton, Dorothy Dix, William Worthington, Lloyd
Ingraham, Warren Hymer.

69) 05-31-34
Allez Oop
Educational/20th Century-Fox
Director: Charles Lamont
Cast: Buster Keaton, Dorothy Sebastian, Harry Meyers, George Lawis.

70) 01-11-35
Palooka from Paducah
Educational/20th Century-Fox
Director: Charles Lamont
Cast: Buster Keaton, Joseph Keaton, Myra Keaton, Louise Keaton,
Dewy Robinson, Bull Montana.

71) 02-22-35
One Run Elmer
Educational/20th Century-Fox
Director: Charles Lamont
Cast: Buster Keaton, Lona Andre, Dewy Robinson.

72) 03-15-35
Hayseed Romance
Educational/20th Century-Fox
Director: Charles Lamont
Cast: Buster Keaton, Jane Jones, Dorthea Kent.

73) 05-02-35
Tars and Stripes
Educational/20th Century-Fox
Cast: Buster Keaton, Vernon Dent, Dorthea Kent, Jack Shutta.

74) 08-09-35
The E-Flat Man
Educational / 20th Century-Fox
Director: Charles Lamont
Cast: Buster Keaton, Dorthea Kent, Broderick O'Farrell, Charles
McAvoy, Si Jenks, Fern Emmet, Jack Shutta.

75) 10-25-35
The Timid Young Man
Educational / 20th Century-Fox
Director: Mack Sennett
Cast: Buster Keaton, Lona Andes, Tiny Sandford, Kitty McHugh,
Harry Bowen.

76) 12-07-35
La Fiesta De Santa Barbara
Louis Lewyn/M-G-M
Director: Louis Lewyn
Cast: Buster Keaton, Chester Conklin, Gary Cooper, Harpo Marx,
Maria Gambarelli, Warner Baxter, Leo Carillo, Adriene Ames, Robert
Taylor, Mary Carlisle, Edmund Lowe, Toby Wing, Ida Lupino, Irvin S.
Cobb, Ted Healy.
The was essentially a boating party going to a Mexican carnival. All
of the above stars were seen briefly on the boat or at the carnival, but the
music and revelry are the main attraction.

77) 01-02-36
The Invader
British & Continental/M-G-M
Director: Adrian Brunel
Cast: Buster Keaton, Lupita Tovar, Lyn Harding, Webster Booth,
Andrea Malandrinos, Hilda Moreno, Clifford Heatherly.

78) 01-03-36
Three On A Limb
Educational / 20th Century-Fox
Director: Charles Lamont
Cast: Buster Keaton, Lona Andes, Harold Goodwin, Grant Withers,
Brabra Bedford, John Ince, Fern Emmett, Phyliss Crane.

79) 02-21-36
Grand Slam Opera
Educational/20th Century-Fox
Director: Charles Lamont
Cast: Buster Keaton, Diana Lewis, Harold Goodwin, John Ince, Melrose Coakley, Bud Jamison.

80) 08-21-36
Blue Blazes
Educational/20th Century-Fox
Director: Raymond Kane
Cast: Buster Keaton, Arthur Jarrett, Rose Kessner, Patty Wilson, Marlyn Stuart.

81) 10-09-36
The Chemist
Educational/20th Century-Fox
Director: Al Christie
Cast: Buster Keaton, Marlyn Stuart, Earl Gilbert, Don McBride, Herman Loeb.

82) 01-20-36
Mixed Marriage
Educational/20th Century-Fox
Director: Raymond Kane
Cast: Buster Keaton, Eddie Lambert, Marlyn Stuart, Eddie Hall, Jimmie Fox, Walter Fenner.

83) 01-08-37
Jail Bait
Educational/20th Century-Fox
Director: Charles Lamont
Cast: Buster Keaton, Harold Goodwin, Betty Andre, Bud Jamison, Matthew Betz.

84) 02-12-37
Ditto
Educational/20th Century-Fox
Director: Charles Lamont
Cast: Buster Keaton, Barbara Bewster, Gloria Brewster, Harold Goodwin, Lynton Brent, Al Thompson, Bud Ellsworth.

85) 03-26-37
Love Nest on Wheels
Educational/20th Century-Fox
Director: Edward Sedgwick
Cast: Buster Keaton, Myra Keaton, Louise Keaton, Harry Keaton, Al St. John, Lynton Brent, Diana Lewis, Bud Jamison.

86) 06-16-39
Pest From the West
Columbia
Director: Del Lord
Cast: Buster Keaton, Lorna Gray, Gino Cozzado, Richard Fiske, Bud Jamison, Eddie Laughton.

87) 08-11-39
Mooching Through Georgia
Columbia
Director: Jules White
Cast: Buster Keaton, Monty Collins, Bud Jamison, Jill Martin, Lynton Brent, Jack Hill, Stanley Mack.

88) 10-13-39
Hollywood Cavalcade
Darryl Zannuck/20th Century-Fox
Director: Irving Cummings
Cast: Alice Faye, Don Amache, J. Edward Bromberg, Alan Curtis, Stuart Erwin, Jed Prouty, Donald Meek, George Givot, Chick Chandler, Russell Hicks, Robert Lowery, Bud Weldon.
Guests appearing as themselves: Buster Keaton, Ben Turpin, Chester Conklin, Al Jolson, Mack Sennett, the Keystone Cops.

89) 01-19-40
Nothing But Pleasure
Columbia
Director: Jules White
Cast: Buster Keaton, Dorothy Appleby, Beatrice Blinn, Bud Jamison, Richard Fiske, Robert Sterling, Jack Randall.

90) 03-22-40
Pardon My Birth Marks
Columbia
Director: Jules While
Cast: Buster Keaton, Dorothy Appleby, Richard Fiske, Vernon Dent.

91) 06-28-40
The Taming of the Snood
Columbia
Director: Jules White
Cast: Buster Keaton, Dorothy Appleby, Elsie Ames, Richard Fiske,
Bruce Bennett.

92) 07-18-40
New Moon
M-G-M
Director: Richard Z. Leonard
Cast: Jeannette MacDonald, Nelson Eddy, Mary Boland, George
Zucco, H.B. Warner, Grant Mitchell.

93) 09-20-40
The Spook Speaks
Columbia
Director: Jules White
Cast: Buster Keaton, Elsie Ames, Dorothy Appleby, Don Beddue,
Bruce Bennett.

94) 10-11-40
The Villain Still Pursued Her
Franklin-Blank Productions/R-K-0
Director: Eddie Cline
Cast: Buster Keaton, Hugh Herbert, Anita Louise, Alan Mowbray,
Richard Cromwell.

95) 11-01-40
Li'l Abner
Vogue/R-K-0
Director: Albert S. Rogell
Cast: Buster Keaton, Granville Owen, Martha O'Driscoll, Mona Ray.

96) 12-13-41
His Ex Marks the Spot
Columbia
Director: Jules White
Cast: Buster Keaton, Elsie Ames, Dorothy Appleby, Matt McHugh.

97) 02-21-41
So You Won't Squak
Columbia
Director: Del Lord
Cast: Buster Keaton, Eddie Featherstone, Matt McHugh, Bud Jamison, Hank Mann, Vernon Dent, Edmund Cobb.

98) 09-18-41
General Nuisance
Columbia
Director: Jules White
Cast: Buster Keaton, Elsie Ames, Dorothy Appleby, Monty Collins, Bud Jamison, Lynton Brent, Nick Arno, Harry Semels.

99) 11-20-41
She's Oil Mine
Columbia
Director: Jules White
Cast: Buster Keaton, Elsie Ames, Monty Collins, Eddie Laughton, Bud Jamison.

100) 03-26-43
Forever and A Day
Produced & Directed: Rene Clair, Edmund Goulding,
Sir Cedric Hardwicke, Frank Lloyd, Victor Seville, Robert Stevenson and Herbert Wilcox.
Cast: Anna Neagle, Ray Milland, Claude Raines, C. Aubrey Smith, Dame Mae Whiity, Gene Lockhart, Ray Bolger, Edmund Gwynn, Lumsden Hare, Stuart Robertson, Claude Allister, Ben Webster, Alan Edmiston, Patrick Knowles, Bernie Sell, Halliwell Hobbes, Helen Pichard, Doris Lloyd, Lionel Belmore, Louise Bessinger, Clifford Severn, Charles Coburn, Alec Craig, Ian Hunter, Jesse Matthews, Charles Laughton, Montague Love, Reginald Owen, Sir Cedric Hardwicke, Noel Madison, Ernest Cossart, Peter Godfrey, Buster Keaton, Wendy Barrie, Ida Lupino. Brian Aherne, Edward Evertt Horton, Isobel Elsom, Wendal Hulet, Eric Blore, June Duprez, Mickey Martin, Queenie Leonard, May Beatty, Merle Oberon, Una O'Conner, Nigel Bruce, Anita Bolster, Marta Gale, Roland Young, Gladys Cooper, Robert Haydn, Emily Fitzroy, Odette Myrtil, Elsa Lanchester, Sara Allgood, Vangie Beilby, Robert Coote, Art Multiner, Ivan Simpson, Pax Walker, Lola Vanti, Bill Cartledge, Charles Hall, Percy Snowden, Donald Crisp, Ruth Warrick, Kent Smith, June Lockhart, Lydia Bilbrook, Billy Bevan, Herbert Marshall, Victor McLaglen, Harry Allen, Ethel Griffies, Gabriel Canzona, Joy Mary Gordon, Evelyn Beresford,

Moyna MacGill, Arthur Treacher, Anna Lee, Cecil Kellaway, Stuart Hall, Barry Heenan, Barry Norton, Daphne Moore.

A wartime paean to the noble British spirit instigated mainly by Sir Cedric Hardwicke. Buster plays Hardwicke's assistant – they are two plumbers installing a bathtub.

Stars contributing their talent included most of the British Colony in Hollywood. The story traces the building of a stately home by C. Aubrey Smith in 1804 and what happens to the subsequent generations who live in it.

101) 09-29-44
   San Diego, I Love You
   Universal
   Director: Reginald Le Borg
   Cast: John Hall, Louise Allbritton, Edward Everett Horton, Eric Blore, Buster Keaton, Irene Ryan, Rudy Wissler, Gerrald Perraau.

102) 06-01-45
   That's the Spirit
   Universal
   Director: Charles Lamont
   Cast: Peggy Ryan, Jack Oakie, June Vincent, Gene Lockhart, Johnny Coy, Andy Devine, Arthur Treacher, Irene Ryan, Buster Keaton, Victoria Horne, Edith Barrett.

Buster has a bit role in a fantasy about a man whose spirit is allowed to come back to earth.

103) 09-28-45
   That Night With You
   Universal
   Director: William A. Seitzer
   Cast: Franchot Tone, Susanna Foster, Louise Allbritton, David Bruce, Jacqueline de Witt, Irene Ryan, Barbara Sears, Anthony Caruso, Julian Rivero, Teddy Infuhr, Janet Ann Gallow, Buster Keaton, Thomas Fadden, Howard Freeman.

Zany farce about a girl who tells a producer that she's the result of his one day marriage many years before. Buster plays a short-order cook.

104) 05-18-46
God's Country
Action Pictures/Screen Guild Productions
Director: Robert Tansey
Cast: Robert Lowery, Helen Gilbert, Buster Keaton.
Outdoor film with Buster as an animal lover.

105) 08-02-46
El Moderno Barba Arul
Also Films (Mexico)
Director: Jamie Salvador
Cast: Buster Keaton, Angel Garasa, Virginia Seret, Luis Bareiro,
Fernando Solto.
Buster is a prisoner of the Mexicans who send him to the moon.

106) 05-11-49
The Lovable Cheat
Skyline Pictures/Film Classics, Inc.
Director: Richard Oswald
Cast: Charles Ruggles, Peggy Ann Garner, Richard Ney, Alan Mow-
bray, Iris Adrian, Minera Urecal, Buster Keaton.

107) 06-23-49
In the Good Old Summertime
M-G-M
Director: Robert Z. Leonard
Cast: Judy Garland, Van Johnson, Buster Keaton, Spring Byington,
S.Z. Sakal.

108) 07-16-49
You're My Everything
20th Century-Fox
Director: Walter Lang
Cast: Dan Dailey, Anne Baxter, Ann Revere, Stanley Ridges, Shari
Robinson, Henry O'Neill, Selena Royle, Alan Mowbray, Robert Arthur,
Buster Keaton, Phyliss Kennedy, Chester Jones.
Musical comedy about the early days of sound in Hollywood. Buster
plays a butler.

109) 08-04-50
Sunset Boulevard
Paramount
Director: Billy Wilder
Cast: William Holden, Gloria Swanson, Erich von Stroheim, Nancy Olson, Fred Clark, Jack Webb, Lloyd Gough, Ruth Clifford.

Appearing as themselves: Cecil B. DeMille, Hedda Hopper, Buster Keaton, Anna Q. Nilsson, H.B. WArner, Ray Evans, Jay Livingston, Sidney Skolsky.

Buster is seen in a card game with Gloria Swanson, Anna Q. Nilsson, and H.B. Warner.

110) 09-07-50
Un Duel A Mort
Film Azur (France)
Director: Pierre Blondy
Cast: Buster Keaton, Antonin Berval.

This short captures on film a skit which Buster used for years at the Cirque Medrano in Paris. He is a comic duelist.

111) 04-22-51
Screen Snaphots: Memories of Famous Hollywood Comedians
Columbia
Directed & Compiled: Ralph Staub
Narrated: Joe E. Brown
Cast: Fatty Arbuckle, Zasu Pitts, Laurel & Hardy, W.C. Fields, Charley Chase, Andy Clyde, Buster Keaton, Louise Farenda, Ben Turpin, The Marx Bros., Olson & Johnson.

A compilation of deleted scenes and off-screen candid footage of many stars.

112) 10-15-52
Paradise for Buster
Wilding Pictures, for Deere & Co. (Shot in 16mm private company film)
Director: Del Lord
Cast: Buster Keaton.

In this industrial short, Buster plays in pantomime an unsuccessful bookkeeper who inherits an old rundown farm and turns it into a well-stocked lake used by fishermen.

113) 10-22-52
Limelight
Celebrated Films/United Artists
Director: Charles Chaplin
Cast: Charles Chaplin, Claire Bloom, Sidney Chaplin, Andre Eglevsky, Melissa Hayden, Charles Chaplin, Jr., Wheeler Dryden, Nigel Bruce, Norman Lloyd, Buster Keaton, Marjorie Bennett, Geraldine Chaplin, Michael Chaplin, Victoria Chaplin.
Buster plays a piano accompanist to Chaplin's performance as a clown.

114) 06-14-53
L'Incantevole Nemica
Orso Films (Italy)
Director: Claudio Gora
Cast: Silvana Pampanini, Robert Lamoureux, Carlo Campanini, Raymond Bussieres, Buster Keaton.
Buster appears in a brief sketch.

115) 07-14-54
Douglas Fairbanks Presents: The Awakening
Television Productions
A television show based on Gogolls "The Overcoat."
Buster plays a timid individual beset by troubles.

116) 10-13-54
Best of Broadway: The Man Who Came To Dinner
Television Production
Director: David Alexander
Cast: Buster Keaton, Sylvia Field, Zasu Pitts, Frank Tweddle, Margaret Hamilton, Merle Oberon, Monty Wooley, Howard St. John, Joan Bennett, Reginald Gardiner, Bert Lahr, Catherine Doucet, William Price.
Television adaptation of the Kaufman/Hart play. Buster plays Dr. Bradley.

117) 10-10-55
Eddie Cantor Theater: The World of Alonzo Pennyworth
Television Production
Director: Unknown
Buster plays Alonzo Pennyworth, a bashful travel agent who himself has never been anywhere and who is doing badly romantically as well.

118) 12-21-55
Screen Director's Playhouse: The Silent Partner
Television Production
Director: George Marshal
Cast: Bob Hope, Joe E. Brown, Buster Keaton, Zasu Pitts, Jack Elam.

119) 03-06-56
Martha Raye Show
Television Production
Director: Unknown
Cast: Buster Keaton, Paul Douglas, Harold Arlen.

120) 09-17-56
Producers' Showcase: The Lord Don't Play Favorites
Television Productions
Producer: Hal Stanley
Cast: Buster Keaton, Robert Stack, Kay Starr, Dick Haymes, Louis Armstrong, Nelsa Ates, Mike Ross, Arthur Q. Bryan.

121) 10-17-56
Around the World in 80 Days
Michael Todd Company/United Artists
Director: Michael Anderson
Cast: David Niven, Caninflas, Robert Newton, Shirley MacLaine, Charles Boyer, Joe E. Brown, Martin Carol, John Carradine, Charles Coburn, Ronald Coleman, Melville Cooper, Noel Coward, Finnlay Currie, Reginald Denny, Andy Devine, Marlene Dietrich, Luis Miguel, Dominguin, Fernandel, Sir John Gielgud, Hermione Gingold, Jose Greco, Sir Cedric Hardwicke, Trevor Howard, Glynis Johns, Buster Keaton, Evelyn Keyes, Beatrice Lillie, Peter Lorre, Edmund Lowe, Victor McLaglen, Tim McCoy, A.E. Mathews, Mike Mazurka, John Mills, Alan Mowbray, Robert Morley, Edward R. Murrow, Jack Oakie, George Raft, Gilbert Roland, Cesar Romero, Frank Sinatra, Red Skelton, Ronald Squire, Basil Sidney, Harcourt Williams, Ava Gardner.

122) 06-05-58
Playhouse 90: The Innocent Slap
Television Production
Director: Franklin Schaffner
Cast: Buster Keaton, Hope Lange, Dennis King, John Ericson, Hope Emerson.

123) 12-24-58
The Donna Reed Show: A Very Merry Christmas
Cast: Donna Reed, Carl Betz, Buster Keaton, Shelly Fabres, Paul Peterson.
Buster plays a philanthropist who provides the money for the annual party at the children's ward in a hospital, and who is talked into playing Santa Claus by Donna Reed.

124) 02-02-60
Sunday Showcase: After Hours
Television Production
Director: Alex March
Cast: Buster Keaton, Christopher Plummer, Sally Ann Howes, Robert Emhardt, Phillip Abbott, Natalie Schafer, Paul McGrath, John Fielder.
A comedy of mistaken identity in which Buster plays Santa Claus.

125) 03-29-60
When Comedy Was King
Ro-Co Productions/20th Century-Fox
Produced & Selected: Robert Youngston
Cast: Charles Chaplin, Laurel & Hardy, Buster Keaton, Harry Langdon, Ben Turpin, Fatty Arbuckle, Wallace Beery, Gloria Swanson, Mabel Norman, etc.
A compilation of great moments from many films from the silent era. No new footage.

126) 06-17-60
The Adventures of Huckleberry Finn
M-G-M
Director: Michael Curtiz
Cast: Tony Randall, Eddie Hodges, Archie Moore, Patty McCormack, Neville Brand, Buster Keaton.
Buster has a small role as a lion tamer.

127) 09-15-60
The Devil to Pay
(Educational research film for the National Association of Wholesalers)
Director: Herb Skoble
Cast: Buster Keaton, Ralph Dunne, Ruth Gillette, Marion Morris, John Rodney.
Buster plays the devil.

128) 1961
The History of Motion Pictures: The Sad Clowns
Produced & Narrated: Saul Terrel & Paul Killiam
Editor: Bill Everson
Cast: Charles Chaplin, Harry Langdon, Buster Keaton.
A compilation of clips from their silent films.

129) 12-15-61
The Twilight Zone: Once Upon A Time
Television Production
Director: Norman Z. McLeod
Cast: Buster Keaton, Stanley Adams, Milton Parsons, Jesse White, Gil Lamb, James Flavin, Michael Ross.

130) 1962
Ten Girls Ago
Am-Can Productions (Canada)
Filmed in 1962 but never released.
Director: Harold Daniels
Cast: Dion, Austin Wills, Jan Milner, Jennifer Billingsley, Risella Bain, Buster Keaton, Bert Lahr, Eddie Foy, Jr.

131) 04-20-62
The Scene Stealers
March of Dimes Production
Director: Unknown
Cast: Buster Keaton, Jimmy Durante, Ed Wynn.
The three comedians get involved in rehearsals of the March of Dimes Show and mess things up.

132) 09-28-62
Route 66: Journey to Nineveh
Director: Unknown
Cast: Buster Keaton, George Maharis, Mattin Milner, Joe E. Brown, Gene Raymond, Jenny Maxwell, John Astin, John Davis, Chandler, John Durren.
Buster plays the town jinx.

133) 12-20-62
   The Great Chase
   Saul Terrel & Paul Williams/Janus Films
   Producer/Editor: Harvey Cort
   Cast: Douglas Fairbanks, Sr., William S. Hart, Mack Sennett, Mabel
Normand, Buster Keaton.
   Compilation of scenes involving chases.

134) 01-19-63
   Mr. Smith: Think Mink
   Television Production
   Director: Unknown
   Cast: Buster Keaton, Jesslyn Fax, Fess Parker,
   Sandra Warner.
   Television show with Buster and Fax playing a couple who discover
how to breed mink much faster by feeding them a special stew.

135) 02-12-63
   Thirty Years of Fun
   20th Century-Fox
   Produced & Written: Robert Youngston
   Cast: Charles Chaplin, Buster Keaton, Laurel & Hardy, Andy Clyde,
Billy Baven, etc.
   Compilation of vintage scenes from comedy classics. Buster is seen
in excerpts from *Cops*, *Day Dreams*, and *The Balloonatic*.

136) 03-25-63
   The Triumph of Lester Snapwell
   Eastman Kodak Company
   (Private comedy film; 16mm)
   Director: James Calhoun
   Cast: Buster Keaton.
   Buster traces the highlights of the delevopment of the
   camera in his comic style.

137) 11-07-63
   Its A Mad, Mad, Mad, Mad World
   Stanley Kramer/United Artists
   Director: Stanley Kramer
   Cast: Spencer Tracey, Milton Berle, Sid Caesar, Buddy Hackett, Ethel
Merman, Mickey Rooney, Dick Shawn, Phil Silvers, Terry-Thomas,
Jonathan Winters, Edie Adams, Dorothy Provine, Rochester, Jim Backus,
Ben Blue, Alan Carney, Bernie Chase, William Demarest, Peter Falk, Paul

Ford, Leo Gorcey, Edward Everett Horton, Buster Keaton, Don Knotts, Carl Reiner, Moe Howard, Larry Fine, Joe De Rita, Joe E. Brown, Andy Devine, Sterling Holloway, Marvin Kaplan, Charles Lane, Charles McGraw, Zasu Pitts, Madlyn Rhue, Arnold Stang, Jesse White, Lloyd Corrigan, Stan Freeberg, Ben Lessy, Bobo Lewis, Mike Mazurka, Nick Stewart, Sammee Tong, Norman Fell, Nicholas Georgiade, Jimmy Durante, Allen Jenkins, Stanley Clements, Tom Kennedy, Harry Lauter, Doodles Weaver, Chick Chandler, Barbara Pepper, Cliff Norton, Roy Roberts, Eddie Ryder, Don C. Harvey, Roy Engel, Paul Birch, Dale Van Sickle, Jack Benny, Jerry Lewis.

Buster plays a crook.

138) 12-17-63
The Sound of Laughter
Union Film
Director: John O'Shaughnessy
Cast: Bing Crosby, Bob Hope, Danny Kaye, Buster Keaton, etc.
Compilation of early sound comedy. Buster is seen in excerpts from One Run Elmer and Grand Slam Opera.

139)
The Greatest Show On Earth: You're All Right, Ivy
Television Production
Director: Jack Palance
Cast: Buster Keaton, Jack Palance, Stuart Erwin, Lynn Loring, Ted Bessle, Joe E. Brown, Joan Blondell, Barbara Pepper.
Buster and Joan Blondell are veteran performers now reduced to menial work in a circus.

140) 05-08-64
Burk's Law: Who Killed Glory Lee?
Television Production
Director: Unknown
Cast: Gene Barry, Buster Keaton, Gary Conway, Regis Toomey, Joan Blondell, Nina Foch, Ann Helm, Betty Hutton, Gisele McKenzie.
Buster is one of the suspects in a case involving a rigged elevator accident.

141) 06-06-64
Hollywood Palace
Television Production
Director: Unknown
Host: Gene Barry
Guest: Buster Keaton and Gloria Swanson.
Buster and Swanson offer a spoof of Cleopatra.

142) 11-11-64
Pajama Party
American International
Director: Don Weis
Cast: Annett Funicello, Tommy Sand, Elsa Lanchester, Donna Loren, Buster Keaton.
Teenage beach fun mixed with a little science fiction. Keaton plays a villianous Indian chief.

143) 01-17-65
The Man Who Bought Paradise
Studio Unknown
Director: Ralph Nelson
Cast: Buster Keaton, Robert Horton, Angie Dickenson, Paul Lukas, Ray Walston, Hoagy Carmichael, Deloroes Del Rio, Cyril Ritchard, Walter Slazak.
In a foreign country, fugitives from the law live at the Hotel Paradise. Buster plays a knife-wielding lawbreaker.

144) 04-15-65
Beach Blanket Bingo
American International
Director: William Asher
Cast: Frankie Avelon, Annette Funicello, Deborah Walley, Paul Lynde, Buster Keaton.
Buster has a cameo as himself.

145) 06-05-65
Film
Evergreen Theater/Grove Press
Director: Alan Schneider
Cast: Buster Keaton.

146) 07-14-65
How Too Stuff A Wild Bikini
American International
Director: William Asher
Cast: Annette Funicello, Dwayne Hickman, Brian Donlevy, Mickey
Rooney, Beverly Adams, Buster Keaton, Frankie Avelon, Irene Tsu.
Another rock-and-roll beach frolic. Buster's cameo role is of a witch
doctor.

147) 08-18-65
Sergeant Deadhead
American International
Director: Norman Taurog
Cast: Frankie Avelon, Deborah Walley, Cesar Romero, Fred Clark,
Gale Gordon, Reginald Gardiner, Buster Keaton, Eve Arden.
Buster plays a private at a missle base who pushes some wrong
buttons at a crucial moment.

148) 10-02-65
The Railrodder
National Film Board (Canada)
Director: Gerald Patterson
Cast: Buster Keaton.
Buster on a railroad handcart as a guide for a trip through gloroius
Canadian scenery.

149) 10-30-65
Buster Keaton Rides Again
National Film Board (Canada)
Director: John Spotton
Cast: Buster Keaton and Eleanor Keaton.
Documentary about the making of The Railrodder.

150) 01-08-66
The Scribe
Film-Tele Productions (Canada)
(Private 16mm film for Construction Safety Association)
Director: John Serbert
Cast: Buster Keaton.
In this industrial safety film, Buster plays a reporter at a contruction
site doing a story on safety. This is the last film Buster worked on.

151) 10-16-66
A Funny Thing Happened On The Way To The Forum
United Artists
Director: Richard Lester
Cast: Zero Mostel, Phil Silvers, Buster Keaton, Jack Gilford, Michael Crawford, Annette Andre, Patricia Jessel, Michael Hordern.
  In this spoof of ancient Rome, Buster plays Erronius, a man searching for his children who were taken away by pirates.

152) 01-18-67
Due Marines Un General
(Released in U.S. as *War Italian Style*)
Italian International/American International
Director: Luigi Scattini
Cast: Franco Franchi, Ciccio Ingrassia, Martha Hyer, Buster Keaton, Fred Clark.
  Buster plays a german general whom two Italian marines at first outwit, but then get to like.

153) 1968
The Great Stone Face
Funnyman Productions
Director/Editor: Vernon P. Becker
Narrated: Henry Morgan
  Compilation film using stills and excerpts from Buster's silent films to trace his career. Buster is seen in lengthy bits from, among others, *Fatty At Coney Island, Cops, Day Dream, The Balloonatic,* and *The General.*

154) 09-09-70
Four Clowns
20th Century-Fox
Producer: Robert Youngston
Narrator: Jay Jackson
  Compilation film of excerpts from the work of Buster Keaton, Charley Chase, and Laurel & Hardy. The lengthiest Keaton sequence is the chase scene from *Seven Chances.*

155) 11-03-74
 The Three Stooges Follies Columbia
 Director: Jules White
 Cast: The Three Stooges, Vera Vague, Buster Keaton, etc.
 Compilation of Columbia shorts from the 30's and 40's, most of them featuring the Three Stooges. Buster is seen in *Nothing But Pleasure*, one of his 1940 releases.

156) 10-11-75
 Three Comedies
 Jay Ward Productions
 Producer: Raymond Rohauer
 Compilation film made up of three Buster Keaton shorts, with narration and musical score: *The High Sign, The Paleface*, and *One Week*.

157) 11-01-82
 Buster (The Golden Age of Buster Keaton)
 Jay Ward Productions
 Producer: Raymond Rohauer
 Compilation film using clips from many Buster Keaton shorts and features, narrated by Bill Scott.

BIBLIOGRAPHY

Adamson, Joe. 1973. *Groucho, Harpo, Chico and Sometimes Zeppo.* Simon & Schuster, New York.

Anderson, Janice. 1985. *History of Movie Comedy.* Exeter/Simon & Schuster, New York.

Anger, Kenneth. 1975. *Hollywood Babylon.* Dell Books, New York.

Barnouv, Erik. 1983. *Documentary.* Oxford University Press, Oxford.

Bergan, Ronald. 1986. *The United Artists Story.* Crown Publishers, New York.

Brooks, Tim and Marsh, Earle. 1988. *The Complete Dictionary to Prime Time Network TV Shows, 1946-Present.* Bantam Books, New York.

Brown, Peter H. and Pinkston, Jim. 1987. *Oscar Dearest.* Harper & Row, San Francisco.

Brownlow, Kevin. 1968. *The Parades Gone By.* University of California Press, Berkeley.

Bullock, Alan, gen. ed. 1989. *Great Lives of the Twentieth Century.* Charwell Books, Inc.

Butler, Ivan. 1987. *Silent Magic.* The Ungar Publishing Company.

Dardis, Tom. 1979. *Keaton: The Man Who Wouldn't Lie Down.* Charles Scribner's Sons, New York.

Eames, John Douglas. 1982. *The M-G-M Story.* Crown Publishers, New York.

Eastman, John. 1989. *Retakes.* Random House, New York.

Edmonds, Andy. 1989. *Hot Toddy.* William Morrow & Co., Inc., New York.

Fields, Ronald J. 1973. *W.C. Fields: By Himself.* Prentice-Hall, Inc., New York.

Giannetti, Louis. 1982. *Understanding Movies.* Prentice-Hall, Inc., New York.

Halliwell, Leslie. 1979. *Halliwell's Film Companion (4th edition).* Charles Scribners' Sons, New York.

Hirschhorn, Joel. 1983. *Rating the Movie Stars.* Publications International, Ltd.

Jewell, Richard B. and Harbin, Vernon. 1982. *The R-K-O Story.* Arlington House/Crown Publishers, New York.

Katz, Ephram. 1979. *The Film Encyclopedia.* Putnam Publishing, New York.

Keaton, Buster and Samuels, Charles. 1960. *My Wonderful World of Slapstick.* Da Capo Press, Inc./Plenum Publishing Corp., New York.

Kerr, Walter. 1975. *The Silent Clowns.* Da Capo Press, Inc., New York.

Kesselman, Marcia E. 19—. *The Video Directory.* Art Ad House.

Lawson, John Howard. 1964. *Film: The Creative Process.* Hill and Wang, New York.

Leyda, Jay. 1977. *Film Makers Speak.* Da Capo Press, Inc., New York.

Lloyd, Ann, ed. 1982. *70 Years at the Movies.* Crescent Books/Crown Publications, New York.

Maltin, Leonard, ed. 1989. *Leonard Maltin's TV Movies and Video Guide.* Signet Books, New York.

Martin, Mick and Porter, Marsha. 1989. *Video Movie Guide 1990.* Ballantine Books, New York.

Mordden, Ethan. 1988. *The Hollywood Studios.* Alfred A Knopf, Inc., New York.

Morley, Sheridan. 1983. *Tales From the Hollywood Raj.* The Viking Press, New York.

Phantom of the Movies, The. 1989. *The Phantom's Ultimate Video Guide.* Dell Publishing, New York.

Robertson, Patrick. 1985. *Guinness Film Facts and Feats.* Guinness Superlatives, Ltd.

Sennett, Ted. 1986. *Great Movie Directors.* Harry N. Abrams, Inc., New York.

Stuart, Ray. 1989. *Immortals of the Screen.* Bonanza Books, New York.

Thomson, David. 1975. *A Biographical Dictionary of Film.* William Morrow and Company, New York.

Webb, Michael, ed. 1986. *Hollywood: Legend and Reality.* Little, Brown and Company, Boston.

Weis, Elizabeth. 1981. *The Movie Star.* Penguin Press, New York.

Wiener, Tom. 1988. *The Book of Video Lists.* Madison Books.

Zicree, Marc Scott. 1989. *The Twilight Zone Companion.* Bantam Books, New York.

INDEX

A

A Biographical Dictionary of Film, 42
A Country Hero, 26, 174
A Day at the Circus, 141, 142
A Funny Thing Happened on the Way to the Forum, 168, *169*, 202
A Night at the Opera, 107
A Reckless Romeo, 24, 173
A Southern Yankee, 143-144
Abbott and Costello, 31, 131, 140, 141, 148
Academy Awards, The, 18, 95, 151, 152, 154, 157, 158, 160
Adams, Stanley, 163
Adventures of Dollie, The, 18
Agee, James, 71, 146
Alias Jimmy Valentine, 103
Al Jolson Story, The, 134
Allen, Woody, 63
Allez Oop, 133, 185
All the King's Men, 135
Amache, Don, 136
American Film Institute, The, 75
American Legion, The, 151
American Medical Society, The, 159
Anderson, Eddie "Rochester", 164
Andrews, Captain James, 88-91
Anna Christie, 107
An Old Spanish Custom, 129
Anvil Chorus, The, 10
Arbuckle, Roscoe "Fatty", 19-40, 41, 48, 50, 59, 109, 121, 161, 173-176
Arizona, 71, 124
Armetta, Henry, 120
Around the World in 80 Days, 158, 195
Arrowhead Springs, 123-124, 128
Astoria, Queens, New York, 132

Atlanta, Georgia, 78, 88, 90, 91
Audubon, James, 77
Avelon, Frankie, 165

B

Back Stage, 26, 175
Balin, Izzy, 8
Balloonatic, The, 59, 61, 179
Barnes, Frank, 81
Barrymore, Lionel, 103, 112, 181
Bathing Beauties, 143-144
Battling Butler, 47, 72, *73*, 112, 118, 180
Baxter, Warner, 130
Bayside, Long Island, 50
Beach Blanket Bingo, 165, 200
Beauregard, General, 90
Beck, Martin, 14
Beckett, Samuel, 165, 166
Bell Boy, The, 26, 174
Ben Hur, 107
Benny, Jack, 112, 164, 181
Berle, Milton, 132, 198
Berlin, Irving, 8
Bernie, Jason, 163
Beery, Wallace, 104, 182, 196
Best of Broadway, 157, 194
Big Shanty, Georgia, 83, 86, 90
Biograph Studio, 18
Birth of a Nation, The, 18
Blacksmith, The, 55, 112, 137, 178
Blake, Alice, 36
Blesh, Rudi, 10
Bloom, Claire, 151, 194
Blue, Ben, 164
Blue Blazes, 134, 187
Blystone, Jack, 62, 179
Boat, The, 52, 177
Bondy, Pierce, 146

B continued

Booth, John Wilkes, 77
Born Yesterday, 135
Brady, Mathew, 77-78, 84
Brady, Matt, 38
Brandt, Harry, 95
Brandt, Joe, 134
Bridge Over the River Kwai, The, 135
Bridgeport Bridge, 89
Bringing Up Father, 103
Brooklyn, New York, 106
Brown Eyes, 71
Brown, Buster, 4
Brownie Kennedy's Roadhouse, 32
Brown, Joe E., 116, 158, 164
Brown, Michael, 36
Bruckman, Clyde, 41, 81
Buell, General Don Carlos, 89
Burns, George, 8
Buster Keaton Story, The, 132, 154-156
Butcher Boy, The, 19-21, 22-24, 173
Butler, Alfred, 47, 102
Byron, Marion, 101, 102, 180

C

Cain, Jeff, 90
Cain Mutiny, The, 135
Cameraman, The, 108-110, 140, 142, 181
Campbell's Soup, 10
Candid Camera, 160, 161
Capra, Frank, 134
Carillo, Leo , 130, 186
Catalina Island, California, 68
Cavender, Glen, 81
CBC-Film Sales Company, 134
Chaplin, Charles, 18, 21, 25, 41, 42, 72,
    73, 104, 105, 107, 126, 127, 135,
    146, 149, 150, 151,-153, 156, 158,
    194, 196-198
Chaplin, Charlie Jr., 194
Chaplin, Geraldine, 194
Chaplin, Josephine, 194
Chaplin, Michael, 194
Chaplin, Studio, 31
Chaplin, Sidney, 194
Chattanooga, Tennessee, 78, 82, 89
Chemist, The, 134, 187
Chevalier, Maurice, 116, 183
Chickamauga, 90
Christie, Albert, 187
Cirque Medrano, 146

Citizen Kane, 75
Coburn, Charles, 158, 190, 195
Cody, Lew, 114, 182, 184
Cohen, George M., 2
Cohn, Harry, 134, 136, 139
Cohn, Jack, 134
Coleman, Ronald, 154, 158, 195
College, 75, 97-99, 180
Columbia Studio, 126, 134-136, 138
Comedy Circus, 149
Comique Film Corporation, 21, 25, 31, 59,
    121, 173-176
Congressional Cemetery, 78
Convict 13, 47, 176
Cooper, Gary, 130, 183, 186
Cops, 53-55, 178, 202
Cottage Grove, Oregon, 84, 93
Cougat, Xavier, 143
Coward, Noel, 158, 195
Cox, Bill, 162
Crawford, Joan, 112, 116, 181, 182
Crisp, Donald, 103, 179, 190
Crook, The, 26
Culver City, California, 104, 118, 125
Cummings, Irving, 136, 137, 176, 188
Curly, James, 32
Cutler-Bryant 10-Cent Show, The, 1
Cutler, F.L., 1

D

Dali, Salvador, 10
Dalton, Georgia, 91
Damfino, 52
Dana, Viola, 27
Daniels, Bebe, 27-28
Daniels, Harold, 163, 197
Davis, Marion, 103, 112, 181
Day Dreams, 178, 198
Day, Marceline, 109, 181
Days of Thrills and Laughter, 164
Delmont, Bambina Maude, 34, 36
Desmond, Nora, 147
Devine, Andy, 158, 164, 191, 195, 199
Dietrich, Marlene, 158, 195
Dillion, Mick, 168
Dion, 163, 196
Ditto, 134, 187
Dixon, Thomas, 18
Dogwatch, Indiana, 2
Donlevy, Brian, 144, 201
Donna Reed Show, The, 159, 160
Doughboys, 115, 182
Dr. Strangelove, 135

Dressler, Marie, 103-104, 112, 181
Drew, Trilby, 111
Dryden, Wheeler, 151
Dunne, Irene, 116, 182, 196
Dumont, Margaret, 142
Durante, Jimmy, 118, 120-123, 164, 184, 197, 199

E

E-Flat Man, The, 133, 186
Eastman, John, 168
Easy Rider, 135
Eddy Cantor Theater, 156, 194
Eddy, Nelson, 144, 189
Educational Pictures, 131-134
Edwards, Cliff, 114, 181, 182
Edwards, Snitz, 112, 180
Edwards, Ukulele Ike, 118
Electric House, The, 48, 57, 179
El Moderno Barba Azul, 145, 192
England, 129, 130, 146, 157, 159, 183

F

Fairbanks, Douglas Jr., 157, 183
Fairbanks, Douglas, Sr., 18, 46, 103, 117, 198
Famous-Players-Lasky, 21, 31-33
Farley, Jim, 81, 180
Fatty at Coney Island, 24, 174
Faye, Alice, 137-138
F.B.I., 151
Fields, W.C., 8, 193
Film, 165-167, 200
Film Quarterly, 64
First National, 51
Fishbach, Fred, 33-35
Fitzgerald, F. Scott, 106
Fort Sumter, 84, 85
Fox, Virginia, 49, 53
Fox, William, 31
Foy, Eddie Jr., 163, 197
Free and Easy, 112-114
Friendless, 71
From Here to Eternity, 135
Frontier Girl, 131
Frozen North, The, 56, 57, 178
Funicello, Annette, 165
Funt, Alan, 160-161

G

Gable, Clark, 140, 184
Gaboure, Fred, 41, 51
Garage, The, 26, 176
Garbo, Greta, 122
Garland, Judy, 140, 145, 192
General, The, 18, 41, 44, 75-95, 96, 99, 117, 144, 180
General, The, (Script Of), 81-84
General Nuisance, 135, 190
George Eastman Festival of Film Arts, 153
Gilbert, John, 112, 113, 181
Gilda, 134
Gingold, Hermione, 158
Gish, Lillian, 103, 153
Givot, George, 138, 188
Go West, 71, 72, 180
Goat, The, 50, 137, 177
Goldberg, Rube, 162
Gold Ghost, The, 133, 185
Goldwyn Pictures, 108
Gone With the Wind, 75
Good Earth, The, 107
Good Night Nurse, 26, 175
Good, Will B., 40
Goodrich, William B., 40
Goodwins, Les, 163
Grand Slam Opera, 134, 187
Grauman, Sid., 27
Gray, Johnny, 81-88, 92
Graziano, Rocky, 158
Great Locomotive Chase, The, 77
Greenwood, Charlotte, 183
Griffith, D.W., 17, 18, 61, 107

H

Hagney, Frank, 81
Haines, William, 103, 181, 182
Hall, Mordount, 76
Halliwell's Film Companion, 155
Halliwell, Leslie, 155
Hamilton, Lloyd, 131
Hard Luck, 48, 177
Hart, William S., 56
Hatfield and McCoy Feud, 61
Haunted House, The, 47, 48
Haver, Phyllis, 179
Haverhill, Massachusetts, 107
Hayes, Rutherford B., 133

H continued

Hayes, Gabby, 116, 183
Hays Commission, The, 39
Hayseed, The, 26, 175
Hayseed Romance, 133, 185
Hays, Will, 39
Hayworth, Rita, 134
Hearst International Newsreel Company, 109
Hearst, William Randolph, 109
Hearts and Pearls, 63
Heflin, Van, 145
High Sign, The, 48, 49, 177
His Ex Marks the Spot, 135, 189
His Wedding Night, 24, 174
Hollywood Cavalcade, 136, 137, 188
Hollywood Revue of 1929, The, 112, 181
Hoover, J. Edgar, 151
Hope, Bob, 157
Hopper, Hedda, 116, 121, 182, 184, 193
Horkheimer Brothers, The, 25
Horne, James, W., 98, 180
Horse Feathers, 162
Horton, Edward Everett, 132
Houdini, Harry, 2-3, 13
Houghton, Buck, 162, 163
Howard, Trevor, 158, 195
How to Stuff a Wild Bikini, 168, 201
Hughes, Howard, 151
Human Mop, The, 5, 8, 23
Huntsville, Alabama, 89

I

I Blow My Own Horn, 31
Ince, Tom, 51
In the Good Old Summertime, 144, 145
Intolerance, 18, 60
Invader, The, 129-131, 186
Ireland, John, 144
Irving, Reginald, 116
It's A Gift, 162
It's A Mad, Mad, Mad, Mad World, 164, 165, 198

J

Jackson, Andrew, 77
Jailbait, 134, 187
Jersy City, 12
Jessle, George, 8
Johnson, Lawrence, 120

Johnson, Van, 140
Jolson, Al, 2, 8, 137
Jolson Sings Again, 134
Judith of Bethulia, 18

K

KHJ Television, 149
Kaye, Danny, 132, 140, 199
Keaton, Buster Jr., 60
Keaton, James 50, 60
Keaton, Joseph, 9, 14-15, 17, 26, 60, 81, 134, 174-177, 179, 180, 185
Keaton, Louise, 102, 134, 185, 188
Keaton, Myra, 1-5, 9, 12, 15, 17, 134
Keaton, Robert, 50
Keaton Studio, 31, 41-74
Keeley Treatment, The, 132, 133
Kelly, Gene, 113, 140
Kennedy, Griffith, 37
Kettle, Ma and Pa, 131
Keystone Comedies, 10, 21
Keystone Cops, The, 21, 116, 137, 183, 188
King, Hetty, 146
Kingston, Georgia, 90
Kirk, Tommy, 164
Klansman, The, 18
Kramer, Stanley, 164, 198

L

La Fiesta de Santa Barbara, 129-130, 186
Laemmle, Carl, 106, 134
Lahr, Bert, 8, 132, 163, 164, 194, 197
Lake, Alice, 27
Lamont, Charles, 131, 185-187, 131
Lane, Lupino, 131
Langdon, Harry, 127, 132, 196, 197
Lasky, Jesse, 31-32
Last Tycoon, The, 106
Laurel and Hardy, 31, 112, 181, 182, 193, 196, 198, 202
Lawrence of Arabia, 135
Leland, T.B., 37
Le Roi des Champs-Elysees, 129-130, 185
Lessley, Elgin, 42, 64
Lester, Richard, 168, 202
Lewis, Jerry, 130, 199
Life Magazine, 76, 146
Li'l Abner, 138, 189
Lilley, Joseph, 138
Lillie, Beatrice, 158, 195

L'Incatevol Nemica, 156, 194
Lincoln, Abraham, 77
Limelight, 146, *147*, 150-153, 156, 158, 194
Lloyd, Harold, 104, 127, 128, 135, 153
Locan, Clarence, 118
Loew, Marcus, 29, 30, 46, 59, 108
Long Beach, California, 25, 26
Los Angeles, California, 15, 26, 30, 34
Los Angeles Examiner, 37
Love Nest, 59, 156, 179
Love Nest On Wheels, 134, 188
Low, Seth, 8
Lupino, Ida, 130, 186, 190

M

MacDonald, Jeanette, 145
Mack, Marion, 81, 94, 95, 180
Mad Dog Gulch, 26
Mannix, Eddie, 118-119, 125, 140
Marietta, Georgia, 81, 82, 84, 89
Maris, Mona, 120, 184
Mark Strand Theater, 17
Marsh, Mae, 153
Martin and Lewis, 31
Martin, Doctor Harry, 128
Marx Brothers, The, 8, 31, 140-142, 193
Marx, Harpo, 130, 140, 186
Matheson, Richard, 162-163
Mayer, Louis B., 95, 106-108, 117, 118, 120, 122, 123-125
McCarthy, Joseph, 151
McGuire, Katheryn, 66, 112, 179
McLaglen, Victor, 116, 158, 182, 190, 195
McLeod, Norman, 162, 197
McKay, Willie, 61
Memphis and Charleston Railroad, 89
Merry Widow, The, 107
Metro Studios, 30, 46, 51, 62, 63, 65, 108, 176-178
Metro-Goldwyn-Mayer, 65, 99, 103, 106, 108, 111, 112, 122, 129, 134, 139, 178-184
Mexico, 124, 129, 130, 145, 192
Mills, John, 158
Minsk, Russia, 107
Mishawn Manor, Boston, 32
Mississippi, 101
Mitchell, General Ormsby McNight, 89
Mixed Marriage, 134, 187
Mohawk Indian Medicine Company, 1, 2

Monkey Business, 162
Monte Carlo, 121
Montgomery, Robert, 114, 181
Mooching Through Georgia, 135, 188
Moonshine, 26, 175
Moore, Grace, 145
Moran, Polly, 103, 120, 181, 182, 184
Morley, Sheridan, 152
Mostel, Zero, 168, 202
Moving Picture World, 23
Mulligan, Woodrow, 161
Mutiny on the Bounty, 107
My Wife's Relations, 55, 178

N

Nagle, Conrad, 112, 181
National P.T.A., 159
National Variety Artists, 116
Navigator, The, 44, 47, 65, 66, *67*, 69, 78, 112, 179
Neighbors, 47, 177
New Henrietta, The, 46
New Moon, 144, 189
New Yorker Magazine, 76
New York Stock Exchange, 47
New York Times, The, 76
Nilsson, Anna Q., 27
Norris, Eleanor (Keaton) 139, 146, 154, 170, 201
Nothing But Pleasure, 135, 188, 203

O

O'Conner, Donald, 154, *155*, 156
Oh Doctor!, 24, 174
Oliver!, 135
On the Waterfront, 135
One Run Elmer, 133, 185
One Week, 44-46, 117, 148, 176, 203
Oostenaula Bridge, 90
Oregon State National Guard, 93
Orpheum Theater, The, 15
Orsattie, Ernie, 67
Our Gang, 116, 182
Our Hospitality, 44, 60, 61, 63, 179,
Outcault, R.F., 4
Out West, 26, 174

P

Page, Anita, 114, 118, 181, 183
Pagliacci, 114

P _{continued}

Pajama Party, 165, 200
Paleface, The, 44, 53, 162, 178, 203
Palooka From Paducah, 133, 134, 185
Pantages Theater, The, 15
Paramount Studio, 23, 27, 39, 116, 126, 154, 156, 172-176
Pardon My Berth Marks, 135, 188
Paris, France, 129, 130, 146
Parlor, Bedroom and Bath, 116-117, 183
Parson, Louella, 128
Passionate Plumber, The, 120-121, 184
Pastor's Theater, 8
Patsy, The, 103
Patterson, Gerald, 166, 201
Pest from the West, 136, 188
Photoplay, 65
Pickfaire, 117
Pickford, Mary, 18, 46, 153
Piqua, Kansas, 1
Pitts, Zasu, 164, 193
Playhouse 90, 159, 195
Playhouse, The, 42, 51, 112, 177
Poe, Edgar Allan, 77
Polk, James, 77
Prince of Whales, 23
Private Lives, 107
Producers' Showcase, 195
Purple Rose of Cairo, The, 63

R

R-K-0 Studio, 126, 138, 151
Raft, George, 158
Railrodder, The, 168, 201
Rappe, Virginia, 32-37, 39
Rathbone, Basil, 143
Raye, Martha, 158
Regan, Tom, 37
Reliance-Majestic Studio, 18
Requiem for a Heavyweight, 159
Retakes, 168
Riddle, Nelson, 139
Riesner, Charles, 100
Riesner, Dan, 100
Ritchard, Cyril, 200
Ritz Brothers, The, 31
Riverside, California, 68
Roberts, Joe, 49
Robinson, Bill "Bojangles", 12, 13
Robinson, Edward G., 116, 182
Robey, George, 146

Rogers, Buddy, 116, 183
Rogers, Will, 2, 8
Rohauer, Raymond, 166, 167, 203
Roland, Gilbert, 120, 184, 195
Romeo and Juliet, 107
Rooney, Mickey, 140, 198, 201
Rough House, The, 24, 173
Route 66, 164, 197
Rueter's News Service, 129
Ruggles, Charles, 72, 192
Ryan, Irene, 132

S

Sacramento, California, 101
Salame, Where She Danced, 131
Salvador, Jaimie, 145, 192
San Fernando Valley, California, 156
San Francisco, California, 15, 20, 32-38, 131, 158, 161
San Gabriel Canyon, California, 26
Santa Clara, California, 20
Saphead, The, 46, 47, 176
Scarecrow, The, 47, 176
Schary, Dore, 108
Schenck, Joseph, 20-21, 31-32, 41, 42, 50, 51, 59, 66, 75, 76, 103, 105, 107, 177
Schenck, Nicholas, 103, 108
Screen Directors Playhouse, 157, 195
Screen Gems, 135
Scribbins, Mae (Keaton), 4, 124, 128, 134
Sebastian, Dorothy, 111-112, 181
Secret Life of Walter Mitty, 162
Sedgwick, Edward, 112, 120, 181, 182, 184, 188
Seeley, Sybil, 44-46
Selig-Poli Scope Company, 21
Sennett, Mack, 10, 20, 21, 25, 35, 64, 131, 137, 186, 188, 198
Sergeant Deadhead, 168, 201
Seven Chances, 70, 123, 180, 202
Shaw, Robert, 155
Shearer, Norma, 106, 112, 181, 182, 183
Sheldon, Sidney, 155
Sheraton-Palace Hotel, 35
Sherlock, Jr., 42, 44, 63-65, 179
Sherman, Lowell, 33-35
She's Oil Mine, 135, 190
Showpeople, 103
Shubert, Revue, The, 18-20
Sidewalks of New York, 117-118, 183
Sidney, George, 144, 182
Sierra Nevada Mountains, 61

Silvers, Phil, 168, 198, 202
Singing in the Rain, 112, 113
Skelton, Red, 140, 143-144, 195
Slippery Pearls, The, 116, 183
Smith Center, Kansas, 20
Smith, Charles, 81, 180
Smithsonian Institute, 61
Society for the Prevention of Cruelty to Children, 7-8
South Lake Tahoe, California, 61
So You Won't Squawk, 136, 190
Speak Easily, 120, 121-122, 184
Spence, Ralph, 120
Spielberg, Steven, 60
Spite Marriage, 44, 110-112, 181
Spook Speaks, The, 135, 189
St. Clair, Mal, 137, 177
St. Francis Hotel, 33, 35
St. John, Al, 22
Stanwych, Barbara, 116, 183
Starke, Pauline, 103
Steamboat Bill, Jr. 42, 44-45, 58, 75, 103, 180
Stephenson Rocket, The, 61
Stewart, Anita, 108
Stolen Jools, 116, 182
Strange Interlude, 107
Sunday Showcase, 160, 196
Sunset Boulevard, 146, 148, 193
Swanson, Gloria, 147, 154, 167, 193, 196, 200

T

Talmadge, Constance, 51
Talmadge, Natalie (Keaton), 47, 50, 60, 61, 134, 179
Talmadge, Norma, 51, 103, 113, 154
Talmadge, Peg, 50
Talmadge Studio, The, 20, 21, 23, 24
Taming of the Snood, The, 135, 189
Tars and Stripes, 133, 185
Taylor, Robert, 131, 186
Taylor, Zachary, 77
Temple, Shirley, 13
Ten Girls Ago, 163-164, 197
Terre Haute, Indiana, 2
Texas, The, 80, 86-87, 90-91, 94,
Thalberg, Irving, 105, 108, 116-118, 125
Thirty Years of Fun, 164, 198
Thomson, David, 48
Three Ages, 42, 60
Three Keatons, The, 5, 8, 9, 10, 14, 15, 20
Three on a Limb, 133, 186

Three Stooges, The, 135, 164, 203
Tibbett, Lawrenece, 145
Tiffany Films, 114, 182
Timid Young Man, The, 133, 186
Todd, Michael, 158, 195
Todd, Thelma, 121, 122, 184
Tolar, Sidney, 121
Too Hot to Handle, 140
Topper, 162
Treadway, Rollo, 47, 66
Truckee River, 61-63
Turner, Lana, 140
Turpin, Ben, 137, 188, 193
Twentieth Century-Fox, 13, 31, 35, 126, 136
Twilight Zone, The, 161-163, 173, 197
Twyman, Alan, 167
Tyler, John, 77

U

Un Duel a Mort, 193
United Artists, Incorporated, 18, 75, 76, 95, 97, 98, 99, 100, 102, 103, 105, 164, 180, 195, 198
United States Army, 30-31, 115
Universal Film Manufacturing Company, 106
Universal Studio, 126, 191
U.S.S. Buford, 66, 69

V

Van Wych, Mayor R.A., 7, 8
Variety Magazine, 46, 76
Vaudeville, 1, 3, 5, 7, 8, 10, 14, 14, 17, 18, 20, 24, 42, 51-52, 102, 121, 132, 148, 149, 153
Venice Film Festival, 166-167
Viking, The, 103
Villain Still Pursued Her, The, 144, 189
Virtuous Wives, 108
Voice of Hollywood #101, 114, 182

W

Wall Street, 47
Warhole, Andy, 10
Warner Brothers, 31, 126
Warner, H.B., 147, 189
Warner, Jack, 31
Watch the Birdie, 110
Weingarten, Laurence, 108-109

W continued

Western and Atlantic Flyer, 81, 89
What! No Beer?, 120, 122-123, 184
When Comedy Was King, 164, 196
White, Jules, 135
Who Framed Roger Rabbit, 60
Wilder, Billy, 146, 193
Williams, John D., 59
Wind, The, 103
Winter Garden Theater, 18
Wizard of Oz, The, 75
Wray, Fay, 116, 183
Wynn, Ed, 148, 197
Wynn, Keenan, 143

Y

Yankee Stadium, 110

Z

Zanuck, Darryl, 13, 136
Zukor, Adolph, 27-29, 31, 32, 37, 38, 104